Collector's Edition

The **PINBALL** PRICE GUIDE

NINTH **9** EDITION

By Pinballeric™

Publisher
Pinballeric™, LLC
www.pinballeric.com

PINBALLERIC™

THE PINBALL PRICE GUIDE, 9TH EDITION

Copyright © 2013, Pinballeric™, LLC

ISBN: 978-0-615-73153-7

Additional copies of this book can be purchased online at www.pinballeric.com

Interior Book Designer
Sara Chapman
Art Squad Graphics
www.artsquadgraphics.com

Cover Designer
Susan Mathews
Susan Mathews Design
www.stillwater-studio.com

Editor
Deborah Kantor
Kantor Writing & Photography
Kantorwriting@gmail.com

Front Cover Photo
From the Richard M. Bueschel Collection,
currently part of the
Gordon A. Hasse, Jr. Pinball Archives

In memory of my father

Jerome Kantor
1922–2013

INSIDE THE GUIDE

FOREWORD

No matter which era of games you collect—Preflipper, Woodrails, Multi- and Single-player, Electronic, or Digital Age—there are many pinball machines from which to choose. Just as collecting vinyl has made a comeback, so has collecting pinball machines. Today, collectors prize their machines not only for the gameplay, but also for the original artwork on the cabinet, playfield, and backglass. There is definitely a certain amount of prestige in owning pinball machines.

The price values listed in this guide do not reflect fully restored machines, which are sometimes referred to as "mint" or "museum" quality. The cost of a restoration can raise the price of a pinball machine $1000, $5000, and even more. New pinball games are made in limited editions (LE). Depending on condition, gameplay, and the marketplace, new LE games can have immediate collector value.

Prices for many pinball machines have increased. There is more interest in pinball now, due to pinball and arcade shows, competitions, museums, and Internet, TV, magazine, and newspaper coverage. The newer games being made can cost $7000 or more. However, it is difficult to compare newer LE game prices to those of older games because the number of machines made now is relatively small compared to the number of games made, let's say, in the 1990s. For instance, Williams made 13,640 Fish Tales machines in 1992. The number of machines being made today for a new game title is 1000 or less.

Pinballeric™

PREFACE

The author of this book is publishing it as a guide for collectors, buyers, and sellers of pinball games. Its purpose is to promote pinball collecting.

The Pinball Price Guide provides a range of average prices, based on many factors to be considered when buying and selling games. The price values are based on the condition, playability, and collectability of the game.

The guide covers the pricing of games produced for the United States market from 1931 through 2012.

The prices listed in this guide are a compilation of information from the Internet, show sales, auctions, dealers' sales lists, and discussions with collectors and pinball dealers.

This book is not a dealer's price list, although some dealers may use it to assist in pricing. It is an informal reference as to what a collector might pay for a game. The final true value of any pinball game is what someone will pay for it.

ACKNOWLEDGMENTS

Special thanks to—

Dennis Dodel, Gordon A. Hasse, Jr., Rob Hawkins, and Brian Saunders for their generous contributions to *The Pinball Price Guide;*

The Pinball Price Guide book production team of Sara Chapman, Deborah Kantor, and Susan Mathews;

Friends of *The Pinball Price Guide:* Jess Askey, Martin Ayub, Larry Bieza, Michael Cohen, Gene Cunningham, Walter Forman, Roger Hilden, Stacy Jedynak, Jon and Ben Kantor, Raphael Lankar, Lloyd Olson, Rascha, Jimmy Rosen, Jay Stafford, and Steve Young.

WHAT'S NEW
IN THE 9TH EDITION

The Pinball Price Guide by **Pinballeric™** is a valuable resource that answers the following questions:

- Do you know the **current value** of your pinball machine?
- Do you know the **fair purchase price** of a pinball machine?
- Do you know **how much to sell** a machine for?
- Do you know what the **additional costs** are when buying or selling a game?

The *Pinball Price Guide* covers price values on collectible games produced for the U.S. market, **1931–2012.**

Four new articles by industry experts in the "Collector's Corner":

Brian Saunders, a premier pinball dealer specializing in 1960s and 70s games, writes about his love of those games in "Electro-Mechanical Games of the 1960s and 70s."

Gordon A. Hasse, Jr., an author, pinball historian, and recognized expert on woodrails, explains in detail the five determinants that go into pricing these precursors to metal rails in "Woodrail Pricing: The Big Picture."

Rob Hawkins, an author, educator, and collector, shares his expertise about the flipperless games of the 1930s and 40s in "Prewar (Flipperless) Pinball Machines."

Dennis Dodel, legendary pinball dealer, collector, and author, compares the Bingo pinballs from the 1950s, 60s, and 70s to the flipperless games of the 30s and 40s in "Bingo-Style Pinball Machines."

Two new resources: Homemade Pinball and Virtual Pinball.

Pinballeric's™ Price Guide Worksheet helps you get organized and understand the actual costs of buying or selling your games.

Home of the Price Guide—Pinballeric.com is the online place to find all kinds of additional information about pinball.

COLLECTING, BUYING, SELLING

How to Start Collecting

You should collect games that appeal to you. They could be ones that you remember playing in your youth. They could be games that have great play features, appealing artwork, or both. Some collectors specialize in a particular vintage, such as woodrails (1950s) or wedge heads (1960s). Some collect modern solid-state games (1970s–1990s) with sound, music, toys, and ramps. Some collectors have to have the newest games being sold.

Before you purchase the first game you see, you should realize that there are over 2,000 different games to choose from. The best way to make a decision is to acquaint yourself with as many games as possible. A great place to see games and meet collectors is at a pinball or arcade show.

Internet web sites provide a vast wealth of information about pinball. There are also dozens of good pinball books available that provide photo illustrations and written details of games. Pinball museums have also taken off in a big way in the United States and around the world.

How to Buy Games

Once you have decided what game(s) to collect, you'll need to find games for sale. Some sources are the Internet, pinball and arcade shows, dealers, local want ads, pinball publications, auctions, or local game operators.

The surest way to find a game that interests you is by looking at the game in person where you can check it carefully for defects, especially on the backglass. You can also save shipping costs by transporting it yourself. Realize that many older games are hard to find, let alone in Class 1—BEST condition. (See Condition Grading Guide on page 68).

Keeping this in mind, you may have to accept a game in something other than Class 1 shape. For example, if you are looking for a game from the 90s, you may only see one of this particular game in many years' time. So, if you see a game that you want, in acceptable condition and at a fair price, buy it!

If you are unable to see a game first-hand, ask the seller to send you close-up photos of both the backglass and the playfield, so any defects will be apparent.

Of course many games are available at online auction sites, such as eBay. You need to be as informed as possible about the game's condition before you bid.

Remember, too, shipping will add $300–$500 to the price of the game. Prices for games can vary somewhat by geographic location and during holiday seasons.

Some sellers' prices may be higher than those listed in the price guide. Depending on condition and the rarity of the game, the higher price may be justified. Only you can ultimately decide if a game is worth the money.

Proper Storage of Games

The stress of temperature extremes can be damaging to backglasses and playfields. Therefore, avoid outdoor storage in cold climates, as well as direct sunlight. The backglass bulbs give off heat, so if the game will be left on for long periods, a cooler bulb than the standard N44 bulb should be used. On some games, the new LEDs can replace the existing bulbs.

Proper humidity is also important as dryness can cause cracking of the cabinet and the playfield plywood. If you store your games in a basement area, you may want to monitor humidity levels as well as keep your games off cement floors. Recommended temperature is 50–80°F, and ideal humidity levels are from 30–50%.

Reproduction Parts

Many original and reproduction parts are available from pinball suppliers and parts dealers. One part that is easily reproduced is the backglass. A reproduction backglass can cost $275–$350. Check with parts dealers to see what's available. Many parts are listed online.

With reproduction parts, some variations from the originals exist but are usually slight. Most internal parts are available for games. Some cosmetic and plastic parts can be hard to find, but many playfield plastics as well as the playfields are now being reproduced. This trend will probably continue as the value of the more collectible machines continues to rise. Shows are a good source for finding reproduction parts and NOS (New Old Stock) parts.

How to Sell Games

One method of selling would be to list your game, with price and condition, on the Internet or in one of the collector magazines. If you live in a major city or metropolitan area, it may be easier to match your game with a collector of that type of game. Another way to sell is through an online auction such as eBay. You can add photographs to your online auction, which is very helpful to the buyer. Avoid returns by describing your game's condition accurately. Also clearly define shipping arrangements, such as pick-up only or using a major shipping company at the buyer's expense.

Another way to sell a game would be to bring it to a pinball and arcade show, where the game would be set up with the sale price posted on the game. This is a great way for a collector to play the game before buying, and for the seller to answer any questions about the game.

You could also sell to a game dealer. Pinball dealers cannot pay full guide prices, as they have many costs involved, such as travel, advertising, show fees, and inventory. They will generally pay up to 45–50% of the guide price depending on whether they have a ready buyer or your game is in demand. Dealers can be found at many shows.

Rating the Condition of Your Game

In coin collecting, there are different values to a coin depending on how worn it is. This is also true for pinball games. The three major parts listed (backglass, playfield, and cabinet) need to be graded separately to accurately determine the value of your game. The Guide lists values for **Classes 1, 2, & 3**, assuming the condition of the three parts (backglass, playfield, and cabinet) are of similar condition as shown in the Condition Grading Guide (see page 68). If the three parts are not of similar condition, find the closest approximate condition and adjust the price accordingly. The better the condition of the three parts of a game, the more it will be worth. Any game worse than Class 3 condition is considered a parts game.

Parts Games

Games below a **Class 3** rating generally can't be salvaged into a decent looking or running game. Any value left in these games comes from the value of the game parts that can be used. Below is a list of approximate values for parts games, assuming some cosmetic, mechanical, and/or electronic parts are useable.

Remember, two or more parts games could be made into one playable game.

1931–1932 (mechanical)	**$50–200**
1933–1976 (electro-mechanical)	**$75–300**
1977–1991(solid state)	**$200–400**
1992 and newer (dot matrix display)	**$300–500**

PURSUING THE SILVER BALL

Pinball Shows and Museums

If you are a pinball collector or just enjoy playing, then a pinball and arcade show is an ideal place to play great games and make new friends.

The Pinball Expo in Chicago, started in 1984, is the oldest show. The Chicago Expo is where you can rub elbows with the designers, artists, and software engineers of your favorite games. Features of the show include an autograph session, banquet, pinball factory tour, and many seminars on the history and upkeep, as well as what's new with pinball games. There is a large exhibit hall that houses wonderful games, old and new, for playing or buying. There is also a competitive pinball player's tournament. http://www.pinballexpo.net/

Many more shows have been held regionally in the United States and around the world since The Pinball Expo debuted in Chicago. The Pinball Expo in California, which began in 2006, features the largest collection of pinball machines on display in the world. http://www.pacificpinball.org/

The Northwest Pinball and Arcade Show in Seattle, is a family-friendly event that features over 350 pinball and arcade games, all set on free play. Uniquely, the Seattle show provides a "Live Stream" of their seminar speakers over the Internet. http://nwpinballshow.com/home

For a complete calendar listing of all shows, go to *Pinball News* on the Internet at http://www.pinballnews.com/diary/index.html. There is a hyperlink to *Pinball News* on pinballeric.com.

Pinball museums have become the place to go to discover and play many classic games. The museums are found around the world, in such locations as Las Vegas, NV; California; The Jersey Shore; England; France; and Japan. To find a pinball museum, go to http://pinballeric.com/history.html

Competitive and League Play

Competitive pinball tournaments, which can be found at most pinball and arcade shows, offer cash prizes and trophies. Tournaments are also happening in bars, bowling alleys, pool halls, and even skateboard shops.

The Professional and Amateur Pinball Association (PAPA) was founded in 1990 by Steve Epstein, who ran the Broadway Arcade, in New York City, with help from his friend Roger Sharpe, who is responsible for having pinball legalized in New York City. PAPA sponsors international tournaments and has a facility dedicated to competitive pinball in Scott Township, Pennsylvania. In December 2012, PAPA President Kevin Martin donated all of the pinball machines and arcade games at the PAPA World Headquarters to Replay Foundation, a new non-profit organization.

The Free State Pinball Association (FSPA) has been running pinball leagues since 1995 in Maryland; Washington, DC; and Northern Virginia. Playing in a pinball league lets you test your skills against players of your ability, improve your game, and above all, have fun!

Some other competitive pinball organizations include The International Flipper Pinball Association (IFPA), SS Billiards Tournaments, PinBrawl, and the European Pinball Championship (EPC). The United States, the United Kingdom, Canada, France, Ireland, Germany, Hungary, Poland, Australia, Japan, Spain, Sweden, Italy, and the Netherlands all have competitive tournaments.

To join a league near you, search the Internet for "pinball leagues." A list of leagues endorsed by the International Flipper Pinball Association (IFPA) can be found on the Arcade Novelties' web page, Pinball Leagues: http://arcadenovelties.com/cgi-bin/store/cpshop.pl/pinball_leagues.

RESOURCES

The Internet

The Internet has a wealth of information about pinball. Online resources cover just about every topic the pinball enthusiast would find interesting, from pinball history, repair, and games for sale to podcast talk shows.

DATABASES

The Internet Pinball Database

The Internet Pinball Database (www.ipdb.org) began as an idea to bring together in one place an accessible store of data about pinball machines. This year marks the Eleventh Anniversary since we took over the Pinball Pastures original database. We are excited to report that during this time, the site has grown in size from 3,000 images to over 50,000 images. We have added game detail, historical references, and behind-the-scenes stories on the making of the games, often told in the very words of the designers, artists, and programmers who made them. We have strived to show unusual or rare examples of games, as well as subtle design changes between games built in the same production run.

One of our hopes had been to grow our information about preflipper games, especially for the 1930s, and we are happy to report that we have made great strides in both areas. We are also excited to have substantially increased our coverage of games made outside of the USA. For all games, thousands of images have been added for each decade of manufacture.

We believe such growth would not be possible without the participation and kind support of our many users everywhere, who have helped make the IPDB be the largest database of pinball machines on the web today. We know we have much more to do, to make the site even better. As we head into our eleventh year, we will continue to work to earn and keep your confidence.

Thank you!

Christopher Wolf and Jay Stafford
Editors, The Internet Pinball Database

The Internet Pinball Serial Number Database

The Internet Pinball Serial Number Database (www.ipsnd.net) collects serial numbers of pinball machines and publishes them as a database. IPSND makes available online registration on their web site for all pinball machines world-wide. The site has many features, such as hyperlinks to and from the Internet Pinball Database (IPDB), graphs, charts, and interactive features.

There are hyperlinks to both IPDB and IPSND on pinballeric.com.

NEWSGROUPS AND SOCIAL MEDIA

The Google Pinball Newsgroup (rec.games.pinball) is the place on the Internet where collectors can chat about every aspect of pinball. This newsgroup features discussions on collecting, buying, and maintaining pinball machines. Go to: groups.google.com/forum/?fromgroups#!forum/rec.games.pinball

Yahoo's EM Pinball Group (empinbalmachines) is a place where you can communicate with other EM game aficionados and post your photos. Go to: games.groups.yahoo.com/group/empinbalmachines

Yahoo's Prewar Pinball Group (prewarpinball) is the newsgroup for prewar pinball collectors. The group's purpose is to bring together collectors and restorers of pre-1948 pinball machines known as flipperless pinball. Go to: http://games.groups.yahoo.com/group/prewarpinball/

Twitter, Facebook, Google+, KLOV, Linkedin, Reddit, Pinside, and **Craigslist** all have active pinball communities.

OTHER WEB SITES

Pinball News (www.pinballnews.com) from the UK, is a great web site for pinball collectors and players around the world who want to keep current on pinball-related news, trends, products, shows, and competitions. A hyperlink to *Pinball News* can be found at pinballeric.com.

PinWiki (www.pinwiki.com) is a site designed for inputting and reading information about pinball machines, including repair guides, history, tournaments, shows, and more.

Pinball Donut Girl (www.pinballdonutgirl.com) is the web site for the indie movie of the same name. It includes photos from pinball shows and on the making of the movie, by the filmmaker and photographer Anna Newman.

YouTube (www.youtube.com) is a web site where you can upload your pinball-related videos or host your own pinball channel. You can watch pinball machine demos, tours of home game rooms, and videos of games for sale, as well as visit pinball museums on your computer screen. *PinGame Journal*

magazine has a YouTube channel at http://www.youtube.com/pinjournal.

VIEMO (http://vimeo.com). Watch and share your creative pinball and arcade videos.

Books and Magazines

Books about pinball cover many different topics, including games from particular eras. There are also encyclopedias of pinball, art and photography books, repair manuals, price guides, and schematics. Books can be ordered easily online and are available from pinball parts dealers, at shows, and in bookstores.

The pinball magazines are:

PinGame Journal—sold by subscription at www.pingamejournal.com.

Pinball Magazine—sold by the copy at www.pinball-magazine.com.

In Europe, there is *Spinner,* published in Dutch by the Dutch Pinball Association, and *Pinball Wizard Magazine,* published quarterly in the UK for members of the Pinball Owners Association.

Out-of-print books and magazines on pinball and arcade games can be found by searching the Internet.

Homemade Pinball

There are some pinball collectors who make homemade machines, either from scratch or by using an existing machine and modifying it. There are other collectors who upgrade their machine's boards, parts, protectors, and add LCDs, etc. There are many educational sources on the Internet on building and modifying your own pinball machine.

Some suggestions are:

Terry Cumming, "Build Your Own Game," *Pinball News,* Pinball Expo 2008, www.pinballnews.com/shows/expo2008/index5.html.

"Pinball News Learn," www.pinballnews.com/learn/index.html.

Jeri Ellsworth Channel, www.youtube.com/user/jeriellsworth/videos?query=pinball.

Virtual Pinball

Play pinball on your game system, phone, or tablet:

VP Forums, a gaming forum web site dedicated to the preservation of pinball through software simulation. http://www.vpforums.org/

Android Pinball Apps on Google Play.
https://play.google.com/store/search?q=pinball+games&c=apps

Pinball Arcade by Farsightstudio. To find out more, go to
http://www.farsightstudios.com/.

Pinball FX2 from Zen Studio San Francisco. http://www.pinballfx.com/

Pinball HD games are available at the iTunes Store.
https://itunes.apple.com/us/app/pinball-hd-collection/id484550839?mt=8

Pinballride by Massive Finger, Inc. Available for the iPhone, iPad, and Android smart phone or tablet. http://pinballride.com/

Pro Pinball. For more info, go to its Facebook page,
https://www.facebook.com/pro.pinball.

COLLECTOR'S CORNER

Electro-Mechanical Games of the 1960s and 70s

By Brian Saunders

As it always has been, the pinball hobby is in a constant state of transition. Some of us accept it as a natural course that cannot be changed, and some of us refuse to acknowledge it with every fiber of our being. I used to be more like the latter, but I am now gradually accepting the former. It's still hard to do, being the hard-core EM-loving man that I am, yet the times demand it. The simplistic appeal of a well-tuned EM is quite satisfying to some of us, just as much as a fully pimped-out LED-equipped creature machine would be to others. Is one more right to have around than another? No. It's all pinball!

In recent times, there has been much more interest in collecting the 90s games, and quite a few of the 80s machines are also being collected and restored more so than they used to be. Once again, the availability of repro parts has fueled this happening and made it easier for collectors to beautify their prized possessions. Not that the EM world has been left behind as far as repro parts—quite the contrary—there are more and more long-awaited backglasses being redone every year, new plastic sets are coming around especially for the Gottlieb and Bally games, and a few hardware pieces and playfields that have long been needed have finally come into being for the more popular titles that were beat to death in the arcades way back in the day. But the big action seems to be in the 90s machines right now. That being said and grudgingly admitted to, I'll get back on track now for what I was asked to write about: the collector's market for the EM machines and what's going on there.

Current Market for EM Games

All in all, it looks to me as if the typical well-known EMs are holding steady as far as selling prices, unless the game has some special pedigree to it. A few exceptions that I'll get to later are bringing the big bucks, but for commonly found titles, prices are not going down much, if at all, and that's a good sign to gauge the market by. If you take a look at eBay and other Internet sites frequently, you will see that the same titles come around for sale at regular intervals. Usually these are well-known titles that most of us experienced collectors would verify as being "good games," and thus they have value as collectibles, even if a lot of them were manufactured. The reason a game is on eBay is simple enough: when you're selling, you want the most people to see it, so it will get the best price for you. But what is the right price for a certain game even if there's a lot of it around?

FACTORS THAT AFFECT PRICING

The price can swing up and down for several reasons. One reason is **playability**—the game is just plain fun to play, regardless of how it might look. Sometimes it's the **artwork or theme** that is the major attraction. However, **rarity** may factor into the selling price for certain titles, and the overall gameplay is not necessarily the prime reason for owning them. For some titles, thousands were produced, and for others, only a few hundred were made, and this all factors into the selling price. Of course, collectors will argue their points of view about a particular game ad nauseum, and in the end, neither will be able to convince the other party that there is only one correct answer. But that's all part of the fun of collecting! If we all liked the same titles, it would be a dull pinball world, and the prices would always be the same. I always get a chuckle when a group of seasoned collectors will argue back and forth on rec.games.pinball about the attributes of pinball Machine A versus pinball Machine B, and what they ought to sell for. The passion is definitely there for all to see and the arguments are valid most of the time, but at day's end, there can be no clear winner. We all like what we like, and that's the way it is! And as we all know, the old axiom for what a game is worth is whatever somebody is willing to pay for it!

TRANSITION GAMES

My previous writing for this price guide had a section in it about the "transition games"—the ones made in both solid state (SS) and electro-mechanical (EM) versions. Now, I don't like my steaks to be cooked rare, but I definitely like my pinballs on the rare side, so this is an aspect of collecting that I take special interest in. Some of these rare ones came along in the 1976–1979 era, and most of them are getting a lot of collector scrutiny right now. Recently there has been one game coming up for sale that has been a hot topic of conversation—the Bally Mata Hari EM. This game was produced in late 1977 as a test game—or "sample game" if you like that term better—in order to see if the game would do well on chosen test locations before committing to making it in larger quantities. Documentation says that 170 Mata Haris were made in an EM format, and in this instance, the game did do well, so there was another 16,000+ of them manufactured but as solid state SS machines. Obviously, the EM version is the one the collector crowd looks for if they want a game with more collector value to it. This is not to say that the SS version of Mata Hari is looked at as undesirable—not at all. It's a fast-paced and fun drop-target game and maybe plays a tiny bit faster than its EM counterpart, but it's not very hard to find a game with a manufacturing run of 16,000 compared to one with a run of only 170, so the EM version commands a lot more money when one is unearthed. The same holds true for other U.S. manufacturers back then. Each one made a few transition games while they were changing their factories over to produce only solid state machines. In almost every case, the EM version will far outdistance its sister SS model in terms of the price it will bring when put on the open market, even if the game isn't all that great to play according to the preferences of today's players. Are there exceptions to this? Of course…we'll get to those later.

HIGHLY DESIRABLE GOTTLIEB GAMES

I'll change topic here just a little and make a comment on some Gottliebs that are highly desired as far as the collecting world is concerned. Some are transition games, and some are not. The bottom line is if you find a Gottlieb machine made from late 1977 and later that still has score reels in it, consider it a true "rarity." You'd better grab it if you can afford it. Gottlieb was the last to change their entire line to solid state, and this meant that a few extra EM models found their way out of the factory and into the world after the others had stopped making that style of game. Here's the Gottlieb EM machines to put on your list of "must finds" if you like your pinballs rare: Sinbad, Strange World, Cleopatra, Pyramid, Neptune, Eye of the Tiger, Joker Poker, Hit the Deck, Poseidon, Close Encounters of the Third Kind, Dragon, Gemini, Charlie's Angels, Rock Star, Blue Note, Solar Ride, Space Walk, and TKO. Most of these were built in limited numbers, and most were pretty good games to play. Some were not really all that rare if you look at the production numbers, but a lot of that production figure was sent out of the U.S. for various reasons, so the finding won't be all that easy if you're living in America. Still, some of them do come up for sale here in the States from time to time, while other titles almost never come up for sale. To get the book-beating big money for these games, condition is king. However, for any of these, you could piece one that's in rough shape back together and find plenty of market action, and it probably will exceed book value by a long way if two collectors want to fight hard to own it. Most of these titles were not on route all that long, which helps with the condition factor.

OTHER RARE GAMES

What else made back then should you look for? Not too many Williams EM transition games were produced, as this company jumped into the solid state platform pretty hard and didn't look back. Hot Tip EM is one machine that can still be found because the production numbers were comparatively high at 1300 units. It's not a bad player, but the EM value isn't all that different from the SS value. A title Williams did in very small numbers, supposedly around 80 of them, was the Lucky Seven EM, and it's like finding hen's teeth, so there's not much selling data to figure out its true value. Currently, only a couple of them are known about, but there should be a few more in hiding if people dig around enough. Worth a mention and even though it's not a transition game, the 1975 Black Gold is another rare machine with only 55 being built, so if you can land one of those, you've certainly got something unique. Actually, as far as the Williams transition games and their values are concerned, it can work in the opposite way: the SS models of some of their titles are the real hard ones to find. A scant few EM Grand Prix's and EM Aztecs were converted to solid state to test the new Williams SS platforms, and some have been seen displayed at pinball shows in the past, so these are the hot tickets as far as Williams rare transition collectibles of the 70s are concerned. The Bally Bow and Arrow SS also falls into this strange category—supposedly 17 of them were made. So what should you collect? The best answer is "what you like to play." Only you know what types of layouts, themes, playing styles, and eras of machines thrill you the most. But if you've read this far, I have to think that you must like EM machines a lot!

Collectible Rare EM Games

So here we go: for the purposes of collectability and the likely threat of some argument as to what is considered "rare" in the EM world (usually a total production under 300, but not always), I offer my list of the Top 25 1960s and 70s collectible rare EM pinball machines in what I feel is their order of market desirability right now, not necessarily their price:

BRIAN SAUNDERS' TOP 25 EM GAMES

1. Charlie's Angels. . . . . 1978 . . . . . . Gottlieb
2. Evel Knievel EM. . . . . 1977 . . . . . . Bally
3. TKO . . . . 1978 . . . . . . Gottlieb
4. Blue Note/Rock Star. . 1978 . . . . . . Gottlieb
5. Mata Hari EM . . . . . . 1977 . . . . . . Bally
6. Dimension. . . . . 1971 . . . . . . Gottlieb
7. Pleasure Isle. . . . . . . 1965 . . . . . . Gottlieb
8. Space Walk . . . . 1979 . . . . . . Gottlieb
9. Joker Poker . . . . 1978 . . . . . . Gottlieb
10. Neptune . . . . 1978 . . . . . . Gottlieb
11. Challenger. . . . . 1971 . . . . . . Gottlieb
12. Hit the Deck. . . . . . . 1978 . . . . . . Gottlieb
13. Eye of the Tiger . . . . 1978 . . . . . . Gottlieb
14. Close Encounters EM . 1978 . . . . . . Gottlieb
15. Gemini . . . . 1978 . . . . . . Gottlieb
16. Poseidon. . . . . 1978 . . . . . . Gottlieb
17. Black Jack EM . . . . . . 1977 . . . . . . Bally
18. Sinbad EM . . . . 1978 . . . . . . Gottlieb
19. Solar Ride EM . . . . . . 1979 . . . . . . Gottlieb
20. Double-Up . . . . 1971 . . . . . . Bally
21. Black Gold . . . . 1975 . . . . . . Williams
22. Bristol Hills. . . . . 1971 . . . . . . Gottlieb
23. Round Up . . . . 1971 . . . . . . Bally
24. King Rex . . . . 1970 . . . . . . Bally
25. Bali-Hi . . . . 1973 . . . . . . Bally

Author Bio

My first recollection of pinball started sometime in the very early 60s when I was maybe four or five years old. My mother handed me some nickels and sat me on a stool in front of some unknown woodrail machine in a small town restaurant/laundromat so she could be left alone long enough to sit and chat with one of her old childhood friends. Little did she know what she had just created.

This early experience lead to spending any paper route money earned as an eight-to-ten year old on playing all the EMs at the Brown Derby ice cream shop near the town swimming pool in Mattoon, Illinois, where we lived. Most of its machines were Gottliebs, as I recall, and were quite unforgiving to the novice player. Just about anywhere I could find another pinball, I played it without end until I knew it well.

During my teenage years, a nice clean teen recreation center called Mr. D's opened up near the high school. The center had a weekly food reward program for getting the high scores on each of their eight or so machines, which were mostly Ballys. This pretty well kept me fed me all through high school and junior college, as hardly a week would go by that I wouldn't get high score on one or two of them. My favorite game back then was a 1970 Bally Big Valley which featured multi-ball action. It is still my favorite today.

I bought one of the games they had at Mr. D's while I was in college in the late 70s—a Bally Sea Ray—and kept it for about 25 years while I moved through other various interests: fixing and reselling muscle cars of all varieties, playing keyboards and trumpet in the school jazz bands, owning a fast food restaurant in the 1980s, and doing some drag racing all through the 90s.

 When the Internet became available to the masses in the late 90s, I finally signed up and found other pinball people to converse with, and of course, found eBay. This began a gradual movement out of car activities and into pinball collecting, since the machines were getting much easier to locate. After several years of repairing and flipping pins, it began to dawn on me that I was within about 35 of having one of all the 149 Bally EM titles that had been produced since 1963, so I embarked on that journey in earnest about 2004. I made many long road trips all throughout the eastern half of the country where I'd find more games for the collection and helped others out with their needs, too, while doing so.

 At the present, I still haven't found all the Ballys I need, but I'm down to only three to go. All are seriously tough finds of course, being sample games or prototypes, but the last five I've gotten have been, too, and yet here they are. Hope springs eternal!

Today, my wife Teresa, college-student daughter Samantha, and I live just outside the vast metropolis of Lerna, Illinois, population 300. It has been remarked that it has to be some kind of record to have more pinballs than there are people in the town you live in. This is surely the sign of a true "sickness." But as we well know, all true collectors would give anything to catch the disease!

To learn more about Brian Saunders

"Picking up a Bimbo in Boston: A Pinball Collector's Adventures on the High-ways of North America," audio seminar, Hartland Supershow 2008.
http://supershow.popbumper.com/seminars.html

Woodrail Pricing—The Big Picture

By Gordon A. Hasse, Jr.

Preface

While there have been woodrail pinball machines since the game's origin back in the early 1930s, today the term *woodrail* is generally understood to mean domestically made, flipper-equipped pinball machines produced during the post-World War II era—beginning with Gottlieb's HUMPTY DUMPTY in October 1947 and ending with the following games from the indicated manufacturers:

Bally: CARNIVAL (August 1957).

Chicago Coin: CAPRI (August 1956).

Exhibit Supply (ESCO): TRIGGER (January 1951).

Genco: FUN FAIR (March 1958).

Gottlieb: FOTO-FINISH (January 1961).

Keeney: HI STRAIGHT (January 1960).

Marvel: HIT PARADE (August 1948).

United: RED SHOES (November 1950).

Williams: SERENADE (May 1960).

Although many bingo machines, one- and two-ball gambling machines, and pitch and bats made during the postwar years were equipped with woodrails, as a collecting category, the term is typically applied only to traditional five- and three-ball amusement pinballs.

While many pre- and post-WW II flipperless games were housed in woodrail cabinets, and many of them are notable for interesting features and excellent artwork, they are typically not considered to be woodrails within the narrow definition observed by most of today's collectors.

A large number of conversion games housed in woodrail cabinets were produced during and after WW II by companies such as Block Marble Company, Victory Games, NASCO (Nate Schneller), and others. None of these conversion games are considered part of the collectible universe of woodrails.

Finally, while many games with woodrails were manufactured outside of the United States, these games are not generally considered as belonging to the woodrail category that today's domestic woodrail collectors prize and pursue.

There are some rare exceptions to the definition of woodrails as it applies to pinball collecting today. For instance, although Gottlieb's near-bingo WATCH

MY LINE (July 1951) and the kicking post-equipped GUYS DOLLS (May 1953) lack flippers, both games were manufactured for amusement only and released during the woodrail era, so they are ordinarily considered woodrails by collectors. The same logic applies to games like Exhibit's SHORT STOP (May 1948), which substitutes a movable bumper for flippers, and to its flipperless NEW CONTACT (October 1948).

It's with the above definitions in mind that any price discussion of woodrails must take place.

The Woodrail Mystique

Let's start by admitting that woodrails aren't for everyone. People tend to collect the pinball machines that they grew up playing and nostalgia is a prime motivator. The majority of serious woodrail collectors that I've known played these games as children or young adults. For those born before or after the woodrail era, woodrails, like Scotch, are an acquired taste.

However, with the recent rise of retro-arcades and pinball museums, the proliferation of pinball shows, and increasing numbers of major collectors willing to open their woodrail collections to others, pinball enthusiasts of all ages are now getting an opportunity to play woodrail pinball—many of them for the very first time. As the unfamiliar is slowly becoming familiar, the games are increasingly recognized for their intrinsic merit. And their beauty, rarity, and design brilliance have begun to create converts.

We see collectors weaned on electronic games suddenly looking to add a choice woodrail or two to an otherwise modern collection. And while the market for woodrails today is still driven primarily by people who played these games in their youth, the pinball collecting market as a whole is now beginning to take a closer look at woodrails.

There are a multitude of reasons why:

- **The woodrail era represented the coming-of-age of the pinball machine.** By the end of the era, virtually all of the components of the modern game had been introduced and were in place: pairs of flippers, with their tips facing inward; guarding drains and out-holes at the bottom of playfields; pop-bumpers; dead bumpers; cyclonic kickers; slot or recovery shooters; kick-out, trap, and gobble holes; even primitive ramps!

- **Legendary pinball artists Leroy Parker and George Molentin reached the peak of their creativity during the woodrail era.** Between them, they practically defined the look and aesthetic of modern pinball. While computer generated images, photo-realism, and derivative subjects now dominate pinball art, the work of these two masters of the "Golden Age" has never been eclipsed as far as creating exactly the right mood for the subject at hand and engaging the player in an encoded story line.

- **The pioneers of modern pinball design were all active in the industry at this time.** Among them were design geniuses Harvey Heiss, Steve Kordek, Harry Mabs, Wayne Neyens, Sam Stern, and Harry Williams. In a very real sense, everything that came before was prelude and everything that followed was postscript to the games created by these industry giants.

- **Woodrails deal with original rather than derivative themes.** Unlike modern pinball games, which are based on licensed properties, woodrail pinballs feature unique and original themes. Woodrails still drew their subject matter from the surrounding culture but showed originality and inventiveness in interpreting this material and allowing the players to create and embroider their own fantasies surrounding the games' central themes. Call these games naïve, call them innocent, call them simplistic…call them what you will. But today woodrail games resonate strongly with collectors and non-collectors alike as icons of a simpler, often better time, and they stand on their own as original works of the imagination.

- **Woodrail pinball machines are user-friendly and intuitive.** A quick examination of the score and instruction cards on most woodrail machines was all the preparation players needed to fully understand and enjoy the play on games of that era. Two or three games were sufficient to provide the player with a high confidence level about the game's objectives, features, and award structure. In dramatic contrast to modern games, woodrails were designed to encourage trial and repeat play by novice and experienced players alike and provide the casual player with a satisfying play experience for his nickel or dime.

- **Woodrail pinball machines award players with multiple routes to specials and lots of replays.** This is one of the most alluring aspects of woodrails for those familiar with these wonderful games. Modern pinball machines offer very few replays. Free games are awarded only for high scores and the one-in-ten chance of matching numbers. Woodrails are celebrated for the number of ways the player can score replays and the large number of replays that could be won during any single game. For example, Gottlieb's 1952 QUEEN OF HEARTS and 1954 DRAGONETTE offer players five separate ways to win replays. Several of Gottlieb's single gobble hole, multiple special games award from 10 to 12 replays when the gobble hole is lit for EXTRA SPECIAL, and completing all the numbers on SWEET ADD-A-LINE awards 26! Williams' 1951 HAYBURNERS awards 20 replays when your selected horse wins the backbox horse race on the first ball. And countless other woodrails offer both multiple routes to specials and large numbers of replays for achieving them.

- **With the exception of the multi-players, woodrails represent pinball in its purest form.** Single-player woodrail pinball machines feature five actual balls. Each of the five balls is raised onto the playfield manually by the player-operated ball elevator. The player determines the launch speed and trajectory of his shot by pulling the plunger back to the desired mark on the ball shooter gauge and then releasing it. Careful launching of the balls, flipper skills, and shaking abilities alone determine success. Until the introduction of the multi-player, there was an unbroken and almost spiritual bond between the game and the player. This intimacy and deep player engagement disappeared with the advent of the multiple-player game. Sad . . . since the uninterrupted, one-to-one correspondence between man and machine is one of the greatest appeals of woodrails for today's collectors and admirers.

The Determinants of Woodrail Pricing

The five variables that contribute to the price of woodrail pinball machines are similar to those that determine prices for many other collectibles. They are DESIRABILITY, RARITY, CONDITION, AGE, and the prevailing MARKET.

DESIRABILTY

Desirability is, by far, the most important determinant of price when it comes to woodrail pinball machines. Generally speaking, the greater the number of collectors who consider a particular game desirable, the higher the price it will bring to the seller. Accordingly, the 'market' for a particular woodrail is the collective expression of those who deem it desirable, aspire to own it, and have the means to do so.

Gottlieb woodrails have traditionally been desired by woodrail collectors more than the games of the other eight manufacturers. And a small subset of Gottlieb woodrails which includes MERMAID, KNOCKOUT, DRAGONETTE, NIAGARA, SPOT BOWLER, SLUGGIN' CHAMP, DAISY MAY, TWIN BILL, QUEEN OF HEARTS, HAWAIIAN BEAUTY, MARBLE QUEEN, MYSTIC MARVEL, and a handful of others have been desired above all others by today's woodrail collectors.

As the collecting hobby has matured and more woodrail examples from all nine manufacturers have surfaced, there has been a growing appreciation of Williams games with titles such as SKYWAY, ARMY NAVY, COD, SHOOT THE MOON, 4 CORNERS, NINE SISTERS, STAR POOL, RACE THE CLOCK, PERKY, GUSHER, SEA WOLF, WONDERLAND, and a few others which have become increasingly desirable in the eyes of woodrail collectors.

While interest in woodrail games from the remaining seven manufacturers has never been particularly strong, there is growing interest in them as well—especially among beginning collectors who wish to own woodrails but are currently priced out of the market for Gottlieb and Williams games.

There has been little interest in the multi-player woodrails of any of the manufacturers because replays are limited to high score and matching numbers at the game's end. However Gottlieb's 1954 SUPER JUMBO and DELUXE JUMBO and its 1955 DUETTE and DUETTE DELUXE have drawn some collector interest since they are respectively Gottlieb's first four- and two-player games. Williams' first multi-player, the 1955 four-player RACE THE CLOCK, is a little- known but extremely interesting and fun to play woodrail—but it almost never surfaces. Among Gottlieb's multi-player woodrails, its roto-target games like 1957 MAJESTIC and SUPER CIRCUS and 1958 PICNIC are among the most fun to play. As an aside, Gottlieb reserved the four-player format for what it considered to be its best multi-player games, releasing the others as two-players. Player experience did not always prove true to its expectations.

RARITY

While rarity, in itself, doesn't always equate to desirability or high prices, in the case of woodrails it often contributes to both. Good analogies can be drawn between collectible pinball machines and collectible comic books and baseball cards. Comic books from the Golden Age (the late 1930s through the late 1940s) saw the introduction of hugely popular super heroes that remain in great demand to this day (Superman, Batman, Captain America, Wonder Woman, etc.). Surviving copies of these early comics are eagerly sought by collectors, not simply for their historical importance and entertainment value but because they are extremely scarce. Why? Because most comics from this period were donated to paper drives during WW II. In general the Golden Age comics commanding the highest prices are first issues, those introducing new characters (or character 'origin' stories), and those featuring the most popular of the era's numerous superheroes.

In a similar vein, collectors of baseball cards favor the early tobacco- and gum-issued cards because of their historical significance and rarity. Few pre-1950 gum or tobacco baseball cards exist today in large numbers. Original runs prior to the 1950s were a fraction of what they are today, and most early cards were lost, destroyed, or discarded over time. Today's baseball cards are made in huge numbers by many manufacturers and enjoy a broad collectors' market. But because they exist in such abundance, they have little monetary value versus the far rarer surviving pre-1950s cards. There may be tens of thousands of examples of any specific modern baseball card available for sale, while the supply of most pre-1950s baseball cards is severely limited. A prime example is the famous 1911 Turkey Red Cigarettes' Honus Wagner baseball card #206 (once owned by Wayne Gretzky) which sold for $2.8 million in 2007. Another is the 2008 sale of a 1914 Babe Ruth rookie baseball card produced by The Baltimore Sun newspaper (one of just three known to exist) that sold for $517,000 in 2008.

Given the mind set of collectors, it seems safe to say that the prices of woodrail pinball machines can be expected to continue rising, not simply because they are desirable, but because they are also quite rare. While few woodrail collectors view their collections as investments, many enjoy the cachet and exclusivity of owning truly rare games.

- **A very limited number of woodrail titles were produced.** Keeney made just four different titles! Marvel made just six. Even mighty Bally released just nine woodrail flipper models, concentrating its efforts on bingos and one- and two-ball gambling pinballs at the time. United made just 23 titles before turning its full attention to bingos and shuffle alleys. Exhibit Supply produced just 25 before exiting pinball entirely with TRIGGER in early 1951. Genco made about 30 and Chicago Coin made 31. Mighty Gottlieb, the powerhouse producer during the immediate post-WW II years, released 147 woodrail titles if you include flipperless GUYS DOLLS and WATCH MY LINE. That's almost 20% more game models than its nearest rival, Williams, who produced 124.

  If you add together all the woodrail flipper game titles made by the nine U. S. manufacturers that produced them in the post-WW II years, it totals just 399 models! Even if this accounting is off by as much as 5% there are unquestionably less than 425 game titles in the universe of woodrail flipper games.

  As of this writing, The Internet Pinball Database (IPDB) currently provides photo documentation of 5,429 pinball game models. Even if there are as many as 425 woodrail titles, they represent less than 8% of the photo-identified pinball games listed on the IPDB.

Mueting and Hawkins identified more than 6,000 different pinball titles in the last edition of their *Pinball Collectors Resource*. Based on their findings, our 425 woodrail titles represent just over 7% of that number!

And while most woodrail collectors favor Gottlieb games, those 147 Gottlieb woodrail titles represent less than 3% of the game models pictured on the IPDB and barely 2.5% of the game titles identified by Meuting and Hawkins!

It's also worth mentioning that of the 147 Gottlieb woodrail games, 30 of them are the far less desirable multi-players which are seldom collected. Because, as previously mentioned, except for the 1958 two-player PICNIC, the only way to win replays on Gottlieb multi-player woodrails was by accumulating points or matching numbers at game's end.

Despite the fact that Gottlieb's multi-player woodrails sported some superb Parker art on their backglasses and playfields, their play value pales in contrast to Gottlieb's multi-featured single-players of the period.

Since Gottlieb pinball machines have traditionally been the overwhelming favorites of woodrail collectors, it now becomes clear that the 'Cadillacs' of the woodrail era are the 117 Gottlieb single-player games made between 1947 and 1961, which represent less than 2% of the game titles identified by Meuting and Hawkins!

No matter how you cut it, woodrails are in short supply and the most popular titles have attracted buyers from across the collecting spectrum.

- **The production runs of the great majority of woodrails were short.**
  Not only are the number of woodrail models severely limited, most models were produced in rather limited numbers. By the 1970s Gottlieb, Williams, and Bally were all enjoying record breaking production runs. Gottlieb's ROYAL FLUSH (March 1976) sold more than 12,000 units, while SINBAD (February 1978) came very close to that number. Williams sold more than 11,000 SPACE MISSIONS in May of 1976 and more than 19,000 units of FLASH in January 1979. Sales of Bally's CAPTAIN FANTASTIC (July 1976) exceeded 16,000, and their EIGHT BALL (September 1977) topped 20,000.

Not so in the days of the woodrails.

In most cases, Gottlieb's woodrail production runs were the longest of any of the manufacturers. But even its top-10 selling games of the 1950s, at the peak of pinball's "Golden Age," were puny relative to sales of later games. Their #1 selling pinball machine during the 1950s was ROYAL FLUSH (April 1957). It sold 3,400 units. Their #10 best seller of the decade, GRAND SLAM (April 1953), sold 1,800.

But typical Gottlieb production runs from that era were in the 1,000 to 1,500 range with many games selling far less. In fact some, like GLAMOR and 4-BELLES, sold as few as 300 and 400 units respectively! Evidence strongly suggests that production runs of other game manufacturers during the woodrail era were a fraction of the Gottlieb numbers in most cases!

It's interesting to note that **very few items requiring sophisticated manufacturing techniques were made in quantities as small as the production runs of individual woodrail titles.** Notable exceptions were the production runs of the 1957 and 1958 Cadillac Eldorado Brougham. Just 400 of these super deluxe automobiles were made in 1957 and a mere 304 were produced in 1958.

Today, while the majority of those 704 Cadillac Eldorado Broughams still exist in the hands of car enthusiasts and collectors, the overwhelming majority of woodrail pinball machines have long since vanished.

- **A very small percentage of the original production run of any specific woodrail pinball machine survives today in the domestic market.** Limited survival rates of these more than half-century-old games add further to the scarcity of woodrails already limited by small production runs and a small universe of models.

While consumers were the target market for those super-luxury Cadillac Eldorado Broughams mentioned earlier, the amusement operator was the target for sales of woodrail pinball machines, and there's a world of difference.

Although woodrail pinball machines were relatively durable and fairly simple for operators to maintain and repair, they were viewed as readily disposable as soon as their ability to earn on location fell below a certain threshold. Unlike today's games, the average street life of a woodrail pinball machine was usually less than three years.

Both Gottlieb and Williams were releasing a new woodrail title nearly every month. The constant supply of new titles played to the operators' need to continuously offer novelty and sustained income to their locations. But it also contributed to the rapid turnover of woodrail operators' game inventories.

When an operator bought a new woodrail from a distributor, he would first place it in one of his best locations. This usually meant a business that was clean and well kept and enjoyed heavy traffic and lots of customer turnover. As soon as the 'take' from this new game dropped below a certain threshold, the operator would move the game to another location. As time went on, the now aging machine would be placed in less and less desirable locations until its earning power was exhausted or it was no longer fit to play.

At that point the operator would either attempt to sell his 'used' game to a smaller, less affluent operator or to a distributor for overseas shipment. Alternatively, he would use older, tired games as 'donors' (stripping them of parts to use as replacements on newer games) or, in many cases, simply destroy them. (As a kid I saw piles of woodrail pin games put out for trash by operators!)

Because most operators during the woodrail era were paranoid about the possibility of local competition, sales to private homes and individuals were almost non-existent. And the few games that wound up in basements or rec rooms were often put out for the trash man when they stopped working. The miles of wire and dozens of switches and relays were intimidating to most homeowners and very few operators were interested in doing service calls.

Serial numbers of surviving woodrails compiled by Steve Young, Sam Harvey, and others suggest the likelihood that **just 1–2% of woodrail pinballs survive today in the domestic market.** Many woodrails left the United States at the time of manufacture, and many used machines were shipped to Canada and abroad after they had rotated through an operator's route locations. Others met their ends domestically in city dumps, leaky storage, at the hands of vandals, and in some cases, as the result of confiscation by local police.

As a result, we might expect to find somewhere in the range of 22 to 44 surviving examples of Gottlieb's iconic 1952 QUEEN OF HEARTS production run of 2,200 games and just 6-12 surviving examples of Gottlieb's run of 600 MERMAIDS from 1951. By way of contrast, roughly half of the 1957 and 1958 Cadillac Eldorado Broughams mentioned earlier survive, and meticulously restored examples typically sell for six figures.

AGE

Generally speaking the later woodrails are more exciting to play and offer a greater number of features than the early ones. Collector experience with Gottlieb games is rather typical. Desirability and prices tend to generally increase in line with technical advances and added play features.

While demand remains high for HUMPTY DUMPTY, the world's first flipper game, there is not a lot of interest in the other six Gottlieb games in the "Fairy Tale" series. But popularity among collectors immediately begins to increase after the six-flipper Fairy Tale games, beginning with BARNACLE BILL.

Desirability further increases for Gottlieb woodrails following the introduction of the 'pop' bumper on BOWLING CHAMP in February 1949, and grows more interesting still with the advent of two flippers in the 'normal' tips-adjacent position guarding the outhole, first featured on JUST 21 in January 1950. The four consecutive machines (JUST 21, SELECT-A-CARD, BUFFALO BILL, and BANK-A-BALL), which debuted pairs of flippers in the 'normal' position, were turret-shooter games which proved to be a fad and are not highly sought by today's collectors (despite the fact that BUFFALO BILL and BANK-A-BALL are extremely rare!). However, the 'new' flipper positioning on these games paved the way for the reappearance of 'normally' positioned flippers on other games from 1950, like ROCKETTES in August, THE 4 HORSEMEN in September, and SPOT BOWLER in October—the latter being perhaps the best-playing game of the early flipper era!

Gottlieb 'woodies' took another step forward in desirability when coil-controlled reset banks replaced hand-activated push chutes on TRIPLETS in July of 1950, and another level of play and collectability accompanied the advent of 'cyclonic' kickers on DOUBLE FEATURE in December of that year.

From mid-1950 through the introduction of the multi-players, Gottlieb reigned supreme and its woodrails from this era tend to attract considerable collector interest. Almost any game Gottlieb made during the four-year period, from SPOT BOWLER in October 1950 through the introduction of four-player SUPER JUMBO in October 1954, warrants serious collector attention, and many of these games command some of the highest woodrail prices. And, from this collector's perspective, deservedly so.

Once multi-players were introduced into the mix, Gottlieb began alternating them on the production line, making single-players one month and multi-players the next. For the most part, Gottlieb's multi-player woodrails hold little interest for current collectors and are priced accordingly.

On the other hand, many collectors find the superb run of centrally-located gobble hole, multiple special games of 1955, 1956, and 1957 (GYPSY QUEEN, SWEET ADD-A-LINE, WISHING WELL, FRONTIERSMAN, EASY ACES, HARBOR LITES, DERBY DAY, CLASSY BOWLER, and WORLD CHAMP) to be among the most desirable of any of the Gottlieb woodrails. FRONTIERSMAN from November 1955, CLASSY BOWLER from July 1956, and WORLD CHAMP from August 1957 are excellent examples of this genre and tend to command premium prices.

The introduction of roto-targets on MAJESTIC ushered in another period of highly desirable Gottlieb woodrails beginning with the production of 3,400 units of the card game ROYAL FLUSH in May, 1957. Collector interest remains relatively high on Gottlieb woodrail single players from that point until the introduction of single-player reel scoring on MISS ANNABELLE in August 1959 and then falls off to some extent until the woodrail era ends with a partial run of FOTO-FINISH in woodrail cabinets in January 1961.

While Williams made some very beautiful games in the late 1940s and early 1950s, they are less exciting and less valued by today's collectors than its later games which replace the impulse flippers they used previously with flippers powered by double-wound coils. The resulting increase in flipping power and the ability to catch balls on upright flippers add tremendously to the value and desirability of later Williams woodrails.

The desirability of woodrails made by other manufacturers tends to follow a timeline similar to Gottlieb in most cases, with each new playfield feature or action component increasing collector interest and pricing accordingly.

CONDITION

Other things being equal, a woodrail in excellent condition is worth multiples of a woodrail in poor condition. That said, the market has changed significantly in the last two decades. Today resources exist that did not exist in the past. In the early days of woodrail collecting, collectors would tend to shun games with badly flaking backglasses or heavily worn playfields. Curled playfield plastics were another huge barrier to purchase since, like backglasses, they were specific to each woodrail model.

In today's market, products exist and techniques have been developed that permit collectors to restore even seemingly terminal woodrail cases to excellent cosmetic and mechanical condition. Lack of restoration parts, materials, and expertise is no longer the critical issue. Now the main barrier to woodrail restoration is adequate money, time, or a combination of the two.

Parts and supplies are readily available from The Pinball Resource and other vendors. Reproduction backglasses are available for many of the most popular woodrails (especially Gottlieb) from The Shay Arcade Group, Ron and Nancy Webb, and others. The same is true for reproduction bumper caps (The Pinball Resource) and playfield plastics (our friends Lee and Gordon at Pinball Rescue in Australia and the Shay Group here at home). And recently the final frontier has been crossed as a limited number of woodrail playfields have now been reproduced.

Several people associated with the pinball collecting hobby also provide professional backglass, playfield, cabinet, and electro-mechanical restorations, and many hobbyists (in particular Clay Harrell, the late Russ Jensen, and others) have researched, developed, and generously shared their own techniques for accomplishing these tasks.

The providers, materials, parts, supplies, information, and techniques required to professionally restore woodrails now exist in relative abundance. And almost any woodrail owner wishing to upgrade pieces in his or her collection must necessarily look to them for help at some point along the way.

Generally speaking, this involves the exchange of cash for products and/ or services. And all of the things that go into a professional restoration have sizeable price tags.

Depending upon the number of pieces in a set of reproduction plastics, the price tag can reach $125 or more. Reproduction backglasses typically run from $265 to $300. And replacement bumper caps are priced in the range of $3 to $12 apiece. When available, reproduction playfields can be extremely pricey.

Work by professional woodrail restorers is usually billed on an hourly basis and can add up quickly. But do not confuse price with value. The prices charged for professional restoration products and services are more than fair, given the skill required and the limited scope of the market served. It's just important to be aware of the potential costs involved before purchasing a game that needs extensive restoration.

As you can readily see, there is ample justification for the difference in price between an excellent original or well-restored woodrail and a basket case. But because of the relative scarcity of surviving woodrails in any condition, the difference in price between a machine in excellent condition and one in poor condition may well be less than you'd expect.

Since the number of survivors of virtually every woodrail title is in the low two figures, it just goes to reason that scarcity will drive prices up on the existing examples in any condition— particularly for titles that are highly desirable.

MARKET

Market conditions will always impact the price of woodrails, sometimes in surprising ways. One of the most interesting is what's referred to as a 'generational' dynamic.

At the moment a significant representation of the best woodrails are in the hands of larger collectors and a few museums and retro arcades. In most cases these games will not return to the market until their owners pass on, downsize their living arrangements as they age, or, in the case of the museums and retro-arcades, close their doors.

As a result, a meaningful percentage of all available woodrails are effectively off the market— many for decades to come. And, given the small percentage of surviving examples of any specific woodrail title, this puts additional upward pressure on price for the few examples that do come to market.

Another market dynamic operating in woodrail collecting is the 'discovery' factor. The last woodrail was made in January 1961, 51 years ago at the time of this writing, and the earliest woodrails are now 64 years old!

During the intervening years most of the surviving woodrails in the domestic market have been unearthed. The large caches in the warehouses, barns, and storage sheds of ex-operators and distributors have long since been discovered. In fact, it's quite likely that most of the still undiscovered woodrails are now in private homes and that they are likely few and far between.

In 1977 a cache of 22,000 Golden Age comic books in superb original condition, known as "The Mile High" collection, was unearthed in Colorado. This discovery set new standards of price and condition for these highly desirable collectibles and dramatically increased the number of issues available to hungry collectors of ultra-rare titles such as *Batman #1, Superman #1, Action Comics #1,* and a host of others.

Sadly, I don't believe that we're likely to discover a "Mile High" cache of pristine woodrails now, or anytime in the future, except in the existing collections of the largest collectors.

Therefore, anyone interested in adding a woodrail to his/her collection today should be prepared for prices that reflect a very limited supply.

But there is some good news. While the largest collectors have cherry picked the woodrail market and cornered most of the highly desirable Gottlieb and Williams games, for the most part, their collections are complete (or nearly so) and their appetites sated. In addition, since several collectors purchased more than one example of many of the games in their collections and melded two or more to create one pristine "keeper," their duplicates sometime come to market at affordable prices.

In addition, there are a reasonable number of woodrails available for purchase from time to time from the seven manufacturers other than Gottlieb and Williams.

The Future

What does the future hold for the prices of woodrails?

I expect to see a continued escalation driven by several factors:

- **Smaller woodrail collectors will want to add to their collections** as space and finances permit. I expect that to be a continuing trend.

- **Completists looking to round out their collections will also be vying for the scarce woodrails available.** By completists, I mean those who are trying to achieve closure on a pre-determined goal. For example, they may wish to own one game from every decade or one game from every post-war manufacturer or as many non-pitch and bat baseball pinballs as possible. A collector of Blackiana or minstrel items might find a Gottlieb MINSTREL MAN or an Exhibit BANJO the crown jewel of his or her collecting interest. While those interested in futurism might covet a Williams SKYWAY, a Gottlieb ROCKET SHIP, or a Genco FLYING SAUCERS. In the most extreme cases a completist may seek to own one of every woodrail of a given manufacturer.

- **Pinball collectors of every description will continue to expand their purview.** As indicated earlier, as more people discover woodrails, a percentage of them express interest in ownership. I expect this number to grow as opportunities to play woodrails at shows, retro-arcades, museums, and in private collections continue to increase.

- **New pinball collectors will continue to enter the market.** The last decade has seen a dramatic rise in the number of people joining the collecting hobby. Also, as noted earlier, we have seen a gratifying increase in the number and types of parts and services available to woodrail owners. As a result, in most cases, new collectors (as well as established ones) can purchase woodrails with the expectation that, given the financial resources and/or requisite skills, they can accomplish high levels of restoration. Stated another way, woodrails that a decade ago were passed over as 'basket cases' today represent quite viable candidates for restoration to excellent working and cosmetic condition. This translates to increased demand and higher prices on woodrails in any condition.

- **People with no direct interest in pinball will discover woodrails and purchase them for motives quite different than pinball collectors.** I foresee a time, in the not too distant future, when woodrail pinballs will become recognized and actively sought after by a broader audience as quintessential examples of our rich popular culture heritage. Like carousel horses, player and reproducing pianos, barber chairs, Packards, Cords, Dusenbergs, and hundreds of other artifacts from our material past, woodrail pinball machines will reach a broader market of discerning buyers who may have little or no interest in pinball per se but recognize the iconic virtues of these beautiful old machines. Lovers of the fine and graphic arts, decorators, designers, collectors of other types of games and other forms of coin-op, even lovers of 1940s and 50s furniture and other décor items will enter and expand the market.

In closing I'd offer the following advice to prospective buyers of woodrail pinballs. Never buy these games as investments, even though they may someday be worth multiples of their current value. Buy them because you enjoy owning, playing, repairing, restoring, admiring, and sharing them. Buy them because they enhance your living space and increase your enjoyment of time spent there. That way, you'll never feel as though you paid too much or received too little when you decide to add a woodrail to your home or office.

GORDO'S FAVORITE WOODRAILS

A chronological list of my favorite woodrails follows. While play value was always paramount for me, I was also heavily influenced in my selection of favorites by the artwork of the games I played.

GOTTLIEB
OLD FAITHFUL, December 1949
JOKER, November 1950
KNOCK OUT, December 1950
MERMAID, May 1951
NIAGARA, December 1951
CROSSROADS, May 1952
CHINATOWN, October 1952
CORONATION, November 1952
QUEEN OF HEARTS, December 1952
FLYING HIGH, February 1953
(4-player)
GRAND SLAM, April 1953
MARBLE QUEEN, June 1953
ARABIAN KNIGHTS, November 1953
MYSTIC MARVEL, February 1954
HAWAIIAN BEAUTY, May 1954
DRAGONETTE, June 1954
DAISY MAY, June 1954
4-BELLES, September 1954 (same design as DRAGONETTE)
DIAMOND LILL, December 1954
TWIN BILL, January 1955
SLUGGIN' CHAMP, April 1955
FRONTIERSMAN, November 1955
HARBOR LITES, February 1956
CLASSY BOWLER, July 1956
AUTO RACE, September 1956
ACE HIGH, February 1957
ROYAL FLUSH, March 1957
WORLD CHAMP, August 1957
LIGHTNING BALL, October 1959

WILLIAMS
SHOOT THE MOON, November 1951
FOUR CORNERS October 1952
TWENTY GRAND, December 1952
C.O.D., September 1953
ARMY NAVY, October 1953
DEALER, December 1953
SKYWAY, February 1954
WONDERLAND, April 1954
STAR POOL, July 1954
RACE THE CLOCK, March 1955
FUN HOUSE, August 1956 (4-player)
PERKY, September 1956

BALLY
BALLS-A-POPPIN', August 1956

Author's Bio

Gordon A. Hasse, Jr., aka "Gordo," has been intimately involved in the world of pinball machines since playing them as a boy in the candy stores, soda fountains, bowling alleys, pool halls, and amusement arcades of his native Philadelphia during the 1950s.

He owned his first pinball, a 1953 Williams Army Navy, at age 12. Today that game remains part of a 240-piece collection of 1940s and 1950s woodrail pinball machines that he donated to the Pacific Pinball Museum in 2009.

That collection is notable for containing at least one of every D. Gottlieb & Company single-player woodrail, from Gottlieb's first post-WWII Stage Door Canteen of 1945 through the last single-player to be released with a portion of its production in a woodrail cabinet—Foto-Finish of 1961.

Hasse and his business partner in Silverball Amusements, Steve Young, were the editors and publishers of the first-ever magazine dedicated exclusively to the interests of pinball collectors, players, and historians.

The Pinball Collectors' Quarterly *was published during 1983 and 1984 and, though it anticipated by several decades today's strong interest in all aspects of pinball, the pioneering publication was a lightning rod for a diverse and geographically dispersed group of pinball collectors and enthusiasts previously unknown to each other. In fact, subscribers to* The Pinball Collectors' Quarterly *served as the mailing list for invitations to Chicago's initial Pinball Expo in 1984, the first annual gathering of pinball collectors, players, and enthusiasts from around the world.*

Hasse wrote the first seminar/lecture for the first Chicago Pinball Expo. This hour-long illustrated presentation examined the artwork of legendary pinball artist Roy Parker and was so well received that he later wrote and delivered several other presentations at subsequent Chicago Expos.

In addition to his Chicago Expo presentations, Hasse delivered an illustrated speech on the popular culture significance of 1950s pinball art to an academic audience at the joint convention of the Popular Culture Association and the American Culture Association in Toronto during the spring of 1990.

More recently he has made presentations at three of the previous Pacific Pinball Museum Pinball Expos, in Marin County, California—the world's largest pinball show.

Hasse served as consultant, proofreader, editor, and co-publisher with

Steve Young of the first two volumes of Dick Bueschel's planned five-volume Encyclopedia of Pinball. *Upon Bueschel's untimely death, he assumed responsibility for writing and publishing the remaining three volumes—a retirement project he hopes to address soon.*

During the last several decades, under the pen name Gordo, he has written more than 50 articles, book reviews, editorials, and blogs on pinball, related coin-operated amusement machines, and other popular culture topics for publications both here and abroad.

Hasse has served as a consultant, in the pinball category, for the Warman's Price Guide *series and has been quoted extensively in collector, hobbyist, and mainstream books and publications, including a feature article on pinball collecting in the autumn 1996 issue of Cigar Aficionado.*

His 12-page "100 Milestones in the Early Development of Pinball Collecting," which appears as the conclusion to Michael Shalhoub's 2008 The Pinball Compendium: Electromechanical Era *is considered the most authoritative history to date of the beginnings of the North American collecting community.*

He is currently at work on a mass-market book on the subject of pinball art, a definitive woodrail glossary, and a comprehensive, illustrated manual for collectors covering the subject of woodrail pinball restoration

A major three-month long holiday exhibit of portions of his antique pinball collection, related memorabilia, and extensive pop-culture commentary filled 20 floor-to-ceiling display cases in the lobby of the Park Avenue Atrium in midtown Manhattan from December 1993 through February 1994.

The New York Times *and other New York media provided extensive coverage of the three-month long exhibit,* Remember Pinball. *The presentation of pinball as art and a mirror of contemporary popular culture drew thousands of interested visitors. It was also deemed to be the most successful show ever mounted in the lobby display area of the J. Walter Thompson headquarters building by Olympia & York's longtime Corporate Curator Ludwig Datene.*

A portion of Hasse's vast collection also provided retro-theming during one of the prestigious Philadelphia Antiques Show, held annually at the West Philadelphia Armory.

Hasse is widely known as an expert on the woodrail pinball machines of the post-WW II era and is constantly answering inquiries about his favorite subject that arrive daily from around the globe.

In 2009, Hasse, along with California mega-collector Richard Conger, received the Pacific Pinball Museum's Lifetime Achievement Award for his "contributions in promoting the history and preservation of pinball."

Hasse spent most of his career as an advertising agency Creative Director in New York City and is currently a Professor of Advertising and Marketing at two Orlando, Florida, colleges.

He is a graduate of Cal's Coin College in Nicoma Park, Oklahoma, where he learned to repair and restore vintage pinball machines, and the Army Cook & Baker's School in Fort Lee, Virginia. He also holds a degree in English literature from Duke University and an MBA in marketing from the University of Pennsylvania's Wharton School of Finance and Commerce.

To learn more about Gordon A. Hasse, Jr.

"Pinball Before Licensing: When Imagination Was King!"
The concluding audio seminar by Gordon from the 2011 Pacific Pinball Expo on *Pinball News*.
http://www.pinballnews.com/shows/ppe2011/index.html

Russ Jensen, "Pinball Expo '86—The Second 'Hurrah.'" See section on Backglass Restoration by Steve Young and Gordon A. Hasse, Jr.
http://www.pinballcollectorsresource.com/russ_files/expo86.html

Pinheads: The Story of the Pacific Pinball Museum.
http://www.30lbsskunk.com/2010/11/04/pinheads-the-story-of-the-pacific-pinball-museum/

Prewar (Flipperless) Pinball Machines

By Rob Hawkins

What exactly is a *prewar* pinball machine?

There are some discrepancies and confusion as to the dates that are used to define prewar games. When using the term *prewar*, questions as to which war, or when during World War II, are you referring? The obvious answer (if you're a U. S. citizen) is any game manufactured prior to December 7, 1941, which was the date the U. S. was drawn into World War II. However, the answer is not that clear-cut. Several other possibilities exist. For example, in May 1942, the War Production Board (WPB) required that the production of "Amusement Machines" be halted and all materials used in that industry be put toward the production of products used to win the war. However, this is not the generally accepted definition for prewar games. This ban was lifted in May of 1945. Perhaps, this date, that signals the end of the war, should be considered the end of the time period that includes prewar games.

Getting a precise definition for games that fall into this prewar date category is difficult. Even the members of the Yahoo Group that uses the title "Prewar Pinball" offer a variety of cut-off dates. In a poll, members of this group made suggestions, ranging from the date of the end of purely mechanical games to anything made prior to the date the flipper was developed.

For my purposes in this article I will use the term *flipperless* games and not just prewar games. This extends the date from December 1941 to December 1947. Gottlieb's Humpty Dumpty is generally considered to be the first flipper game and was actually introduced in October 1947. But, most manufacturers' games did not begin to introduce the flipper until the end of the year.

What makes the games produced prior to the development of the flipper so interesting?

One of the attractions is the mechanical acrobatics of the non-electric games. **People who collect games from this era find the mechanical works one of the most interesting features.** Rockola's World's Fair Jigsaw is an example of the extent of mechanical complexity. In this game the challenge to the player is to complete a jigsaw picture puzzle of the 1933 Chicago World's Fair displayed in the center of the playfield. Simply using the action of the ball to trigger a complex system of mechanical devices under the playfield allows this to be accomplished without the use of electricity. A mechanically ingenious set of springs and levers allows the puzzle pieces to flip into place as various scoring objectives are achieved by well-executed marble placement shot from the plunger. This feature appears to be the primary attraction for the three most popular games in the results of the Prewar Pinball Group's poll.

A second attraction of games from this time period is the number of games that fall into the category of "firsts," as in, the first game with bumpers, the first game to use an electric bell, or perhaps the first game to use a solenoid to propel the ball across the playfield. These examples and many other "firsts" were incorporated into games made prior to the introduction of the flipper, which in itself is probably the most important first!

A third attraction for the time period is the art and motifs used to decorate these games. The designs used to attract players varied from Victorian designs to futuristic and often science fiction themes. Themes and the art work varied with world events. Many games made just prior to WWII displayed war-related themes. Card themes frequented and dominated entire playfields. Sports-related themes have always been highly sought after design themes. And, pretty girls have often been used in pin game art work and even to title the game!

Another interesting area of focus for collectors in this time period is the wartime conversion. Several people, Russ Jensen and Terry Cumming, to name two, have done extensive research and written a lot about the history of converting an existing model of a pinball machine into a different game. Russ's article "Pingame Conversions" was originally published in the August/September 1983 issue of *Coin Slot*. This article covered all types of conversions from board replacements made during the infancy years of pinball in the early 1930s through the time of the publication of the article. He included all types of conversions and even included some arcade games. His entire article can be found on our web page at http://www.pinballcollectorsresource.com/russart. html. All of Russ's articles are included on the site and are listed in date order, so scroll down to the end of 1983 (83/08–09) and then look for the title "Pingame Conversions." Terry Cumming has published two editions of his book *Pinball and World War II*. The second edition, which was updated in 1998, includes information exclusively about pinball games and pinball conversions made just prior to the War, as well as games up through 1946. The volume includes extensive photos and related information about the pinball industry in and around the time of World War II.

In order to follow the history behind conversion machines, I will pick up the story with the United State's involvement in World War II, since this time period caused an explosion of this type of collectible game. The ensuing ban on the production of new amusement and gambling devices by the War Production Board (WPB), caused an upsurge of companies focusing on the redesigning of games to meet the public's demand for ever-changing challenges in this form of entertainment. These companies would convert games manufactured prior to the ban by redesigning or modifying the backglass and/or the playfield. They would essentially create a "new game" to satisfy the public's demands and stay within the WPB laws. There has been no thorough research completed on conversion games. The practice of creating a "new game" by simply changing out the playfield has been around as long as pinball machines have existed. If you perform an advanced search on the Internet Pinball Database (IPDB) (http://www.ipdb.org/search.pl) and use "<48" for the date and under "Specialty," use the dropdown menu to select "Converted Game," the result will be 131 individual games. Thirteen of these are dated prior to the War Production Board's ban. I know for a fact there are many others that are "conversions" from this time period that have not been labeled as a "converted game" simply because of a lack of time and diligent research by anyone to document these games. According to the data in Appendix A of our book, *Pinball Collectors Resource,* there were approximately 76 companies producing over 349 games that involved some type of conversion using materials from an older game. This version of the book was published in 2000. Our current data shows 78 companies producing 369 games. So, in 12 years we have found two additional companies and 20 more games to include in the list of converted games. For additional information on converted games, I have begun the lengthy process of documenting manufacturing companies and their games on our web site on the "Conversions" page at http://www. pinballcollectorsresource.com/conver.html. This article was initiated several years ago and is yet to be completed. But, it is a start!

Note—conversion prices are not included in The Pinball Price Guide *due to incomplete and unverified information.*

There is a group for that.

As alluded to above, one of the Yahoo groups is devoted to games from the prewar pinball era. I conducted two polls of this group's 200 members. One asked about the date that terminates this group's interest and the other about their favorite games. The opinions of this group about the dates that encompassed the prewar era are quite varied, with answers ranging from "purely mechanical games only" to "anything without flippers." The results of this poll simply reflect the actual dates of interest of its members. I selected a wider time period for this article simply because it offers the exploration of a wider variety of machines.

Rather than rely on my personal likes and limit this article to games I have been exposed to, I felt that asking for the expertise of those who have been immersed in collecting, restoring, and documenting these games would provide a broader outlook and overview of games from this time period. For these reasons, I decided to ask the members of this group to provide a list of their favorite games and to provide comments about what would attract them to add a particular game to their list. The resulting list of pinball games and comments are reproduced on the next page.

The Prewar Pinball Group's Favorite Pinball Games

Game Name	Mfr.	Year-Month	# of Lists	Features/Comments
World's Series (Gray) (Black)	ROC	1934-05	14	Innovative base running/play Fun/Realistic/Elegant/Unusual
Army and Navy (Gold) (Brown)	ROC	1934-12 early version	14	Mechanics/Castings/Ingenious mechanism/Graphics
World's Fair Jigsaw	ROC	1932-08	13	Unique scoring mechanism/ Challenging
Sportsman	ODJ	1934-02	6	Slot Like/Great art & front casting
Baffle Ball	GOT	1931-11	4	Harder than it looks
Contact	PAM	1933-11	4	Harry Williams design
Chicago Express	DAV	1935-01	4	Art/Play innovative
Neontact	PAM	1935-02	4	Neon lighting
Bumper	BAL	1936-12	4	Scoring bumpers
Ballyhoo	BAL	1932-01	3	
Big Broadcast	GOT	1933-01	3	Great ball trap covers
Airway	BAL	1933-02	3	I love the "toilet seats"
Fleet	BAL	1934-06	3	Best use of catapults/Clever
Major League	PAM	1934-07	3	Harry Williams design
Turf Champs	STO	1936-01	3	Real world simulation
Metro	GNC	1940-10	3	Art/Interesting play
Log Cabin	CBC	1903-01	2	First with pinball traits
Cloverleaf	GOT	1932-10	2	
Mat-Cha-Skor	PEO	1933-01	2	Ingenious use of pneumatics
Rocket	BAL	1933-10	2	Fun to race two balls
Kings of the Turf	HCE	1935-02	2	Great horse race mechanics
Confucius Say	RTG	1936-00	2	Unique/Play fun/Rotating PF
Stop and Go	KEE	1936-10	2	
Chicago Express	DAV	1938-01	2	
Ballyround	BAL	1932-04	1	
Daisy	PEO	1932-04	1	
Five Star Final	GOT	1932-08	1	
Eight and Six	SSM	1932-10	1	
Big Broadcast	BAL	1933-01	1	Great ball trap covers
Bank A Ball	UNT	1933-04	1	

Game Name	Mfr.	Year-Month	# of Lists	Features/Comments
Silver Cup	GNC	1933-07	1	
Leland	STO	1933-09	1	
Pennant	BAL	1933-12	1	High in fun factor
Baby Leland	STO	1933-12	1	
Lightning	EXS	1934-04	1	
American Beauty	DAV	1934-06	1	First catapult, First electrical tilt
Cannon Fire	MIL	1934-12	1	
Merry-Go-Round	GOT	1934-08	1	Roto discs
Football	ODJ	1934-10	1	QB catch & shoot
Skyscraper	BAL	1934-12	1	Casting/Scoring
Beacon	STO	1934-12	1	
Criss Cross A-Lite	GNC	1935-01	1	
Builder Upper	GML	1935-03	1	Change target based on previous shot
All Stars	ABT	1935-01	1	Art/Light animation
Cavalcade	STO	1935-04	1	
Play Ball	EXS	1935-06	1	Art/Features/Play
Flying Turf	ODJ	1935-08	1	
Spit Fire	GNC	1935-08	1	Super-raised ball tracks
Derby	BAL	1935-12	1	
Lite-A-Line	ANS	1935-12	1	
Short Sox	STO	1936-07	1	
Railroad	MIL	1936-09	1	
Center Smash	WEP	1936-11	1	Art/Pay out
Deauville	LBE	1937-03	1	Art
Entry	BAL	1938-02	1	
Bambino	BAL	1938-06	1	
Softball	MIL	1938-09	1	Chrome playfield
Chubbie	STO	1938-11	1	
Sky Rocket	EXS	1939/1941	1	Uncertain Date
Fifth Inning	BAL	1939-04	1	Art/Mirrored backglass
Spinning Reels	MIL	1940-01	1	
Sporty	CCM	1940-04	1	
Pla-Mor	VPD	1944-00	1	Great conversion
Rola-Ball			1	

The games on this chart are first sorted by the total number of times that a game was mentioned in all lists submitted by the Group and secondly by date. As an example, if you look at the "# of Lists" column, you will see that the first two entries were mentioned on 14 lists. Then looking under the "Date" column, you will see those two games are listed so that the oldest game appears first.

Some of the games on this chart are one of a kind. Others can be found in a variety of locations: eBay, Craigslist, auction houses across the country, antique stores, garage sales, and online classified ads. Numerous online pinball restoration sites also sell games from this time period.

For additional information on games from this time period, below are some excellent books. Some are out of print but can still be found on the Internet:

Bueschel, Richard. *Pinball One: Illustrated Historical Guide to Pinball Machines.* Wheat Ridge, CO: Hoflin Publishing, Ltd., 1988. 0-86667-047-5.
http://www.crowriver.com/books/bk090.htm

Bueschel, Richard. *Encyclopedia of Pinball, Vol. 1.* Silverball Amusements, 1998. 1-889933-01-5.
http://www.pbresource.com/books.html

Cumming, Terry. *Pinball Ad Catalog Volume I, 1931–33, 2nd Edition.* 2002.
http://www.crowriver.com/books/bk126.htm

Author's Bio

Rob Hawkins has been working together with Don Mueting documenting and compiling information about all pinball machines since 1977. They published the first documented list of pinball games, manufacturers, and dates of introduction in 1979. Don began to gather pinball machine information and compile a list of machines in 1972. As part of Rob's research for his Master's thesis, "The History of the Pinball Machine," he started gathering information in 1973. They both are still active in gathering information and photographs of pinball machines and maintaining a web site devoted to their research at pinballcollectorsresource.com. At this site, they offer their publication, Pinball Collectors Resource, *for sale and have several web pages devoted to pinball repair, historical and educational information, as well as a tribute to Russ Jenson's work and his contributions to the story of pinball. They have all of Russ's articles available and are in the process of adding the original color images to his articles as they were included in black and white with each original article. They are happy to answer inquiries about machines and offer this service free of charge for people who have acquired their book. Their database continues to expand and includes many new entries as they are able to research and document new primary sources.*

To learn more by Rob Hawkins

"Conversion Games." The intent of this article is to expand the information available about pinball conversions and revamps produced between 1936 and 1946.
http://www.pinballcollectorsresource.com/conver.html

"Kings of the Turf: How Many Kings?"
http://www.pinballcollectorsresource.com/history.html

Bingo-Style Pinball Machines

By Dennis Dodel

Whether you love them or hate them, bingo-style pinball machines are the only games left on location that replicate playing pinball as it was in the 1930s and 40s, before flippers and pop bumpers were invented. Some are still set on a nickel per game. Many pinball collectors have never seen or played bingo-style games, also known as In-Line Games or 25 Holers.

My introduction to bingo machines began in St. Louis, Missouri, in 1967 when my friend Joe Babcock's dad Boyd sold, for $15, a Bally Gayety bingo that had been sitting in his basement gathering dust to our mutual friend Tim Courtwright. Joe and Tim loaded the game onto Tim's Western Flyer wagon and towed the monster down the street to Tim's basement. Tim had a knack for fixing mechanical things, but even he had trouble trying to get the bingo to come to life. Luckily, one of his neighbors happened to be a telephone repairman. He recognized some of the bingo's step units as being similar to telephone switching equipment at the time and was able to get the game somewhat working. Tim figured out how to get the game working 100% and eventually became a bingo repairman later on in life. He is one of the top bingo mechanics around today. Joe, Tim, and I (sounds like that song "Timothy" by The Buoys) started playing bingos at a local greasy spoon, the Concord Grill, and played such games as Circus Queen, Roller Derby, and County Fair. I purchased my first bingo in 1981, a United Caravan, which I still own. Today I have a total of 26 bingos in my collection.

Types of Bingos

There are many different types of bingos, but most have one common goal: try to place at least three balls in a row on a numbered playfield that corresponds to a numbered bingo card in the backglass. The majority of bingo games have a 25-hole playfield, although the late 60s and 70s brought us 20-hole and even an 18- and 28-hole game. However, the 25-hole games made by Bally and United remain the most popular by far. United was a competitor of Bally, but its games were never as popular as Bally's were. The early bingos were very simple with 1–3 cards on the backglass.

As each successive game was built, more features were added, including Extra Balls, Super Cards, and moving screens.

Most Desirable Bingos Today

The most sought after bingos today are the Bally Magic Screen games from the late 50s and early 60s. There are many other unique and fun-to-play bingos from Bally, United, and a small handful of other bingo manufacturers, but for playing and collectability, the Magic Screen games are by far the most sought after.

For more detailed bingo game operation, see one of Jeffrey Lawton's books on the subject: *Bally Bingo Machines,* http://www.crowriver.com/books/bk031.htm, and *The Bingo Pinball War,* http://www.pbresource.com/books.html. There is also a great bingo web site at http://bingo.cdyn.com, as well as a few other sites dedicated to bingos.

Bingo Pricing

As far as value goes, prices of early 50s bingos continue to stagnate as the bingo-playing population grows older and dies out. Sadly, the bingo gene has not been passed on in most instances. The same is true for 60s and 70s 20-hole and 6-card games. These games were only legal in a few states and overseas, and while they do have a small following, their prices continue to plummet. It's no secret that most locations pay out under the counter for replays. With the proliferation of legalized gambling casinos in most states, the bingo machine is no longer "the only game in town." Magic Screen games with the OK feature and Turning Corners games continue to increase in value as these games in nice, working condition become harder to find. These types of bingos in Class 1 and 2 condition are very hard to find and command high prices when they do show up. However, some of these games have been on location for up to 50 years or more and are in deplorable condition with cabinets severely scraped and smashed in. A Bally Magic Screen game in Class 1 condition would be a very, very rare find! Some of the early games, particularly United's, do turn up in remarkable condition from time to time, but even they do not usually command a very high price.

Top 25 Bingos According to Current Value

The following is a list of what I personally think are the top 25 bingos, according to their current value. A personal list of my *favorite* bingos would be different. You will notice that all but one of the top 25 are Bally bingos. That is a tribute to Don Hooker, the mastermind designer behind the Bally bingos. The book on this genius has not yet been written. As I mentioned earlier, it is rare to find a bingo in Class 1 condition. The following prices are based on an above-average restored game in working condition. If a bingo does turn up in original Class 1 condition, you could probably double these values. Conversely, a bingo's value drops considerably as its condition deteriorates. Most as-found, non-working bingos will typically sell in the $100–300 range or less. Again, these prices are based on what I have seen in the market place in the last year or so. These prices are not set in stone.

Dennis Dodel's Top 25 Bingos

Bingo Game	Mfr.	Year	Price Range
Bounty	Bally	1962	$2500–2800
Golden Gate	Bally	1962	$1800–2000
Silver Sails	Bally	1962	$1800–2000
Bikini	Bally	1961	$1500–1800
Lido	Bally	1961	$1500–1800
Circus Queen	Bally	1960	$1400–1600
Can-Can	Bally	1961	$1400–1600
Roller Derby	Bally	1960	$1400–1600
Malibu Beach	Bally	1979	$1400–1600
Laguna Beach	Bally	1960	$1200–1400
County Fair	Bally	1959	$1200–1400
Beach Time	Bally	1958	$1200–1400
Sun Valley	Bally	1957	$1200–1400
Carnival Queen	Bally	1958	$800–1000
Sea Island	Bally	1959	$800–1000
Double Header	Bally	1956	$800–1000
Ballerina	Bally	1959	$700–900
Big Show	Bally	1956	$700–900
Key West	Bally	1956	$700–900
Cypress Gardens	Bally	1958	$700–900
Show Time	Bally	1957	$700–900
Playtime	United	1957	$700–900
Miss America DeLuxe	Bally	1977	$700–900
Miss America Supreme	Bally	1976	$600–800
Miss America	Bally	1957	$600–800

There are still a few places operating bingos in the St. Louis area. Most are still a nickel a game. I don't get out to play them much anymore, but when I do, I still get the same thrill as I did when playing them back in the 60s.

Author's Bio

Dennis Dodel was born in St. Louis, Missouri, in 1952. He has been interested in pinball machines since 1965, when his father brought home a Gottlieb Cover Girl and a Sweethearts that he had purchased from a bowling teammate who happened to be a game route operator.

Dennis has bought, refurbished, and sold over 2000 games. In the 1980s Dennis and his friend Jon Mueller operated The Pinball Shop in St. Louis. In addition to selling games and game supplies, they refurbished and supplied pinball machines to Hollywood movies and local live plays.

From 1986 to 1990 Dennis was publisher and editor of The Pinball Trader, *a magazine for pinball enthusiasts with subscribers in 49 states and many foreign countries. He has written articles for many hobbyist magazines including* The Coin Slot, Gameroom, Pinhead Classified, *and* Pinball Journal. *Dennis was interviewed for a pinball feature in* Smithsonian *magazine. His game collection has been featured in the* St Louis Post-Dispatch *newspaper, on KSDK-TV, and in the documentary "Pinball: From Bagatelle to Today" by collector and historian Ed Nickels, which won a cable TV Ace award. Dennis was also a member of the late Dick Beuschel's pricing panel for Dick's* Encyclopedia of Pinball.

In 1997 he started Dennis Dodel's Special Delivery, a cross-country game delivery service that gave him the unique opportunity to deliver games to and meet with pinball collectors in 48 states. Through this business, he was able to view some of the largest pinball collections in the United States, which also gave him a sneak peek at which games collectors were buying and how much they were selling them for.

Today Dennis is retired but occasionally restores and sells games.

To learn more about Dennis Dodel

"Dracula's Pinball," a video about the game built by pinball legend Dennis Dodel. The cabinet is made from a real casket.

https://www.youtube.com/watch?v=Ubh-hcTuZB0

An Artist Named ART:
Art Stenholm

Original electro-mechanical (EM) games with artwork by Art Stenholm are classic and very collectible. After the death of Gottlieb's pinball artist Roy Parker in 1965, Art Stenholm was hired by Advertising Posters, the Chicago company where its staff artists provided the artwork and screen printing for Gottlieb games. During the 60s and early 70s, Art Stenholm's artwork appeared on many Gottlieb games, such as Moulin Rouge 1965, Subway 1966, Super Score 1967, PlayMates 1968, Spin-A-Card 1969, and Baseball 1970.

Featuring Art Stenholm's imaginative artwork, The King of Diamonds 2010, manufactured by Retro Pinball LLC, has the finest 60s art and design, combined with today's digital electronics. This game is a retro-version of the 1967 King of Diamonds by Gottlieb. Priced reasonably, this limited edition King of Diamonds from Retro Pinball (http://retropinball.net/index.html) will certainly increase in value in the future.

THE PINBALL COLLECTOR MARKET REPORT

In an interview at the 2012 Texas Pinball Festival on *CBS Dallas/Fort Worth News*, pinball designer George Gomez says he is optimistic about the future of pinball, "We're at the genesis of a bit of a renaissance. I think pinball is definitely coming back." Bally's **Corvette 1994** and **Attack from Mars 1995**; Williams' **Monster Bash 1998**; Stern's **Playboy 2002, The Sopranos 2005, Transformers 2011**, and **The Avengers 2012** are some of the fantastic games designed by George Gomez.

New pinball manufacturing has been revving up since the 8th Edition of *The Pinball Price Guide* came out in 2010. Leading the way is Stern with **Avatar** in 2010, **The Rolling Stones** in 2011, and **X-Men** in 2012. Retro Pinball's **The King of Diamonds 2010** has the best price for a new game. Whizbang Pinball's **Whoa Nellie! Big Juicy Melons**, with only four games produced, is sure to be a collector's treasure. Many machines are being manufactured, such as Jersey Jack's **The Wizard of Oz**; PinBall Manufacturing's new version of Capcom's 1996 game, **Kingpin**; and **The P³ Machine** from Multimorphic. P³ pinball is so advanced it could be the pinball machine of the future. Heighway Pinball is a new entry into the pinball manufacturing marketplace.

When buying older games, find games that have available parts to purchase. Backglasses are remade, as well as plastics, caps, ramps, circuit boards, and playfields. You can make one good game out of parts from two or more of the same game. There are many pinball services that can restore your machine to like-new condition. If you can restore a pinball machine yourself, all the better. As long as a Class 1, Class 2, or Class 3 pinball game is fun to play, then it would be fun to own

Reality television, with its very high viewership, has been featuring all types of pinball machines. These shows have uncovered many games sitting in basements, attics, back rooms, and barns—games now coming on the market. So be on the lookout for preflipper, 50s, 60s, 70s, and 80s games surfacing in your neighborhood. Keep in mind when buying to use the Condition Grading Guide on page 68 because sometimes the prices shown for the games on TV can be unrealistically on the high side.

The following pages in The Pinball Market Report section are broken down by different eras in the history of pinball, based on the most notable type of machine for that time period. For each era, there is a chart, arranged by price, that lists some of the most desirable games to collect.

Prewar or Flipperless Pinballs
(1931–1947)

Many collectors are adding **prewar** or **flipperless** games to their collections. Once the flipper was introduced in 1947, these games were considered to be obsolete. Some pinball operators added flippers to the playfield, and because the games were engineered to be flipperless, the addition of flippers really never worked well. To get a good hands-on feel of how these games look and play, go to a pinball museum or show. Flipperless games are showing up for sale at shows, on the Internet, and even in local neighborhoods.

Rock-Ola's **Gold Top Army and Navy 1935** and **Army and Navy 1934** football-themed games take the number one and two spots respectively. A new addition to the guide, **Confucius Say 1936** by Rotor Table Games, is a cocktail table game and comes in at number three. At number four, **Dutch Pool 1931** by A.B.T. Manufacturing is a tabletop model featuring a billiards theme. **Neontact 1935** by Pacific Amusement Company has red-colored neon backbox lighting and places at number five.

There are other valuable collectible flipperless games, such as **World's Fair Jig-Saw 1933** by Rock-Ola, which features playfield animation of a jigsaw puzzle created from a map of the 1933 Chicago World's Fair. **Bambino 1938** by Bally, **World's Series 1934** by Rock-Ola, **Major League 1934** by Pacific Amusement, and **Short Stop 1940** by Exhibit Supply are all baseball-themed games. Payout games include **Rocket 1933** by Bally; **Sportsman 1934, Red Man 1936**, and **Flying Turf 1935** by O.D. Jennings & Co.; **One-Two-Three 1938** by Mills Novelty Co.; and **Stop and Go 1936** by J.H. Keeney & Co. There are two versions of Gottlieb's **Speedway 1933**: the original, manufactured in September, was a three-lap model; in October, a second model was released with a longer cabinet, allowing the cars to advance five laps.

Remember that "Quality Is King" and since parts are harder to find for these games, it would be best to buy games that are in Class 1 condition. Complete games in Class 2 or Class 3 condition can be restored.

Games with metal figures on the playfield, which were made in the mid-1930s, such as **Soccer 1936** by GM Labs, are good finds to add to your collection.

For more in-depth information about this type of game, read "Prewar (Flipperless) Pinball Machines" by Rob Hawkins on page 35 of this guide.

Prewar or Flipperless Pinballs

Rank	Game	Mfr.	Year	Class 1 Price
1	Gold Top Army and Navy	ROC	1935	$5,850
2	Army and Navy	ROC	1934	$5,700
3	Confucius Say	RTG	1936	$3,800
4	Dutch Pool	ABT	1931	$2,700
5	Neontact	PAM	1935	$2,650
6	World's Fair Jig-Saw	ROC	1933	$2,200
7	All Stars	ABT	1935	$2,200
8	Bambino	BAL	1938	$2,200
9	Sportsman	ODJ	1934	$2,150
10	Speedway (5 laps)	GOT	1933	$2,000
11	Skyscraper	BAL	1934	$2,000
12	Rocket	BAL	1933	$1,800
13	World's Series	ROC	1934	$1,800
14	Speedway (3 laps)	GOT	1933	$1,800
15	Soccer	GML	1936	$1,750
16	Big Ten	HCE	1935	$1,675
17	Red Man	ODJ	1936	$1,625
18	Flying Turf	ODJ	1935	$1,600
19	Congo	EXS	1940	$1,550
20	Gold Star	GOT	1940	$1,525
21	Major League	PAM	1934	$1,500
22	One-Two-Three	MIL	1938	$1,500
23	Short Stop	EXS	1940	$1,450
24	Cannon Fire Jr	MIL	1934	$1,400
25	Stop and Go	KEE	1936	$1,375

Woodrail Pinballs
(1948–1960)

Gottlieb takes the number one through number five spots and has the most games in the top 25 of highly desirable woodrail games. **Mermaid 1951** has shown the greatest dollar value increase (168%) since the 8th Edition of *The Pinball Price Guide* came out in 2010, carrying the woodrail category to number one. **Buffalo Bill 1950**, featuring Gottlieb's turret shooter and oscillating rangefinder, comes in at number two. **Knock Out 1950**, which includes playfield animation with fighting boxers, scores the number three position. **Dragonette 1954**, which parodied *Dragnet*, the Jack Webb radio and TV series, and includes two cyclonic kickers, comes in at number four. **Minstrel Man 1951**, the first Gottlieb pinball with drop targets, taps in to the number five spot.

If you enjoy pop bumpers, **Nags 1960** by Williams features a horse race theme with a six-jet bumper turntable and a mechanical backbox with racing horses. **Fun House 1956** by Williams features a trap door which scores bonus points. **Balls-A-Poppin 1956** by Bally was the first flipper game to feature multi-ball. **Sea Wolf 1959** by Williams features a disappearing jet bumper and backglass light animation. **Hot-Rods 1949** by Bally is a flipperless game.

The other Gottlieb woodrails in the top 25 include: **Niagara 1951, Queen of Hearts 1952, Arabian Knights 1953, 4-Belles 1954, Daisy May 1954, Diamond Lill 1954, Mystic Marvel 1954, Twin Bill 1955, Sluggin' Champ 1955, Sluggin' Champ Deluxe 1955, Sittin' Pretty 1958, Rocket Ship 1958, Roto Pool 1958, Universe 1959**, and **Lightning Ball 1959**.

For more information on woodrails, see "Woodrail Pricing: The Big Picture" by Gordon Hasse on on page 16 of this guide.

Woodrail Pinballs

Rank	Game	Mfr.	Year	Class 1 Price
1	Mermaid	GOT	1951	$15,000
2	Buffalo Bill	GOT	1950	$4,000
3	Knock Out	GOT	1950	$4,000
4	Dragonette	GOT	1954	$3,225
5	Minstrel Man	GOT	1951	$3,100
6	Nags	WIL	1960	$2,900
7	Sluggin' Champ Deluxe	GOT	1955	$2,650
8	Niagara	GOT	1951	$2,625
9	Hot-Rods	BAL	1949	$2,500
10	4-Belles	GOT	1954	$2,450
11	Rocket Ship	GOT	1958	$2,350
12	Fun House	WIL	1956	$2,300
13	Daisy May	GOT	1954	$2,175
14	Sluggin' Champ	GOT	1955	$2,125
15	Roto Pool	GOT	1958	$2,050
16	Universe	GOT	1959	$2,025
17	Twin Bill	GOT	1955	$2,000
18	Sittin' Pretty	GOT	1958	$2,000
19	Mystic Marvel	GOT	1954	$1,975
20	Diamond Lill	GOT	1954	$1,950
21	Balls-A-Poppin	BAL	1956	$1,900
22	Queen of Hearts	GOT	1952	$1,850
23	Arabian Knights	GOT	1953	$1,825
24	Sea Wolf	WIL	1959	$1,825
25	Lightning Ball	GOT	1959	$1,800

Multi-Player Pinballs
(1948–1978)

Rare games take the one, two, and three spots on the multi-player pinball chart. Jumping the finish line at the number one spot is the **EM** (electro-mechanical) version of **Evel Knievel 1977** by Bally. Only about 155 were made before Bally switched to **SS** (solid state). **Grand Prix 1976** by Williams zooms in at number two with an **SS** prototype version of which only about two were made before switching over to **EM**. The number three spot goes to **Mata Hari 1977** by Bally, which made only 170 **EM** models before switching over to **SS**. In the number four spot is **Fireball 1972** by Bally with zipper flippers. Finishing at number five, **Flying Turns 1964** by Midway is a widebody auto racing game featuring a turret shooter and backbox mechanical animation of cars racing around a track.

Coming in at number six is the **EM** version of **Charlie's Angels 1978** by Gottlieb, based on the TV show. The head-to-head two-player game **Challenger 1971** by Gottlieb is in the number seven spot. **Captain Fantastic 1976** by Bally, with the X-rated backglass, takes the number eight position. The **SS** version of **Evel Knievel 1977** by Bally follows at number nine. Dropping in at number ten is **Captain Fantastic 1976** by Bally, which is based on the movie *Tommy* and features Elton John playing a pinball in his oversized boots on the backglass.

Bally has the most games on the chart, finishing with **Bulls Eye 1965, Bow and Arrow 1974, Playboy 1978, Wizard! 1975, Nip-It 1973, Four Million B.C. 1971, Strikes and Spares 1978, Eight Ball 1977,** and **Power Play 1978. Race Way 1963** by Midway is a widebody auto racing game. **Nugent 1978** by Stern features the rock star and hunter himself playing and shooting a guitar gun on the backglass. Gottlieb charts with four more games: **Royal Flush 1976, Joker Poker 1978, Pleasure Isle 1965,** and **Close Encounters 1978**.

To find out more about games of this era, see page 10 for "Electro-Mechanical Games of the 1960s and 70s" by Brian Saunders.

Multi-Player Pinballs

Rank	Game	Mfr.	Year	Class 1 Price
1	Evel Knievel (EM)	BAL	1977	$3,125
2	Grand Prix (SS)	WIL	1976	$2,675
3	Mata Hari (EM)	BAL	1977	$2,600
4	Fireball	BAL	1972	$2,275
5	Flying Turns	MWY	1964	$2,125
6	Charlie's Angels (EM)	GOT	1978	$2,000
7	Challenger	GOT	1971	$1,975
8	Captain Fantastic (x-rated backglass)	BAL	1976	$1,875
9	Evel Knievel (SS)	BAL	1977	$1,775
10	Captain Fantastic	BAL	1976	$1,675
11	Bull's Eye	BAL	1965	$1,575
12	Royal Flush	GOT	1976	$1,575
13	Joker Poker (EM)	GOT	1978	$1,525
14	Bow and Arrow	BAL	1974	$1,500
15	Playboy	BAL	1978	$1,500
16	Wizard!	BAL	1975	$1,450
17	Nip-It (moving alligator)	BAL	1973	$1,375
18	Four Million B.C.	BAL	1971	$1,325
19	Strikes and Spares	BAL	1978	$1,300
20	Pleasure Isle	GOT	1965	$1,275
21	Race Way	MWY	1963	$1,250
22	Eight Ball	BAL	1977	$1,250
23	Power Play	BAL	1978	$1,250
24	Nugent	STN	1978	$1,200
25	Close Encounters (EM)	GOT	1978	$1,150

Single-Player Pinballs
(1960–1978)

The single-player category of pinball games was built during the "Boomer Generation." With only 55 games made, Bally's motorcycle-themed **Double-Up 1970** takes first place. However, Gottlieb single-player games from this era lead the pinball world and dominate the remaining slots on the top 25. **Buckaroo 1965**, played by Elton John in the movie *Tommy*, comes in at number two. **Cow Poke 1965** scores the number three spot.

The woodrail version of **Flipper 1960**, at fourth place, was the first Add-A-Ball game. **Slick Chick 1963** takes fifth place. The wedgehead and metal rail version of **Flipper 1960** places sixth. **Kings & Queens 1965**, with a card game theme, takes the number seven spot. **Flipper Cowboy 1962**, with Add-A-Ball and a cowboy shooting at a target, rides into number eight. **Majorettes 1964**, featuring Add-A-Ball, marches to number nine on the chart. **Flipper Clown 1962** is in tenth place with a backglass featuring mechanical animation of a clown hitting a bell at a circus sideshow.

El Dorado 1975 has a bank of five and a bank of ten drop targets. **Flipper Fair 1961** and **Flipper Parade 1961** are both Add-A-Ball games with mechanical backglass animation. **World Fair 1964** has a "Spin Disc" feature and was made for the New York World's Fair. **Gold Strike 1975, Foto Finish 1961, Dimension 1971, Sweet Hearts 1963, Cross Town 1966, Subway 1966, Bank-A-Ball 1965**, and **Hurdy Gurdy 1966** round out the top 25 single-player games. The restoration of single-player pinballs in Class 2 and Class 3 condition has been made easier due to the availability of re-production backglasses, plastics, and playfields.

To find out more on games from this era, see "Electro-Mechanical Games of the 1960s and 70s" by Brian Saunders on page 10 of this guide.

Single-Player Pinballs

Rank	Game	Mfr.	Year	Class 1 Price
1	Double-Up	BAL	1970	$2,500
2	Buckaroo	GOT	1965	$2,350
3	Cow Poke	GOT	1965	$2,300
4	Flipper (woodrail)	GOT	1960	$2,200
5	Slick Chick	GOT	1963	$2,050
6	Flipper	GOT	1960	$1,925
7	Kings & Queens	GOT	1965	$1,850
8	Flipper Cowboy	GOT	1962	$1,800
9	Majorettes	GOT	1964	$1,750
10	Flipper Clown	GOT	1962	$1,650
11	El Dorado	GOT	1975	$1,600
12	North Star	GOT	1964	$1,550
13	King of Diamonds	GOT	1967	$1,550
14	Gold Strike	GOT	1975	$1,525
15	Foto Finish	GOT	1961	$1,500
16	Flipper Fair	GOT	1961	$1,425
17	Hit the Deck	GOT	1978	$1,425
18	Flipper Parade	GOT	1961	$1,400
19	World Fair	GOT	1964	$1,400
20	Cross Town	GOT	1966	$1,375
21	Subway	GOT	1966	$1,375
22	Dimension	GOT	1971	$1,300
23	Sweet Hearts	GOT	1963	$1,275
24	Bank-A-Ball	GOT	1965	$1,275
25	Hurdy Gurdy	GOT	1966	$1,250

1st Electronic Age Pinballs
(1975–1989)

Rare games sometimes have a unique story to tell. The top collectible electronic age pinballs manufactured from 1975 to 1989 are no exception. A particular feature of the early electronic era was the introduction of music and voice in many of the games.

Ranked number one is **Loch Ness Monster 1985** by Game Plan. Only one prototype was produced before Game Plan closed operations in 1985. With only ten test games produced, **Krull 1983** by Gottlieb takes the number two spot. The boxing-themed **T.K.O. 1979** by Gottlieb punches high in the number three spot. Striking in at number four is **Thunderball 1982** by Williams, which never went into production, and only ten test models were made. Rocking out at number five are the sights and sounds of **Kiss 1979** by Bally.

The motorcycle racing game **Banzai Run 1988** by Williams crosses the finish line at number six. The head-to-head game **Joust 1983** by Williams tilts in at number seven. At number eight is the multiball underwater adventure **Fathom 1981** by Bally. Sylvester Stallone's **Rocky 1982** by Gottlieb hit the number nine spot. Dancing to number ten with the hit songs "Satisfaction," "Jumpin' Jack Flash," "Miss You," and "When the Whip Comes Down," is **Rolling Stones 1980** by Bally.

Varkon 1982 by Williams, **Iron Maden 1981** by Stern, and **Haunted House 1982** by Gottlieb all have unique playfield designs. **Eight Ball Deluxe 1981** by Bally has a bank of seven drop targets, four-in-line drop targets, and one standalone drop target. William's **Black Knight 1980, Black Knight 2000 (1989), F14 Tomcat 1987**, and **Fire! Champagne Edition 1987**; Bally's **Centaur 1981, Elvira and the Party Monsters 1989**, and **Evel Knievel 1977**; and Data East's **Playboy 35th Anniversary 1989** are all licensed theme games. Gottlieb made ten prototype games of **Goin' Nuts 1983**; however, the game never went into production. Baseball fans have their very own **Chicago Cubs Triple Play 1985** by Gottlieb/Premiere.

As games transitioned from the **EM** (electro-mechanical) to **SS** (solid state), the technology lent itself to the addition of sound and speech. The production teams went from basically the designer and artist to many more professionals, working on animation, mechanics, music, sound, software, etc. A complete list of team members for each game can be found online at the Internet Pinball Database at http://www.ipdb.org. There is a hyperlink to The Internet Pinball Database on Pinballeric.com.

1st Electronic Age Pinballs

Rank	Game	Mfr.	Year	Class 1 Price
1	Loch Ness Monster	GPN	1985	$20,327
2	Krull	GOT	1983	$8,750
3	T.K.O.	GOT	1979	$5,750
4	Thunderball	WIL	1982	$5,000
5	Kiss	BAL	1979	$3,750
6	Banzai Run	WIL	1988	$3,400
7	Joust	WIL	1983	$3,350
8	Fathom	BAL	1981	$3,175
9	Rocky	GOT	1982	$3,000
10	Rolling Stones	BAL	1980	$2,625
11	Varkon	WIL	1982	$2,175
12	Iron Maiden	STN	1981	$2,100
13	Elvira and the Party Monsters	BAL	1989	$2,050
14	Centaur	BAL	1981	$2,025
15	Goin' Nuts	GOT	1983	$2,000
16	Haunted House	GOT	1982	$1,950
17	Black Knight 2000	WIL	1989	$1,875
18	Evel Knievel	BAL	1977	$1,775
19	Chicago Cubs Triple Play	GPRE	1985	$1,750
20	Eight Ball Deluxe	BAL	1981	$1,700
21	Black Knight	WIL	1980	$1,650
22	Fire! Champagne Edition	WIL	1987	$1,650
23	Fireball Classic	BAL	1985	$1,600
24	F14 Tomcat	WIL	1987	$1,600
25	Playboy 35th Anniversary	DE	1989	$1,575

2nd Electronic Age Pinballs
(1990–2001)

During the last decade of the 20th Century, pinball manufacturers continued the trend of producing games based on popular culture, with licensed artwork. Games from this era are characterized by high quality game play, dazzling graphics, and music. Several also have novelty features. This period also saw a downturn in manufacturing, with companies eliminating or selling off their pinball divisions or closing their doors altogether. By the end of 1999, only Stern Pinball continued to manufacture pinball machines.

With only nine machines made, **Kingpin 1996** by Capcom is ranked number one. At number two is **Big Bang Bar 1996** by Capcom, with 14 prototype machines made as the Capcom Pinball division ceased operations. **Cactus Canon 1998** by Bally, at number three, features a moving toy train. At number four, **Monster Bash 1998** by Williams's features rockin' old time monsters. **King Kong 1990** by Data East, with only nine machines made, climbs to the number five spot.

Bally's **Addams Family Gold 1994**, "Special Collector Edition," with gold-colored accents and a gold numbered plate, enters the number six spot. **Medieval Madness 1997** by Williams, featuring the voice of *30 Rock*'s Tina Fey, is in the seventh spot. **Cirqus Voltaire 1997** by Bally, with the wisecracking ringmaster's head, is in the number eight position. Based on the TV series by Rod Serling, **Twilight Zone 1993** by Bally, with five multi-ball modes, comes in at number nine. **Safe Cracker 1996** by Bally dispenses tokens and cracks the number ten spot.

Monopoly Platinum 2001 by Stern, **Indiana Jones: the Pinball Adventure 1993** by Williams, **Monopoly 2001** by Stern, and **Scared Stiff, Elvira 1996** by Bally are all licensed themes. **Golden Cue 1998** by Sega, featuring Kelly Packard of the TV show *Baywatch*, is a test game of which only ten were made. **NFL 2001** by Stern featured customized team backglasses, which could be ordered with the helmet and logo of your favorite NFL team. The outer space themed **Revenge from Mars 1999** by Bally was the first to use the Williams Pinball 2000 system that overlays interactive video on the mechanical playfield. **South Park 1999** by Sega, based on the TV show of the same name, has lots of toys. In **No Good Gofers! 1997** by Williams, you try to play nine holes of pinball golf while two gophers pop-up and wreak havoc during gameplay. **The Champion Pub 1998** by Bally features a bar brawl theme with a huge toy boxer. **Corvette 1994** by Bally pays tribute to the beloved American sports car.

Funhouse 1990 by Williams stars Rudy the Talking Head, following your every shot in real time.

One of the most licensed corporate brands and logos is Harley-Davidson Motorcycles. There are three Harley pinballs on this chart: **Harley-Davidson 1999** by Stern, **Harley-Davidson 1999** by Sega, and **Harley-Davidson 1991** by Bally.

2nd Electronic Age Pinballs

Rank	Game	Mfr.	Year	Class 1 Price
1	Kingpin	CAP	1996	$28,500
2	Big Bang Bar	CAP	1996	$24,500
3	Cactus Canyon	BAL	1998	$10,825
4	Monster Bash	WIL	1998	$9,550
5	King Kong	DE	1990	$9,250
6	Addams Family Gold	BAL	1994	$8,600
7	Medieval Madness	WIL	1997	$8,550
8	Cirqus Voltaire	BAL	1997	$6,775
9	Twlight Zone	BAL	1993	$4,700
10	Safe Cracker	BAL	1996	$4,550
11	Monopoly Platinum	STN	2001	$4,500
12	Indiana Jones: The Pinball Adventure	WIL	1993	$4,050
13	Monopoly	STN	2001	$3,800
14	Scared Stiff, Elvira	BAL	1996	$3,550
15	NFL	STN	2001	$3,350
16	Harley-Davidson	STN	1999	$3,225
17	Golden Cue	SEG	1998	$3,050
18	Revenge From Mars	BAL	1999	$3,025
19	Harley-Davidson	SEG	1999	$3,000
20	South Park	SEG	1999	$3,000
21	No Good Gofers!	WIL	1997	$2,925
22	Champion Pub, The	BAL	1998	$2,925
23	Corvette	BAL	1994	$2,900
24	Harley-Davidson	BAL	1991	$2,825
25	Funhouse	WIL	1990	$2,800

3rd Electronic Age Pinballs
(2002–2010)

The games from this era attract high prices, despite being relatively new, because they were produced in limited numbers of only a few hundred. These limited edition games are fun to play and the themes are funny or dark. The number one and two ranking games are **Big Bang Bar (Gold) 2006** and **Big Bang Bar 2006** by PinBall Manufacturing. These Limited Editions are considered two of the top collectible pinballs ever made.

Stern has an unbelievable lineup of games that reach out to everyone. **Spider-Man (Black) LE 2007** crawls to the number three spot. **Avatar LE 2010**, based on James Cameron's futuristic world, mines the number four spot. **Iron Man 2010** takes the number five spot.

Pirates of the Caribbean 2006 seizes the number six spot, and **Lord of the Rings LE 2009** conquers number seven. **Elvis Gold 2004**, which comes with a Certificate of Authenticity, is in the house at number eight. **Avatar 2010** obtains the number nine spot, and **Spider-Man 2007** slides down to hold the number ten spot.

The rest of the games on the list also are licensed theme games and come in many categories—music: **Elvis 2004**; sports: **NBA 2009, Harley-Davidson Third Edition 2004, Dale Jr 2007**, and **Big Buck Hunter Pro 2010**; TV: **24 2009, The Sopranos 2005, Family Guy 2007, CSI 2008**, and **The Simpsons Pinball Party 2003**; and movies: **Indiana Jones 2008, Batman 2008, Lord of the Rings 2003**, and **Shrek 2008. King of Diamonds 2010** is a solid-state conversion by Retro Pinball of Gottlieb's 1967 electro-mechanical game.

3rd Electronic Age Pinballs

Rank	Game	Mfr.	Year	Class 1 Price
1	Big Bang Bar (Gold)	PMI	2006	$18,000
2	Big Bang Bar	PMI	2006	$15,000
3	Spider-Man (Black) LE	STN	2007	$7,700
4	Avatar LE	STN	2010	$5,550
5	Iron Man	STN	2010	$5,375
6	Pirates of the Caribbean	STN	2006	$5,225
7	Lord of the Rings LE	STN	2009	$5,000
8	Elvis Gold	STN	2004	$4,900
9	Avatar	STN	2010	$4,850
10	Spider-Man	STN	2007	$4,675
11	Indiana Jones	STN	2008	$4,425
12	NBA	STN	2009	$4,400
13	Batman	STN	2008	$4,300
14	24	STN	2009	$4,275
15	Family Guy	STN	2007	$4,150
16	Lord of the Rings	STN	2003	$4,125
17	CSI	STN	2008	$4,125
18	Elvis	STN	2004	$4,025
19	Sopranos, The	STN	2005	$3,975
20	Simpsons Pinball Party, The	STN	2003	$3,950
21	Harley-Davidson Third Edition	STN	2004	$3,925
22	Dale Jr	STN	2007	$3,900
23	Big Buck Hunter Pro	STN	2010	$3,725
24	King of Diamonds	RP	2010	$3,700
25	Shrek	STN	2008	$3,650

Digital Age Pinballs
(2011–2012)

Pinball, as well as books, cameras, computers, newspapers, and magazines, are going through changes in the digital age. It's no surprise that Stern Pinball takes this category by producing the top games, with music and comic book themes and in limited editions. **AC/DC Back in Black LE 2012, AC/DC Let There Be Rock LE 2012**, and **AC/DC Premium 2012** take the top three spots. **Avengers LE 2012** and **Avengers Hulk LE 2012** reach the number four and five spots.

X-Men Magneto LE 2012 and **X-Men Wolverine LE 2012** come in at six and seven. **Transformers Decepticon Violet LE 2011** and **Transformers Autobot Crimson LE 2011** are in at eight and nine. **The Rolling Stones LE** is sound at number ten.

Transformers LE (Combo) 2011, Transformers (Pro) 2011, Disney Tron: Legacy (Pro) 2011, The Rolling Stones 2011, AC/DC Pro 2012, X-Men Pro 2012, Avengers Pro 2012, and **Disney Tron Legacy LE 2011** round out the 18 games from Stern Pinball.

In 2012, PinballControllers.com introduced the modular, multi-game **P³ Pinball Platform**, designed by Gerry Stellenberg. The P³ contains many never-seen-before features, including an interactive virtual playfield where the ball interacts with images on an LCD. To find out more, go to http://www.multimorphic.com/.

Digital Age Pinballs

Rank	Game	Mfr.	Year	Class 1 Price
1	AC/DC Back in Black LE	STN	2012	$8,500
2	AC/DC Let There Be Rock LE	STN	2012	$8,500
3	AC/DC Premium	STN	2012	$7,700
4	Avengers LE	STN	2012	$7,400
5	Avengers Hulk LE	STN	2012	$7,400
6	X-Men Magneto	STN	2012	$7,200
7	X-Men Wolverine LE	STN	2012	$7,200
8	Transformers Decepticon Violet LE	STN	2011	$7,150
9	Transformers Autobot Crimson LE	STN	2011	$7,050
10	Rolling Stones LE, The	STN	2011	$6,600
11	Transformers LE (Combo)	STN	2011	$6,375
12	Tron: Legacy (Pro), Disney	STN	2011	$5,850
13	Rolling Stones, The	STN	2011	$5,700
14	AC/DC Pro	STN	2012	$5,175
15	Transformers (Pro)	STN	2011	$4,975
16	X-Men Pro	STN	2012	$4,975
17	Avengers Pro	STN	2012	$4,900
18	Tron: Legacy LE, Disney	STN	2011	$4,700

PRICING

The Value of a Game

Rarity can influence the value of a game. For example, when Capcom's Pinball Division closed its doors in 1996, only 14 Big Bang Bar pinball games had been made. In 2007, Gene Cunningham of Pinball Manufacturing Inc. (PMI) produced a limited edition of 191 Big Bang Bar games selling for $4,500 each. Since these games are signed and numbered limited editions (LE), they are rare and command a top dollar resale price. PMI's Big Bang Bar is now selling for $15,000.

The prices listed in this guide are a compilation of data from the Internet, auctions, show sales, dealers' sales lists, and discussions with collectors and pinball dealers.

The guide lists the current fair value of each pinball machine. Keep in mind that the current market determines the price of any machine. For example, when the EM flipper was introduced in 1947 with Gottlieb's woodrail, Humpty Dumpty, flipperless games from the 1930s and 40s were considered obsolete. Today, flipperless games are very collectible.

Don't forget to fill out Pinballeric's™ Pinball Price Guide Worksheet on page 69 for each game you buy or sell to see the actual cost, which includes such extras as shipping and restoration.

Prices for pinball conversion games are not fully included in *The Pinball Price Guide* due to incomplete and unverified information.

Antique, Vintage, or Collectible?

The traditional definition of an antique is that it must be 100 years old (with the exception of automobiles). Bagatelle pin games that were made starting in the mid to late 1860s qualify as antiques. However, the first pinball games, made in 1930, will not be considered antiques until 2030. So, calling a pinball game "vintage" or "collectible" is currently more accurate.

Star Power: Bally Games of the 70s

Bally produced pinball games in the 70s with star power, which are still highly sought after by collectors today. Bally came out with Wizard in 1975 and Captain Fantastic in 1976. Both games are based on the 1975 movie *Tommy*, starring The Who, Ann Margret, Elton John, Eric Clapton, Tina Turner, and Jack Nicholson.

Other Bally games of the 70s with star power are 1977 Eight Ball, featuring The

Fonz; 1977 Evel Knievel; 1978 Power Play, featuring NHL Star Bobby Orr; 1978 Playboy with Hugh Hefner and his Playboy Bunnies; 1979 Dolly Parton; and 1979 Kiss. Kiss is very popular in the United States and worldwide in Argentina, Austria, Belgium, Canada, Chile, France, Germany, Luxembourg, Netherlands, New Zealand, Portugal, South Africa, Sweden, and the United Kingdom.

Top 25 Collectors' Favorites

Rank	Game	Mfr.	Year	Class 1 Price
1	Monster Bash	Williams	1998	$9,550
2	Pirates of the Caribbean	Stern	2006	$5,225
3	Avatar, James Cameron's	Stern	2010	$4,850
4	Twilight Zone	Bally	1993	$4,700
5	Safe Cracker	Bally	1996	$4,550
6	Family Guy	Stern	2007	$4,150
7	Indiana Jones: The Pinball Adventure	Williams	1993	$4,050
8	Theatre of Magic	Bally	1995	$3,975
9	Simpsons Pinball Party, The	Stern	2003	$3,950
10	Monopoly	Stern	2001	$3,800
11	Wheel Of Fortune	Stern	2007	$3,375
12	South Park	Saga	1999	$3,000
13	Corvette	Bally	1994	$2,900
14	World Cup Soccer	Bally	1994	$1,800
15	Pin-Bot	Williams	1986	$1,450
16	Eight Ball	Bally	1977	$1,250
17	Star Trek	Bally	1979	$1,250
18	Swords of Fury	Williams	1988	$1,125
19	Jungle Lord	Williams	1981	$875
20	Quicksilver	Stern	1980	$725
21	Baseball	Gottlieb	1970	$675
22	Circus	Gottlieb	1980	$650
23	Metro	Williams	1961	$625
24	Flying Chariots	Gottlieb	1963	$550
25	Lady Luck	Williams	1968	$475

HAVE A FAVORITE GAME? Email it to eric@pinballeric.com.

Condition Grading Guide

BACKGLASS

Class 1 No more than 1/4 square inch of paint missing. The defect should be in an unlit area, which allows for easy touch-up. Games from the1930s should have a perfect glass if they have one.

Class 2 No more than 1 square inch of paint missing in an opaque area.

Class 3 No more than 3 square inches of paint missing, the majority in an opaque area.

PLAYFIELD

Class 1 Can have some ball marks (tiny half-moon cracks), but has to have a shiny finish and no missing paint. Games from the 1930s should have a perfect playfield.

Class 2 Small areas of worn-through paint around pop bumpers, kickout holes, or flippers. Main wear in 1930s games would be in the shooter lane.

Class 3 Heavier wear, with paint worn off in a circle around pop bumpers or bald spots worn from kickout holes. Also, flipper arc paths that have worn through the playfield paint. Games from the 1930s would have moisture damage or staining.

CABINET

Class 1 Cabinet is clean with minor scratches. All plastic light shields and pop bumpers are in perfect shape. All mechanical and electronic parts are complete. Game is in good working order. Games from the 1930s should have a close-to-perfect cabinet.

Class 2 Plastic light shields have small areas of paint missing, scratches, or warping. Paint is beginning to peel and flake off many areas of cabinet. Mechanically and electronically complete and working. May need cleaning. Games from the 1930s may have somewhat warped wood and metal parts may need polishing, but they should be working.

Class 3 Bumper caps have small burn marks on them. Plastic light shields are moderately warped, scratched. Ramps and toys are cracked or broken. Cabinet is re-painted to another design or solid color, or large areas of paint are gouged or flaked off or artwork is faded. Minor electronic or mechanical parts are missing. Game is not working.

BEST — CLASS 1   GOOD — CLASS 2   OK — CLASS 3

Pinballeric's™
Pinball Price Guide Worksheet

This worksheet may be copied for your personal use.

MACHINE NAME

YEAR MADE

MANUFACTURER

SERIAL #

DATE PURCHASED

LOCATION

Fill in dollar amounts that apply:

PURCHASE PRICE	$ _____
SALES TAX	$ _____
PICK UP	$ _____
SHIPPING CRATE	$ _____
DELIVERY	$ _____
SET-UP	$ _____
WARRANTY	$ _____
PARTS AND SERVICE	$ _____
RESTORATION	$ _____
BUYER'S PREMIUM	$ _____
MISCELLANEOUS	$ _____
TOTAL	$ _____

NOTES: _____

_____

_____

USING THE PRICE CHARTS

This price guide covers values for pinball games that were produced for the United States market from **1931–2012**. The first step in determining pricing is to identify the manufacturer of the game because different manufacturers often had similarly named games. The manufacturer's name is generally somewhere on the backglass, playfield, or inside the game.

Next, you also need to know the exact name of the specific game. You can find the name on the backglass in large letters, or on the scorecards at the bottom of the playfield, or printed on the playfield itself. Once you've located the name, look in the price chart under the name of that specific game.

Then, use the grading section of this book to determine the class/condition of the game. The condition of the game is extremely important in deciding the value of the game. Don't assume that the game is in Class 1 condition because it looks "Good." It's necessary to read the grading section carefully.

The price charts are organized left to right as follows:

Game	Manufacturer	Year	# Made
Sky Jump	Gottlieb	1974	4200
Sky Kings	Bally	1974	2000

1st column: Lists in alphabetical order the names of the games with footnotes for any significant features, such as Add-A-Ball. Games with numerical names (e.g., "2001," "4 Queens," etc.) are listed as if the numbers were spelled out. For example, "24" can be found where "Twenty-four" would be listed.

2nd column: Shows the manufacturer's name.

3rd column: Shows the year of introduction—when the first one of this particular game was produced.

4th column: Shows the number of games produced (if known). It may be an approximate number.

Type	Play	Designer	Artist	Class 1	Class 2	Class 3
EM	1	EK	GOM	$750	$500	$275
EM	1	JP	DIW	$625	$425	$225

5th column: Shows a code for the type of game:
M = Mechanical,
EM = Electro-Mechanical
EMP = Electro-Mechanical Pay
SS = Solid State
VID = Video

6th column: Shows the number of players.

7th column: Lists codes for the designers who worked on the game (if known).

See the Designers key on pages 186 and 187.

8th column: Lists codes for the artists who worked on the game (if known).

See the Artists key on page 188.

9th, 10th, 11th columns: Shows the value of the game according to the three classes of condition.

Refer to the Condition Grading Guide, page 68.

Game	Manufacturer	Year	# Made
A-Go-Go	Williams	1966	5100
A. G. Football	Alvin G.	1992	500
A.G. Soccer-Ball	Alvin G.	1991	500
ABC Bowler	Gottlieb	1941	N/A
Abra-Ca-Dabra	Gottlieb	1975	2825
AC/DC Back In Black LE	Stern	2012	300
AC/DC Let There Be Rock LE	Stern	2012	200
AC/DC Premium	Stern	2012	N/A
AC/DC Pro	Stern	2012	N/A
Ace	Bally	1935	N/A
Ace High	Gottlieb	1957	2100
Aces & Kings	Williams	1970	N/A
Aces High	Bally	1965	1275
Across the Board	Rock-Ola	1938	N/A
Action	Chicago Coin	1969	N/A
Action Jr.	Bally	1934	N/A
Action Sr.	Bally	1934	N/A
Addams Family	Bally	1992	20270
Addams Family Gold	Bally	1994	1000
Af-Tor	Wico	1984	N/A
Agents 777	Game Plan	1984	400
Air Aces	Bally	1975	3085
Air Circus	Exhibit Supply	1942	N/A
Air Derby	Western Equipment	1937	N/A
Air Lane	Bally	1936	N/A
Airborne	Capcom	1996	1350
Airborne Avenger [1]	Atari	1977	350
Airliner	Exhibit Supply	1939	N/A
Airport	Genco	1939	N/A
Airport	Gottlieb	1969	1900
Airway	Bally	1933	N/A
Airway	Bally	1937	N/A
Aladdin's Castle	Bally	1976	4155
Alamo	Rock-Ola	1936	N/A
Algar	Williams	1980	349
Ali	Stern	1980	2971
Ali Baba	Stoner	1939	N/A
Ali Baba	Gottlieb	1948	1700
Alice in Wonderland	Gottlieb	1948	1000

1. Widebody

Type	Play	Designer	Artist	Class 1	Class 2	Class 3
EM	4	NC	JK	$725	$500	$275
SS	2	JA/MG	TE	$1,925	$1,275	$675
SS	2	JA/MG	TE	$1,925	$1,275	$675
EM	1	HM	RP	$600	$400	$225
EM	1	JB	GOM	$700	$475	$250
SS	4	SR	N/A	$8,500	$5,625	—
SS	4	SR	N/A	$8,500	$5,625	—
SS	4	SR	N/A	$7,700	$5,100	—
SS	4	SR	N/A	$5,175	$3,425	—
EM-P	4	N/A	N/A	$875	$575	$300
EM	1	WN	RP	$1,475	$975	$525
EM	4	SK	N/A	$450	$300	$175
EM	4	TZ	AS	$425	$300	$150
EM-P	1	N/A	N/A	$750	$500	$275
EM	1	N/A	CM	$450	$300	$175
EM	1	HW	N/A	$375	$250	$150
EM	1	HW	N/A	$425	$300	$150
SS	4	LD/PL	JY	$5,425	$3,575	$1,900
SS	4	LD/PL	JY	$8,600	$5,675	$3,025
SS	4	N/A	N/A	$550	$375	$200
SS	4	EC	DIW	$450	$300	$175
EM	4	JP	DC	$825	$550	$300
EM	1	N/A	N/A	$625	$400	$225
EM-P	1	N/A	N/A	$1,000	$675	$350
EM-P	1	N/A	N/A	$1,625	$1,075	$575
SS	4	CF	HV	$1,925	$1,275	$675
SS	4	SR	GO	$450	$300	$175
EM	1	N/A	N/A	$625	$400	$225
EM	1	N/A	N/A	$600	$400	$225
EM	2	EK	AS	$625	$400	$225
M	1	HGB	N/A	$850	$575	$300
EM	1	N/A	N/A	$625	$400	$225
EM	2	GK	CM	$700	$475	$250
EM-P	1	N/A	N/A	$1,025	$675	$375
SS	4	TK	COM	$750	$500	$275
SS	4	HW	BT	$775	$525	$275
EM	1	N/A	N/A	$750	$500	$275
EM	1	HM	RP	$1,175	$775	$425
EM	1	HM	RP	$1,450	$950	$525

Game	Manufacturer	Year	# Made
Alien Poker	Williams	1980	6000
Alien Star	Gottlieb	1984	1065
All American	Chicago Coin	1940	2344
All-Star Basketball	Gottlieb	1952	1000
All Stars [1]	A.B.T. Mfg.	1935	N/A
Alligator	Bally	1968	N/A
Aloha	Gottlieb	1961	1700
Alpine Club [2]	Williams	1965	1200
Alps, St. Moritz [3]	Chicago Coin	1938	225
Amazon Hunt	Gottlieb	1983	1515
Amazon Hunt II	Gottlieb	1987	781
American Beauty	Daval	1934	N/A
Amigo	Bally	1973	4325
Anabel	Stoner	1940	N/A
Andromeda	Game Plan	1985	500
Apollo	Williams	1967	3100
Apollo 13	Sega	1995	2000
Aquacade	United Mfg.	1949	N/A
Aquarius	Gottlieb	1970	2025
Arabian Knights [4]	Gottlieb	1953	700
Arcade [5]	Bally	1938	N/A
Arcade	Williams	1951	N/A
Arena	Gottlieb/Premier	1987	3099
Argentine	Genco	1941	N/A
Argosy	Williams	1977	2052
Arizona, Yuma	United Mfg.	1950	N/A
Arlington	Bally	1937	N/A
Armada	Stoner	1941	N/A
Army and Navy [6]	Rock-Ola	1934	N/A
Army Navy [7]	Williams	1953	N/A
Around the World [2]	Stoner	1937	N/A
Around the World	Gottlieb	1959	800
Arrow Head [8]	Williams	1957	N/A
Arrowhead	Bally	1938	N/A
Arrowhead	J. H. Keeney and Co.	1962	N/A
Ascot Derby	Western Equipment	1938	N/A
Asteroid Annie and the Aliens	Gottlieb	1980	211
Astro	Gottlieb	1971	500
Astronaut	Chicago Coin	1969	N/A

1. Manikin players 2. Light animation 3. Free Play 4. Knob selects hole 5. Mechanical animation targets
6. Mechanical animation 7. Williams' first scoring reels 8. One-million-points shot

Type	Play	Designer	Artist	Class 1	Class 2	Class 3
SS	4	ET	TR	$825	$550	$300
SS	4	JT	LD	$550	$375	$200
EM	1	N/A	N/A	$650	$425	$225
EM	1	WN	RP	$1,900	$1,275	$675
EM	1	N/A	N/A	$2,200	$1,475	$775
EM	4	TZ	JK	$625	$425	$225
EM	2	WN	RP	$500	$350	$175
EM	1	SK	AS	$600	$400	$225
EM	1	N/A	N/A	$550	$375	$200
SS	4	EK	LD	$550	$375	$200
SS	4	EK	LD	$575	$375	$200
M	1	RF	N/A	$800	$550	$300
EM	4	GK	DIW	$525	$350	$200
EM	1	N/A	N/A	$475	$325	$175
SS	4	EC/MK	PF	$725	$500	$275
EM	1	NC	AS	$900	$600	$325
SS	6	JK/JOEB	MR/JB	$2,125	$1,400	$750
EM	1	N/A	N/A	$475	$325	$175
EM	1	EK	AS	$550	$375	$200
EM	1	WN	RP	$1,825	$1,200	$650
EM	1	N/A	N/A	$1,150	$750	$400
EM	1	HW	GM	$750	$500	$275
SS	4	RT	COM	$700	$475	$250
EM	1	N/A	N/A	$550	$375	$200
EM	4	CO	N/A	$475	$325	$175
EM	1	N/A	GM	$525	$350	$200
EM-P	1	N/A	N/A	$1,075	$725	$400
EM	1	N/A	N/A	$550	$375	$200
M	1	BHU	N/A	$5,700	$3,775	$2,000
EM	1	HW	GM	$850	$575	$300
EM	1	N/A	N/A	$1,000	$675	$350
EM	2	WN	RP	$950	$625	$350
EM	1	HW	GM	$850	$575	$300
EM	1	N/A	N/A	$500	$325	$175
EM	1	EK	N/A	$475	$325	$175
EM	1	N/A	N/A	$550	$375	$200
SS	1	JB	GOM	$1,175	$775	$425
EM	1	EK	GOM	$725	$475	$250
EM	2	ALS/JEK/JG	CM	$450	$300	$150

Game	Manufacturer	Year	# Made
Atarians, The	Atari	1976	N/A
Atlantis	Gottlieb	1975	2225
Atlantis	Bally	1989	1501
Atlas	Gottlieb	1959	950
Attack from Mars	Bally	1995	3450
Attention	Bally	1940	N/A
Attila the Hun	Game Plan	1984	500
Austin Powers	Stern	2001	N/A
Auto Derby	Genco	1937	N/A
Auto Race	Gottlieb	1956	1500
Autobank	A.B.T. Mfg.	1934	N/A
Avalon [1]	Exhibit Supply	1939	N/A
Avatar, James Cameron's	Stern	2010	N/A
Avatar LE, James Cameron's	Stern	2010	250
Avengers LE	Stern	2012	250
Avengers Hulk LE	Stern	2012	250
Avengers Pro	Stern	2012	N/A
Aztec	Williams	1976	10150
Aztec	Williams	1976	10
Baby Face	United Mfg.	1948	N/A
Baby Leland [2]	Stoner for Chicago Coin	1933	N/A
Baby Pac-Man	Bally	1982	7000
Back to the Future	Data East	1990	3000
Bad Cats	Williams	1989	2500
Bad Girls	Gottlieb/Premier	1988	2500
Baffle Ball [2]	Gottlieb	1931	N/A
Baffle Card	Gottlieb	1946	1860
Balance	Mills Novelty Co.	1935	N/A
Bali-Hi	Bally	1973	80
Ball Fan	Stoner	1935	N/A
Ball Park [3]	Chicago Coin	1937	N/A
Ballerina	Bally	1948	N/A
Ballot	Pacific Amusement	1936	N/A
Balls-A-Poppin [4]	Bally	1956	750
Bally Hoo	Bally	1969	2115
Bally Supreme	Bally	1939	N/A
Ballyhoo [2]	Bally	1932	75000
Ballyhoo	Bally	1947	N/A
Ballyround [5]	Bally	1932	N/A

1. Wonder star lights   2. Tabletop   3. One-ball payout   4. Multiple balls   5. Tabletop/legs optional

Type	Play	Designer	Artist	Class 1	Class 2	Class 3
SS	4	BJ	GO	$375	$250	$150
EM	1	JB/EK	GOM	$950	$625	$325
SS	4	PP	PM	$900	$600	$325
EM	2	WN	RP	$725	$475	$275
SS	4	BE	DW	$7,700	$5,075	$2,700
EM	1	N/A	N/A	$625	$400	$225
SS	4	JT	N/A	$525	$350	$200
SS	4	LR/JONB	N/A	$2,700	$1,800	$950
EM	1	N/A	N/A	$750	$500	$275
EM	1	WN	RP	$1,050	$700	$375
EM	1	N/A	N/A	$1,300	$875	$475
EM	1	HW/LYD	N/A	$1,175	$775	$425
SS	4	JONB/LR	KO	$4,850	$3,200	$1,700
SS	4	JONB/LR	KO	$5,550	$3,675	$1,950
SS	4	GEG	N/A	$7,400	–	–
SS	4	GEG	N/A	$7,400	–	–
SS	4	GEG	N/A	$4,900	–	–
EM	4	N/A	N/A	$625	$425	$225
SS	4	N/A	N/A	$900	$600	$325
EM	1	N/A	GM	$400	$275	$150
M	1	N/A	N/A	$650	$450	$250
SS	2	CF	MH	$900	$600	$325
SS	4	EC/JK	PF	$1,500	$1,000	$525
SS	4	BO	PA	$1,200	$800	$425
SS	4	JN	COM	$1,000	$650	$350
M	1	DG	N/A	$650	$450	$250
EM	1	HM	RP	$475	$325	$175
EM	1	N/A	N/A	$550	$375	$200
EM	4	TZ	CM	$1,075	$725	$375
EM	1	WB	N/A	$1,200	$800	$425
EM-P	1	N/A	N/A	$1,200	$800	$425
EM	1	N/A	N/A	$650	$425	$225
EM-P	1	N/A	N/A	$1,500	$1,000	$525
EM	2	N/A	N/A	$1,900	$1,250	$675
EM	4	TZ	CM	$600	$400	$225
EM	1	N/A	N/A	$550	$375	$200
M	1	N/A	N/A	$775	$525	$275
EM	1	N/A	N/A	$550	$350	$200
M	1	RM	N/A	$1,500	$1,000	$525

Game	Manufacturer	Year	# Made
Ballyview	Bally	1938	N/A
Bambino	Bally	1938	N/A
Band Leader	J. H. Keeney & Co.	1948	N/A
Band Wagon	Genco	1940	N/A
Band Wagon	Williams	1955	N/A
Band Wagon	Bally	1965	1840
Bang	Genco	1939	N/A
Banjo	Exhibit Supply	1948	N/A
Bank-A-Ball [1]	Gottlieb	1950	816
Bank-A-Ball [2]	Gottlieb	1965	3400
Bank A Ball [3]	United Mfg.	1933	N/A
Bank Shot	Gottlieb	1976	730
Banzai Run	Williams	1988	1750
Barb-Wire	Gottlieb/Premier	1996	1000
Barnacle Bill	Gottlieb	1948	2500
Barracora	Williams	1981	2350
Barrage	Western Products	1941	N/A
Base Hit	Chicago Coin	1935	N/A
Baseball [4]	Genco	1935	N/A
Baseball	Chicago Coin	1947	1400
Baseball	Daval	1937	N/A
Baseball	Stoner	1940	N/A
Baseball	Gottlieb	1970	2350
Basketball [5]	Exhibit Supply	1938	N/A
Basketball	Gottlieb	1949	1200
Batman	Data East	1991	3500
Batman [6]	Stern	2008	N/A
Batman [7]	Stern	2010	48
Batman Forever	Sega	1995	2500
Batter Up	Genco	1937	N/A
Batter Up [8]	Gottlieb	1970	560
Batting Champ	Gottlieb	1939	N/A
Battle	Bally	1935	N/A
Baywatch	Sega	1995	N/A
Bazaar [9]	Exhibit Supply	1937	N/A
Bazaar [10]	Bally	1966	2925
Be-Bop	Exhibit Supply	1950	N/A
Beach Queens [11]	Bally	1960	950
Beacon [12]	Stoner	1934	N/A

1. Turret shooter 2. Mech. animation 3. Tabletop 4. Electric 5. Light animation 6. Dark Knight 7. Standard
8. Add-A-Ball 9. One-ball payout 10. Zipper flippers 11. One ball/flipperless 12. Battery powered

Type	Play	Designer	Artist	Class 1	Class 2	Class 3
EM	1	N/A	N/A	$550	$375	$200
EM	1	N/A	N/A	$2,200	$1,475	$775
EM	1	N/A	N/A	$400	$275	$150
EM	1	N/A	N/A	$425	$275	$150
EM	4	HW	GM	$600	$400	$225
EM	4	TZ	N/A	$450	$300	$175
EM	1	N/A	N/A	$475	$325	$175
EM	1	N/A	N/A	$500	$350	$175
EM	1	HM	RP	$1,025	$700	$375
EM	1	EK	RP	$1,275	$850	$450
M	1	N/A	N/A	$300	$200	$125
EM	1	EK	GOM	$700	$475	$250
SS	4	PL/LD	MS	$3,400	$2,250	$1,200
SS	4	BP	COM/SCM	$1,350	$900	$475
EM	1	HM	RP	$1,225	$825	$450
SS	4	RS/SE/BO	DW	$750	$500	$275
EM	1	N/A	N/A	$550	$375	$200
EM	1	JW	N/A	$950	$650	$350
EM	1	N/A	N/A	$975	$650	$350
EM	1	N/A	N/A	$600	$400	$225
EM	1	N/A	N/A	$1,075	$725	$400
EM	1	N/A	N/A	$775	$525	$275
EM	1	EK	AS	$675	$450	$250
EM	1	N/A	N/A	$775	$525	$275
EM	1	WN	RP	$1,550	$1,025	$550
SS	4	JK/EC	PF/BF/TF	$1,350	$900	$475
SS	4	GG	KO/MH	$4,300	$2,850	$1,525
SS	4	GG	KO/MH	$2,500	$1,650	$875
SS	6	PL/JK	MW/MR/JB	$1,750	$1,175	$625
EM	1	N/A	N/A	$750	$500	$275
EM	1	EK	AS	$800	$525	$275
EM	1	HM	RP	$625	$425	$225
EM	1	N/A	N/A	$900	$600	$325
SS	6	JK/JOEB	M/JB	$1,625	$1,075	$575
EM	1	BR	N/A	$500	$350	$175
EM	1	TZ	GM	$575	$375	$200
EM	1	N/A	N/A	$400	$275	$150
EM	1	N/A	N/A	$575	$400	$225
EM	1	HS/KK	N/A	$800	$550	$300

Game	Manufacturer	Year	# Made
Beam Lite [1]	Chicago Coin	1935	5703
Beam-Lite Of '37	Chicago Coin	1937	773
Beat the Clock	Bally	1985	500
Beat the Clock [2]	Williams	1963	2100
Beat Time [3]	Williams	1967	2802
Beatniks	Chicago Coin	1967	N/A
Beauty	Bally	1940	N/A
Beauty Contest [4]	Bally	1960	1750
Bee Jay	Pacific Amusement	1936	N/A
Belle Hop	Gottlieb	1941	N/A
Belmont	Bally	1936	N/A
Bermuda [5]	Chicago Coin	1947	2500
Big Bang Bar	Capcom	1996	14
Big Bang Bar	PinBall Mfg. Inc.	2006	190
Big Bang Bar (Gold)	PinBall Mfg. Inc.	2006	1
Big Bank Nite	Rock-Ola	1936	N/A
Big Ben	Williams	1954	N/A
Big Ben [6]	Williams	1975	2900
Big Bertha Jr.	Daval	1934	N/A
Big Bertha Sr.	Daval	1934	N/A
Big Brave	Gottlieb	1974	3450
Big Broadcast Jr.	Gottlieb	1933	N/A
Big Broadcast Sr.	Gottlieb	1933	N/A
Big Broadcast Special	Gottlieb	1933	N/A
Big Buck Hunter Pro	Stern	2010	N/A
Big Casino	Chicago Coin	1936	157
Big Casino	Gottlieb	1961	1600
Big Chief	Genco	1940	N/A
Big Chief	Williams	1965	2950
Big Daddy	Williams	1963	1850
Big Day	Bally	1964	2075
Big Deal	Williams	1963	1350
Big Deal	Williams	1977	7301
Big Flipper	Chicago Coin	1970	N/A
Big Game	Rock-Ola	1935	N/A
Big Game	Stern	1980	2713
Big Guns	Williams	1987	5250
Big Hit	Chicago Coin	1952	N/A
Big Hit	Gottlieb	1977	2200

1. Battery powered 2. Multi-ball 3. Beatles theme 4. Flipperless one-ball game 5. 1st Chicago Coin flipper game 6. Add-A-Ball

Type	Play	Designer	Artist	Class 1	Class 2	Class 3
EM	1	SG	N/A	$600	$400	$225
EM	1	N/A	N/A	$550	$375	$200
SS	4	GC	TR	$800	$525	$275
EM	1	SK	GM	$800	$550	$300
EM	2	SK	JK	$1,000	$675	$350
EM	2	N/A	CM	$525	$350	$200
EM	1	N/A	N/A	$500	$350	$175
EM	1	N/A	N/A	$475	$325	$175
EM-P	1	N/A	N/A	$1,075	$725	$400
EM	1	HM	RP	$450	$300	$175
EM-P	1	N/A	N/A	$725	$475	$250
EM	1	JEK	RP	$525	$350	$200
SS	4	RM	SFP/MAZ	$24,500	$16,175	$8,575
SS	4	RM	SF	$15,000	$9,900	$5,250
SS	4	RM	SF	$18,000	$11,900	$6,300
EM-P	1	N/A	N/A	$725	$500	$275
EM	1	N/A	GM	$650	$425	$225
EM	1	SK	CM	$700	$475	$250
EM	1	N/A	N/A	$1,200	$800	$425
EM	1	N/A	N/A	$1,300	$875	$475
EM	2	EK	GOM	$975	$650	$350
M	1	N/A	N/A	$750	$500	$275
M	1	N/A	N/A	$850	$575	$300
M	1	N/A	N/A	$650	$450	$250
SS	4	JONB	JY	$3,725	$2,450	$1,300
EM-P	1	N/A	N/A	$900	$600	$325
EM	1	WN	RP	$600	$400	$225
EM	1	N/A	N/A	$675	$450	$250
EM	4	SK	N/A	$425	$275	$150
EM	1	SK	N/A	$550	$375	$200
EM	4	TZ	N/A	$475	$325	$175
EM	1	SK	N/A	$525	$350	$200
EM	4	SK	N/A	$625	$425	$225
EM	2	JEK	CM	$375	$250	$150
EM	1	N/A	N/A	$850	$575	$300
SS	4	HW	DW/GS	$775	$500	$275
SS	4	MR/PA	PA	$1,050	$700	$375
EM	1	JEK/AS/JG	N/A	$525	$350	$200
EM	1	EK	GOM	$700	$475	$250

Game	Manufacturer	Year	# Made
Big House	Gottlieb/Premier	1989	1977
Big Hurt, Frank Thomas'	Gottlieb/Premier	1995	1985
Big Indian	Gottlieb	1974	8030
Big League	Genco	1940	N/A
Big League	Bally	1946	N/A
Big Leaguer	Pacific Amusement	1935	N/A
Big Parade	Exhibit Supply	1941	N/A
Big Parlay [1]	J. H. Keeney & Co.	1947	N/A
Big Prize [1]	Western Products	1940	N/A
Big Shot	Gottlieb	1973	2900
Big Show [2]	Bally	1974	1000
Big Show	Gottlieb	1940	N/A
Big Star [2]	Williams	1972	1130
Big Strike	Williams	1966	3600
Big Ten	J. H. Keeney & Co.	1938	N/A
Big Ten [3]	H. C. Evans & Co.	1935	N/A
Big Time	Baker Novelty	1941	N/A
Big Top [2]	Gottlieb	1964	750
Big Top	Genco	1949	N/A
Big Town	Genco	1940	N/A
Big Valley	Bally	1970	2500
Bingo [4]	Bingo Novelty	1931	N/A
Bingo [4]	Gottlieb	1931	N/A
Bingo Ball [4]	Gottlieb	1931	N/A
Bingo Planet Ball [4]	Bingo Novelty	1932	N/A
Birdie	Baker Novelty	1940	N/A
Black Beauty	Genco	1933	N/A
Black Beauty	Gottlieb	1934	N/A
Black Belt	Bally	1986	600
Black Gold	Genco	1949	N/A
Black Gold	Williams	1975	55
Black Hole	Gottlieb	1981	8774
Black Jack [5]	Williams	1960	N/A
Black Jack	Bally	1976	120
Black Jack	Bally	1977	4883
Black Knight [6]	Williams	1980	13075
Black Knight 2000	Williams	1989	5703
Black Knight Limited Edition	Williams	1981	600
Black Pyramid	Bally	1984	2500

1. Full cabinet   2. Add-A-Ball   3. Mechanical animated players   4. Tabletop   5. 1960s-style cabinet
6. Multi-level playfield

Type	Play	Designer	Artist	Class 1	Class 2	Class 3
SS	4	RT	COM/PE	$1,100	$725	$400
SS	4	BIP	SCM/SO/COM	$1,550	$1,025	$550
EM	4	EK	GOM	$850	$550	$300
EM	1	N/A	N/A	$975	$650	$350
EM	1	N/A	N/A	$1,025	$700	$375
EM-P	1	N/A	N/A	$1,075	$725	$400
EM	1	LYD/HW	GM	$550	$375	$200
EM-P	1	N/A	N/A	$750	$500	$275
EM-P	1	N/A	N/A	$675	$450	$250
EM	2	EK	GOM	$850	$575	$300
EM	2	JP	DIW	$500	$350	$175
EM	1	HM	RP	$675	$450	$250
EM	1	SK	CM	$450	$300	$175
EM	1	SK	N/A	$650	$425	$225
EM	1	N/A	N/A	$750	$500	$275
EM	1	N/A	N/A	$1,675	$1,100	$600
EM	1	N/A	N/A	$425	$275	$150
EM	2	WN	RP	$800	$525	$275
EM	1	HH	N/A	$725	$475	$250
EM	1	N/A	N/A	$525	$350	$200
EM	4	TZ	CM	$550	$375	$200
M	1	N/A	N/A	$675	$450	$250
M	1	N/A	N/A	$675	$450	$250
M	1	N/A	N/A	$600	$400	$225
M	1	N/A	N/A	$650	$425	$225
EM	1	N/A	N/A	$550	$375	$200
M	1	N/A	N/A	$550	$375	$200
M	1	N/A	N/A	$400	$275	$150
SS	4	DL	GF	$725	$475	$250
EM	1	HH	N/A	$450	$300	$175
EM	1	SK	N/A	$675	$450	$250
SS	4	AS/JOB	TD	$1,375	$900	$475
EM	1	SK	GM	$550	$375	$200
EM	2	JP	DIW	$1,025	$675	$375
SS	4	JP	DIW	$550	$375	$200
SS	4	SR	TR	$1,650	$1,100	$575
SS	4	SR	DW	$1,875	$1,250	$675
SS	4	SR	TR	$1,375	$900	$500
SS	4	GC	GF	$800	$525	$275

Game	Manufacturer	Year	# Made
Black Rose	Bally	1992	3746
Black Velvet [1]	Game Plan	1978	N/A
Blackout	Williams	1980	7050
Blackwater 100	Bally	1988	3000
Blast Off [2]	Williams	1967	4635
Blondie	Genco	1940	N/A
Blondie	Chicago Coin	1956	N/A
Blue Bird	Bally	1936	N/A
Blue Chip [2]	Williams	1976	2150
Blue Max	Chicago Coin	1975	N/A
Blue Note	Gottlieb	1979	229
Blue Ribbon [3]	Bally	1933	N/A
Blue Ribbon	Bally	1965	875
Blue Skies	United Mfg.	1948	N/A
BMX	Bally	1982	406
Bo Bo	Williams	1961	400
Bola-Way	Chicago Coin	1941	1414
Bomber	Chicago Coin	1951	N/A
Bon Voyage	Bally	1974	1585
Bonanza	Exhibit Supply	1935	N/A
Bonanza	Gottlieb	1964	2640
Bone Busters Inc.	Gottlieb/Premier	1989	2000
Bone Head	Genco	1948	N/A
Bongo	Bally	1963	1050
Bonus	Bally	1936	N/A
Boogie	Allied Leisure	1976	N/A
Boom Town	Success Mfg.	1941	N/A
Boomerang	Bally	1974	2585
Booster [4]	Bally	1937	N/A
Border Town	Gottlieb	1940	N/A
Bosco	Genco	1941	N/A
Boston	Williams	1949	N/A
Bounty [5]	Exhibit Supply	1938	N/A
Bounty Hunter	Gottlieb/Premier	1985	1220
Bow and Arrow	Bally	1974	17
Bow and Arrow	Bally	1975	7630
Bowl A Strike [2]	Williams	1965	1401
Bowling Alley	Gottlieb	1939	N/A
Bowling Champ	Gottlieb	1949	2419

1. Cocktail table 2. Add-A-Ball 3. Car racing theme 4. Baseball theme 5. Free play

Type	Play	Designer	Artist	Class 1	Class 2	Class 3
SS	4	JT/BE	PM	$1,800	$1,200	$650
SS	4	EC	JS	$325	$225	$125
SS	4	CF	COM	$825	$550	$300
SS	4	DN	TR	$1,225	$825	$450
EM	1	NC	AS	$850	$575	$300
EM	1	N/A	N/A	$550	$350	$200
EM	1	JEK/JG/AP/ALS	RP	$475	$325	$175
EM-P	1	N/A	N/A	$1,000	$675	$350
EM	1	GH	LDR	$625	$425	$225
EM	4	JEK/AP/WM	N/A	$500	$350	$175
EM	1	JO	GOM	$850	$575	$300
M	1	HGB	N/A	$950	$650	$350
EM	4	TZ	N/A	$425	$275	$150
EM	1	N/A	N/A	$475	$325	$175
SS	4	WP	GF	$875	$575	$325
EM	1	SK	GM	$475	$325	$175
EM	1	N/A	N/A	$750	$500	$275
EM	1	N/A	RP	$500	$325	$175
EM	1	JP	DC	$600	$400	$225
EM-P	1	N/A	N/A	$725	$475	$250
EM	2	WN	RP	$650	$450	$250
SS	4	RT	COM/BJ	$1,200	$800	$425
EM	1	SK	N/A	$675	$450	$250
EM	2	TZ	N/A	$450	$300	$175
EM-P	1	N/A	N/A	$675	$450	$250
SS	4	JAP	RB	$350	$250	$125
EM	1	N/A	N/A	$325	$200	$125
EM	4	JP	CM	$625	$400	$225
EM	1	N/A	N/A	$1,200	$800	$425
EM	1	HM	RP	$625	$400	$225
EM	1	N/A	N/A	$675	$450	$250
EM	1	HW	GM	$550	$375	$200
EM	1	HW/LYD	N/A	$800	$550	$300
SS	4	JOB	LD	$650	$425	$225
SS	4	GK	CM	$1,500	$1,000	$525
EM	4	GK	CM	$725	$475	$250
EM	1	NC	N/A	$550	$375	$200
EM	1	HM	RP	$400	$275	$150
EM	1	HM	RP	$1,125	$750	$400

Game	Manufacturer	Year	# Made
Bowling League	Gottlieb	1947	1200
Bowling Queen	Gottlieb	1964	2650
Bowl-O	Bally	1970	1050
Box Score	Daval	1935	N/A
Box Score	Daval	1939	N/A
Bram Stoker's Dracula	Williams	1993	6801
Breakshot	Capcom	1996	1000
Bristol Hills [1]	Gottlieb	1971	110
Brite Spot	Stoner	1940	N/A
Brite Star	Gottlieb	1958	800
Broadcast	Bally	1941	N/A
Brokers Tip	Gottlieb	1933	N/A
Broncho	Genco	1947	N/A
Bronco	Chicago Coin	1963	N/A
Bronco	Gottlieb	1977	9160
Bubbles	Genco	1939	N/A
Buccaneer	Gottlieb	1948	3650
Buccaneer	Gottlieb	1976	3650
Buck Rogers	Gottlieb	1980	7410
Buckaroo [2]	Chicago Coin	1939	643
Buckaroo [3]	Chicago Coin	1939	127
Buckaroo [4]	Gottlieb	1965	2600
Budget	Chicago Coin	1936	430
Buffalo Bill	Gottlieb	1950	500
Bugs Bunny's Birthday Ball	Bally	1991	2500
Build Up	Exhibit Supply	1948	N/A
Builder Upper	GM Labs	1935	N/A
Bullfight	Bally	1965	825
Bull's Eye	Bally	1965	80
Bump-A-Lite	Chicago Coin	1937	N/A
Bumper	Bally	1936	N/A
Bus Stop	Bally	1964	825
Buttons	Exhibit Supply	1938	N/A
Buttons and Bows	Gottlieb	1949	2220
C.O.D [5]	Bally	1939	N/A
C.O.D.	Williams	1953	N/A
Cabaret	Williams	1968	3852
Cactus Canyon	Bally	1998	903
Cactus Jack's	Gottlieb/Premier	1991	1900

1. Add-A-Ball 2. Standard 3. Novelty play 4. Mechanical animation 5. Free plays

Type	Play	Designer	Artist	Class 1	Class 2	Class 3
EM	1	HM	RP	$675	$450	$250
EM	1	WN	RP	$1,175	$775	$425
EM	1	MAR	CM	$500	$350	$175
EM-P	1	N/A	N/A	$725	$475	$250
EM	1	N/A	N/A	$625	$400	$225
SS	4	BO/MS	MS	$1,975	$1,300	$700
SS	4	GK	SF	$1,350	$900	$475
EM	2	EK	AS	$650	$425	$225
EM	1	N/A	N/A	$425	$275	$150
EM	2	WN	RP	$725	$500	$275
EM	1	N/A	N/A	$625	$425	$225
M	1	N/A	N/A	$675	$450	$250
EM	1	HH/SK	N/A	$400	$275	$150
EM	2	ALS/JK	RP	$675	$450	$250
EM	4	EK	GOM	$975	$650	$350
EM	1	N/A	N/A	$600	$400	$225
EM-P	1	HM	RP	$1,100	$725	$400
EM	1	EK	GOM	$900	$600	$325
SS	4	JB	GOM	$725	$500	$275
EM	1	N/A	N/A	$925	$600	$325
EM	1	N/A	N/A	$950	$625	$350
EM	1	WN	RP	$2,350	$1,550	$825
EM	1	N/A	N/A	$550	$375	$200
EM	1	HM	RP	$4,000	$2,650	$1,400
SS	4	JT/PA	PA/JY	$1,850	$1,225	$650
EM	1	N/A	N/A	$450	$300	$175
EM	1	N/A	N/A	$1,500	$1,000	$525
EM	1	TZ	N/A	$450	$300	$175
EM	2	TZ	N/A	$1,575	$1,025	$550
EM-P	1	N/A	N/A	$725	$475	$250
EM	1	N/A	N/A	$675	$450	$250
EM	2	TZ	AS	$525	$350	$200
EM	1	HW/LYD	N/A	$900	$600	$325
EM	1	HM	RP	$925	$625	$325
N/A	1	N/A	N/A	$425	$275	$150
EM	1	HW	GM	$825	$550	$300
EM	4	SK	N/A	$400	$250	$150
SS	4	TOK/MC	JY	$10,825	$7,150	$3,800
SS	4	JN/RHB	DM/COM	$1,250	$825	$450

Game	Manufacturer	Year	# Made
Cadet	Bingo Novelty	1932	N/A
Cadet	Chicago Coin	1938	349
Cadillac	Genco	1940	N/A
Camel Caravan	Genco	1949	N/A
Camelot [1]	Bally	1970	1865
Campus	Exhibit Supply	1950	N/A
Campus Queen	Bally	1966	1125
Can Can [2]	Williams	1955	N/A
Canasta	Genco	1950	N/A
Cannon Fire	Mills Novelty Co.	1934	N/A
Cannon Fire Jr. [3]	Mills Novelty Co.	1934	N/A
Cannon Fire Jr.	Shyvers Coin	1934	N/A
Capersville	Bally	1966	5120
Capri	Chicago Coin	1956	N/A
Capt. Card [1]	Gottlieb	1974	675
Captain Fantastic	Bally	1976	16155
Captain Fantastic—X rated [4]	Bally	1976	100
Captain Hook	Game Plan	1985	450
Captain Kidd	Genco	1941	N/A
Captain Kidd	A.B.T. Mfg.	1936	N/A
Captain Kidd	Gottlieb	1960	900
Car Hop	Gottlieb/Premier	1991	1061
Caravan	Genco	1949	N/A
Caravan	Williams	1952	N/A
Caravelle	Williams	1961	425
Card Trix [1]	Gottlieb	1970	1750
Card Whiz	Gottlieb	1976	3250
Cargo	Genco	1937	N/A
Caribbean	United Mfg.	1948	N/A
Caribbean Cruise [5]	International Concepts	1989	377
Carioca	Western Products	1935	N/A
Carnival	Genco	1937	N/A
Carnival	Bally	1948	N/A
Carnival [6]	Bally	1957	N/A
Carolina	United Mfg.	1949	N/A
Carousel	J. H. Keeney & Co.	1947	N/A
Casanova [7]	Williams	1966	3575
Casino	Williams	1958	N/A
Casino	Chicago Coin	1972	N/A

1. Add-A-Ball 2. Full cabinet 3. 1st game with a kicker 4. X-Rated glass 5. Cocktail table
6. Push-up flippers 7. Mechanical animation

Type	Play	Designer	Artist	Class 1	Class 2	Class 3
M	1	N/A	N/A	$500	$325	$175
EM-P	1	N/A	N/A	$550	$375	$200
EM	1	N/A	N/A	$525	$350	$200
EM	1	EC	PL	$475	$325	$175
EM	4	TZ	CM	$425	$275	$150
EM	1	N/A	N/A	$400	$275	$150
EM	4	TZ	N/A	$450	$300	$175
EM	1	HW	GM	$975	$650	$350
EM	1	N/A	N/A	$425	$275	$150
EM	1	KS	N/A	$1,575	$1,050	$550
EM	1	KS	N/A	$1,400	$925	$500
EM	1	KS	N/A	$1,200	$800	$425
EM	4	TZ	JK	$825	$550	$300
EM	1	JEC/JG/AP/ALS	RP	$450	$300	$175
EM	1	EK	GOM	$925	$625	$325
EM	4	GK	DC	$1,675	$1,100	$600
EM	4	GK	DC	$1,875	$1,250	$675
SS	4	EC	N/A	$650	$425	$225
EM	1	N/A	N/A	$600	$400	$225
EM-P	1	N/A	N/A	$1,025	$675	$375
EM	2	WN	RP	$675	$450	$250
SS	4	JN	COM(B)/DM(P)	$1,150	$775	$425
EM	1	N/A	N/A	$475	$325	$175
EM	1	HW	GM	$625	$425	$225
EM	4	SK	GM	$400	$275	$150
EM	1	EK	AS	$675	$450	$250
EM	2	EK	GOM	$800	$550	$300
EM	1	N/A	N/A	$725	$475	$250
EM	1	N/A	N/A	$575	$375	$200
SS	4	JT	DM/COM	$500	$350	$175
EM-P	1	N/A	N/A	$725	$475	$250
EM	1	N/A	N/A	$600	$400	$225
EM	1	N/A	N/A	$625	$425	$225
EM	2	DH	N/A	$750	$500	$275
EM	1	N/A	N/A	$425	$300	$150
EM	1	N/A	N/A	$600	$400	$225
EM	2	SK	N/A	$525	$350	$200
EM	1	HW	GM	$775	$525	$275
EM	4	AP/JEK	CM	$475	$325	$175

Game	Manufacturer	Year	# Made
Catacomb	Stern	1981	N/A
Catalina	Chicago Coin	1948	2700
Cavalcade	Stoner	1935	N/A
Caveman [1]	Gottlieb	1982	1800
Centaur	Bally	1981	3700
Centaur II	Bally	1983	1550
Center Smash [2]	Western Products	1936	N/A
Centigrade 37	Gottlieb	1977	1600
Central Park [3]	Gottlieb	1966	3100
Challenger [2]	Bally	1936	N/A
Challenger [4]	Gottlieb	1971	1109
Champ, The	Gottlieb	1940	N/A
Champ [5]	Midway	1963	N/A
Champ [6]	Bally	1974	4070
Champion	Bally	1934	N/A
Champion	Bally	1939	N/A
Champion	Chicago Coin	1949	N/A
Champion Pub, The	Bally	1998	1369
Champs [7]	Genco	1936	N/A
Charlie's Angels	Gottlieb	1978	350
Charlie's Angels	Gottlieb	1978	7950
Chase	Pacific Amusement	1936	N/A
Checkers	Int'l. Mutoscope	1935	N/A
Checkpoint [8]	Data East	1991	3500
Cheer Leader	Genco	1935	N/A
Cheetah	Stern	1980	1223
Chevron	Bally	1939	N/A
Chicago Cubs Triple Play	Gottlieb/Premier	1985	1365
Chicago Express	Daval	1935	N/A
Chicago Express [9]	Daval	1938	N/A
Chico Baseball	Chicago Coin	1938	1001
Chico Derby	Chicago Coin	1937	1459
Chief	Exhibit Supply	1939	N/A
Chieftain	Pacific Amusement	1935	N/A
Chinatown	Gottlieb	1952	1500
Chubbie	Stoner	1938	N/A
Cinderella	Gottlieb	1948	4000
Cinema	Chicago Coin	1976	N/A
Circa 1933 [10]	Fascination Int'l. Inc.	1979	N/A

1. Video added 2. One-ball payout 3. Mechanical animation 4. Head-to-head play 5. Auto Racing
6. Add-A-Ball 7. Baseball theme 8. 1st DMD 9. Balls in backglass 10. Cocktail table

Type	Play	Designer	Artist	Class 1	Class 2	Class 3
SS	4	JJ	N/A	$950	$650	$350
EM	1	JEK	RP	$400	$275	$150
EM	1	N/A	N/A	$900	$600	$325
SS	4	JOB	TD/DM/RT	$775	$525	$275
SS	4	JP	PF	$2,025	$1,350	$725
SS	4	JP	PF	$1,275	$850	$450
EM-P	1	N/A	N/A	$1,200	$800	$425
EM	1	AE	GOM	$1,125	$750	$400
EM	1	EK	RP	$1,425	$950	$500
EM-P	1	N/A	N/A	$1,150	$750	$400
EM	2	EK	GOM	$1,975	$1,300	$700
EM	1	HM	RP	$550	$375	$200
EM	2	N/A	N/A	$1,200	$800	$425
EM	4	JP	CM	$575	$400	$200
EM-P	1	N/A	N/A	$775	$525	$275
EM	1	N/A	N/A	$625	$400	$225
EM	1	N/A	N/A	$500	$325	$175
SS	4	PEP	LAD/PB	$2,925	$1,925	$1,025
EM	1	N/A	N/A	$1,150	$750	$400
EM	4	AE	GOM	$2,000	$1,325	$700
SS	4	AE	GOM	$650	$450	$250
EM-P	1	N/A	N/A	$1,075	$725	$375
M	1	JF	N/A	$600	$400	$225
SS	4	JK/EC	PF	$1,200	$800	$425
EM	1	N/A	RP	$600	$400	$225
SS	4	HW	N/A	$675	$450	$250
EM	1	N/A	N/A	$475	$325	$175
SS	4	JT	LD	$1,750	$1,150	$625
EM	1	N/A	N/A	$1,800	$1,200	$650
EM	1	N/A	N/A	$1,900	$1,275	$675
EM	1	N/A	N/A	$900	$600	$325
EM	1	N/A	N/A	$600	$400	$225
EM	1	N/A	N/A	$600	$400	$225
EM	1	N/A	N/A	$675	$450	$250
EM	1	WN	RP	$1,350	$900	$475
EM	1	WB	N/A	$450	$300	$175
EM	1	HM	RP	$1,425	$950	$500
EM	4	AP/JEK/WM	LDR	$575	$375	$200
SS	4	N/A	N/A	$400	$275	$150

Game	Manufacturer	Year	# Made
Circus	Genco	1939	N/A
Circus	Exhibit Supply	1948	N/A
Circus [1]	Bally	1957	N/A
Circus [2]	Bally	1973	3550
Circus [3]	Gottlieb	1980	1700
Circus Wagon	Williams	1955	N/A
Cirqus Voltaire	Bally	1997	2704
City Slicker	Bally	1987	300
Class of 1812	Gottlieb/Premier	1991	1668
Classic [4]	Bally	1937	N/A
Classy Bowler	Gottlieb	1956	1100
Cleopatra	Marvel Mfg. Co.	1948	N/A
Cleopatra	Gottlieb	1977	1600
Cleopatra	Gottlieb	1977	7300
Click	J. H. Keeney & Co.	1947	N/A
Clipper	Stoner	1939	N/A
Clocker	Mills Novelty Co.	1939	N/A
Close Encounters	Gottlieb	1978	470
Close Encounters	Gottlieb	1978	9950
Cloverleaf	Gottlieb	1932	N/A
Club House	Williams	1958	N/A
Club Trophy [5]	Bally	1941	N/A
Coed	Exhibit Supply	1947	N/A
College Daze	Gottlieb	1949	2230
College Football	Gottlieb	1936	N/A
College Queens	Gottlieb	1969	1725
Colorama	J. H. Keeney & Co.	1963	N/A
Colors [6]	Williams	1954	N/A
Comet	Williams	1985	8100
Commander [7]	Genco	1933	N/A
Commodore	Chicago Coin	1939	2252
Coney Island	Exhibit Supply	1938	N/A
Coney Island, Old	Game Plan	1979	3000
Confucius Say [8]	Rotor Table Games	1936	N/A
Congo	Bally	1936	N/A
Congo	Exhibit Supply	1940	N/A
Congo	Williams	1995	2129
Conquest	Exhibit Supply	1939	N/A
Contact	Exhibit Supply	1939	N/A

1. Multiple balls 2. Add-A-Ball 3. Widebody 4. Chrome playfield 5. Replay unit 6. 2 midget playfields
7. Tabletop 8. Cocktail table

Type	Play	Designer	Artist	Class 1	Class 2	Class 3
EM	1	N/A	N/A	$675	$450	$250
EM	1	N/A	N/A	$450	$300	$150
EM	2	N/A	N/A	$1,375	$900	$475
EM	4	JP	DIW	$500	$325	$175
SS	4	EK	GOM	$650	$425	$225
EM	2	HW	GM	$625	$425	$225
SS	4	JP/CS	LID	$6,775	$4,475	$2,375
SS	4	GK	PM	$800	$550	$300
SS	4	RT/JK	DM/COM	$1,700	$1,125	$600
EM-P	1	N/A	N/A	$900	$600	$325
EM	1	WN	RP	$1,325	$875	$475
EM	1	N/A	N/A	$525	$350	$200
EM	4	EK	GOM	$900	$600	$325
SS	4	EK	GOM	$800	$525	$275
EM	1	N/A	N/A	$550	$375	$200
EM	1	N/A	N/A	$850	$550	$300
EM-P	1	N/A	N/A	$775	$525	$275
EM	4	EK	GOM	$1,150	$750	$400
SS	4	EK	GOM	$875	$575	$325
M-P	1	N/A	N/A	$1,200	$800	$425
EM	1	HW/SS	GM	$800	$525	$275
EM-P	1	N/A	N/A	$425	$275	$150
EM	1	N/A	N/A	$475	$325	$175
EM	1	WN	RP	$1,000	$675	$350
EM-P	1	N/A	N/A	$975	$650	$350
EM	4	EK	AS	$450	$300	$175
EM	2	N/A	N/A	$400	$275	$150
EM	1	HW	GM	$950	$650	$350
SS	4	BO	PA	$1,075	$725	$375
M	1	N/A	N/A	$425	$275	$150
EM	1	N/A	N/A	$550	$375	$200
EM	1	HW/LYD	N/A	$850	$550	$300
SS	4	EC/RS	DIW	$375	$250	$150
EM	1	N/A	N/A	$3,800	$2,525	$1,350
EM	1	N/A	N/A	$1,400	$925	$500
EM	1	N/A	N/A	$1,550	$1,025	$550
SS	4	JT	KO	$1,675	$1,100	$600
EM	1	N/A	N/A	$550	$375	$200
EM	1	LYD	N/A	$600	$400	$225

Game	Manufacturer	Year	# Made
Contact	Williams	1978	2502
Contact Sr. [1]	Pacific Amusement	1934	N/A
Contention	Gottlieb	1940	N/A
Contest	J. H. Keeney & Co.	1941	N/A
Contest	Gottlieb	1958	1100
Continental Cafe	Gottlieb	1957	1350
Control Tower	Williams	1951	N/A
Coquette	Williams	1962	N/A
Coronation	Gottlieb	1952	1100
Corral	Gottlieb	1961	2000
Corvette	Bally	1994	5001
Cosmic Gunfight	Williams	1982	1008
Cosmos [2]	Bally	1969	2160
Count-Down	Gottlieb	1979	9899
Counterforce	Gottlieb	1980	3870
County Fair [3]	United Mfg.	1951	N/A
Cover Girl	Gottlieb	1945	N/A
Cover Girl	J. H. Keeney & Co.	1947	N/A
Cover Girl	Gottlieb	1962	2100
Cow Poke [3]	Gottlieb	1965	1256
Cowboy	Chicago Coin	1970	N/A
Cracker Jack	Chicago Coin	1936	338
Crazy Ball [4]	Chicago Coin	1948	900
Creature from the Black Lagoon	Bally	1992	7841
Credit	Rock-Ola	1936	N/A
Crescendo	Gottlieb	1970	1175
Criss Cross	Genco	1934	N/A
Criss Cross	Gottlieb	1958	1900
Criss Cross A-Lite	Genco	1935	N/A
Cross Country	Bally	1963	500
Cross Fire	Exhibit Supply	1947	N/A
Cross Town	Gottlieb	1966	2765
Crossroads	Stoner	1935	N/A
Crossroads	Gottlieb	1952	1300
Crossword	Williams	1959	N/A
Crusader [5]	Bally	1933	N/A
CSI	Stern	2008	N/A
Cue	Chicago Coin	1936	351
Cue Junior	Chicago Coin	1936	N/A

1. 4 sizes   2. Light animation   3. Mechanical animation   4. Playfield spinner   5. Large-size only

Type	Play	Designer	Artist	Class 1	Class 2	Class 3
EM	4	SK	CM	$525	$350	$200
EM	1	HW	N/A	$575	$375	$200
EM	1	HM	RP	$500	$325	$175
EM	1	N/A	N/A	$425	$275	$150
EM	4	WN	RP	$650	$425	$225
EM	2	WN	RP	$600	$400	$225
EM	1	HW	GM	$800	$525	$275
EM	1	SK	GM	$450	$300	$175
EM	1	HM	RP	$1,250	$825	$450
EM	1	WN	RP	$875	$575	$300
SS	4	GEG	DH	$2,900	$1,925	$1,025
SS	4	BO	LD(P)/DW(B)	$1,000	$675	$350
EM	4	TZ	JK	$625	$425	$225
SS	4	EK	GOM	$575	$400	$225
SS	4	EK	GOM	$675	$450	$250
EM	1	N/A	N/A	$700	$450	$250
EM	1	N/A	N/A	$625	$425	$225
EM	1	N/A	N/A	$550	$375	$200
EM	1	WN	RP	$725	$475	$250
EM	1	WN	RP	$2,300	$1,525	$825
EM	4	JEK	CM	$550	$375	$200
EM	1	N/A	N/A	$675	$450	$250
EM	1	N/A	RP	$650	$450	$250
SS	4	JT	KO	$3,225	$2,125	$1,125
EM-P	1	N/A	N/A	$850	$550	$300
EM	2	EK	AS	$600	$400	$225
M	1	HH	N/A	$550	$375	$200
EM	1	WN	RP	$1,075	$725	$375
EM	1	HH	N/A	$800	$550	$300
EM	1	TZ	N/A	$875	$600	$325
EM	1	N/A	N/A	$600	$400	$225
EM	1	EK	AS	$1,375	$925	$500
EM	1	N/A	N/A	$725	$475	$250
EM	1	WN	RP	$1,050	$700	$375
EM	1	HW	GM	$900	$600	$325
M	1	N/A	N/A	$500	$325	$175
SS	4	PL	JY/MH	$4,125	$2,725	$1,450
EM	1	N/A	N/A	$750	$500	$275
EM	1	N/A	N/A	$775	$525	$275

Game	Manufacturer	Year	# Made
Cue Senior De Luxe	Chicago Coin	1936	N/A
Cue Ball	Williams	1956	N/A
Cue Ball Wizard	Gottlieb/Premier	1992	5700
Cue-T	Williams	1968	2800
Cue-Tease	Bally	1963	500
Cue-Tee	Williams	1954	N/A
Cybernaut	Bally	1985	900
Cyclone	Delmar Mfg. Co.	1932	N/A
Cyclone	Gottlieb	1935	N/A
Cyclone	Williams	1947	N/A
Cyclone	Gottlieb	1951	800
Cyclone	Williams	1988	9400
Cyclopes	Game Plan	1985	400
Daffie [1]	Williams	1968	2453
Daffy Derby [2]	Williams	1954	N/A
Daily Races	Gottlieb	1936	N/A
Daisy [3]	Peo Mfg. Corp.	1932	N/A
Daisy May [4]	Gottlieb	1954	600
Dale Jr.	Stern	2007	600
Dallas	Williams	1949	N/A
Dancing Dolls [2]	Gottlieb	1960	1150
Dancing Lady [2]	Gottlieb	1966	2675
Dark Horse [5]	Bally	1940	N/A
Darling	Williams	1973	3677
Darts [6]	Williams	1960	N/A
Davy Jones	Stoner	1939	N/A
Daytona	Stoner	1937	N/A
Dead Heat [7]	Western Products	1939	N/A
Deadly Weapon	Gottlieb/Premier	1990	803
Dealer [8]	Williams	1953	N/A
Dealer's Choice [9]	Williams	1974	8850
Deauville	L. B. Elliot Products	1937	N/A
Defender	Williams	1982	369
Defense	Baker Novelty	1940	N/A
Defense	Genco	1943	N/A
De-Icer	Williams	1949	N/A
Delta Queen	Bally	1974	1575
Demolition Man	Williams	1994	7019
Derby	Bally	1935	N/A

1. Zipper flippers 2. Mechanical animation 3. Tabletop 4. Double award 5. Free play
6. 1960s-style cabinet 7. Full cabinet 8. Reel scoring 9. Add-A-Ball

Type	Play	Designer	Artist	Class 1	Class 2	Class 3
EM	1	N/A	N/A	$800	$550	$300
EM	1	HW	GM	$825	$550	$300
SS	4	JN	DM(BG)/COM	$1,675	$1,100	$600
EM	1	NC	CM	$425	$300	$150
EM	2	TZ	N/A	$375	$250	$150
EM	1	HW	GM	$550	$375	$200
SS	4	GK	DW	$800	$525	$275
M	1	N/A	N/A	$1,000	$675	$350
EM	1	N/A	N/A	$600	$400	$225
EM	1	HW	N/A	$550	$375	$200
EM	1	WN	RP	$1,150	$775	$425
SS	4	BO	PA	$1,425	$950	$500
SS	4	RS	SM	$500	$325	$175
EM	1	SK	CM	$450	$300	$175
EM	1	HW	GM	$825	$550	$300
EM-P	1	N/A	RP	$975	$650	$350
M	1	N/A	N/A	$600	$400	$225
EM	1	WN	RP	$2,175	$1,450	$775
SS	4	N/A	N/A	$3,900	$2,575	$1,375
EM	1	HW	GM	$475	$300	$175
EM	1	WN	RP	$1,000	$675	$350
EM	4	EK	AS	$800	$525	$275
EM	1	N/A	N/A	$500	$325	$175
EM	2	SK	CM	$450	$300	$175
EM	1	SK	GM	$375	$250	$150
EM	1	N/A	N/A	$500	$325	$175
EM	1	N/A	N/A	$675	$450	$250
EM-P	1	N/A	N/A	$725	$475	$250
SS	4	JT/JN	COM(B)/DM(P)	$675	$450	$250
EM	1	HW	GM	$1,200	$800	$425
EM	4	NC	CM	$625	$425	$225
EM-P	1	N/A	N/A	$1,800	$1,200	$650
SS	4	BO/JK	COM	$1,450	$950	$525
EM	1	N/A	N/A	$600	$400	$225
EM	1	N/A	N/A	$500	$325	$175
EM	1	HW	GM	$700	$475	$250
EM	1	JP	CM	$600	$400	$225
SS	4	DN	DW/LID	$1,675	$1,125	$600
EM-P	1	BOM	N/A	$900	$600	$325

Game	Manufacturer	Year	# Made
Derby Clock [1]	Western Products	1939	N/A
Derby Day [2]	Gottlieb	1936	N/A
Derby Day	Gottlieb	1956	1600
Derby Day [3]	Williams	1967	N/A
Derby King	Western Products	1938	N/A
Derby Time [1]	Western Products	1938	N/A
Devil's Dare	Gottlieb	1982	3832
Dew-Wa-Ditty	Williams	1948	N/A
Diamond Jack [4,6]	Gottlieb	1967	650
Diamond Lady	Gottlieb/Premier	1988	2700
Diamond Lill [5]	Gottlieb	1954	700
Dimension [6]	Gottlieb	1971	490
Diner	Williams	1990	3552
Ding Dong	Williams	1968	1850
Dipsy Doodle	Williams	1970	N/A
Dirty Harry	Williams	1995	4248
Disco	Stern	1977	815
Disco Fever [7]	Williams	1978	6000
Disco '79 [8]	Allied Leisure	1979	N/A
Discotek	Bally	1965	730
Discovery	Pacific Amusement	1935	N/A
Disk Jockey [9]	Williams	1952	N/A
Ditto	Rock-Ola	1936	N/A
Dixie	Chicago Coin	1940	2297
Dixieland [10]	Bally	1968	1800
Do Re Me	Exhibit Supply	1941	N/A
Dr. Dude	Bally	1990	4000
Doctor Who	Bally	1992	7752
Dodge City [4]	Gottlieb	1965	3175
Dogies	Bally	1968	3670
Dolly Parton	Bally	1979	7350
Dolphin	Chicago Coin	1974	N/A
Domino	Williams	1952	N/A
Domino	Gottlieb	1968	2650
Doodle Bug	Williams	1971	N/A
Doozie	Williams	1968	2150
Double Action	Genco	1951	N/A
Double Action [11]	Gottlieb	1958	1000
Double Barrel	Bally	1946	N/A

1. Full cabinet 2. With clock 3. Mech. horse race 4. Mech. animation 5. Double award 6. Add-A-Ball
7. Banana flippers 8. Cocktail table model 9. Bingo type 10. Bagatelle on playfield 11. Vertical flippers

Type	Play	Designer	Artist	Class 1	Class 2	Class 3
EM-P	1	N/A	N/A	$850	$550	$300
EM-P	1	N/A	N/A	$1,150	$750	$400
EM	1	WN	RP	$1,200	$800	$425
EM	2	SK	CM	$650	$450	$250
EM	1	N/A	N/A	$725	$475	$250
EM-P	1	N/A	N/A	$725	$475	$250
SS	4	TS	DW/DM	$725	$475	$275
EM	1	HW	GM	$550	$350	$200
EM	4	EK	AS	$1,200	$800	$425
SS	4	JN	COM	$600	$400	$225
EM	1	WN	RP	$1,950	$1,300	$700
EM	1	EK	GOM	$1,300	$850	$450
SS	4	MR	MS	$2,075	$1,375	$725
EM	1	NC	CM	$500	$325	$175
EM	4	NC	CM	$550	$375	$200
SS	4	BO	KO/PM	$2,075	$1,375	$725
EM	2	N/A	N/A	$450	$300	$175
SS	4	TK	CM	$500	$350	$175
SS	4	BB	RMT	$350	$250	$125
EM	2	TZ	N/A	$500	$325	$175
EM-P	1	N/A	N/A	$550	$375	$200
EM	1	HW	GM	$775	$500	$275
EM	1	N/A	N/A	$500	$325	$175
EM	1	N/A	N/A	$500	$325	$175
EM	1	TZ	CM	$625	$400	$225
EM	1	N/A	N/A	$425	$275	$150
SS	4	DN	GF	$1,900	$1,250	$675
SS	4	BO/BP	LID	$1,875	$1,250	$675
EM	4	EK	RP	$975	$650	$350
EM	4	TZ	JK	$625	$425	$225
SS	4	GC	DC	$900	$600	$325
EM	2	AP/WM	CM	$425	$275	$150
EM	1	HW	GM	$575	$375	$200
EM-P	1	EK	AS	$700	$450	$250
EM	1	NC	CM	$550	$375	$200
EM	1	SK	CM	$500	$325	$175
EM	1	N/A	N/A	$625	$400	$225
EM	2	WN	RP	$525	$350	$200
EM	1	N/A	N/A	$550	$375	$200

Game	Manufacturer	Year	# Made
Double Barrel	Williams	1961	700
Double Feature [1]	Gottlieb	1937	N/A
Double Feature	Stoner	1940	N/A
Double-Feature [2]	Gottlieb	1950	550
Double Header	Mills Novelty Co.	1936	N/A
Double Play	Exhibit Supply	1941	N/A
Double-Shuffle [3]	Hercules Novelty Co.	1932	N/A
Double-Shuffle	Gottlieb	1949	911
Double Track [4]	Genco	1938	N/A
Double-Up	Bally	1970	55
Doughboy	Baker Novelty	1940	N/A
Dracula	Stern	1979	3612
Dragon	Gottlieb	1978	6550
Dragon	Gottlieb	1978	507
Dragonette [5]	Gottlieb	1954	950
Dragonfist	Stern	1982	N/A
Draw Ball	Rock-Ola	1936	N/A
Dreamy	Williams	1950	N/A
Drop Kick	Exhibit Supply	1934	N/A
Drop-A-Card	Gottlieb	1971	2600
Drum Major	Gottlieb	1940	N/A
Dude Ranch	Genco	1940	N/A
Duette	Gottlieb	1955	326
Duette Deluxe	Gottlieb	1955	736
Dungeons & Dragons	Bally	1987	2000
Duotron	Gottlieb	1974	2525
Duplex	Exhibit Supply	1940	N/A
Dutch Pool	A.B.T. Manfacturing	1931	N/A
Dux [4]	Chicago Coin	1937	1809
Dyn O' Mite	Allied Leisure	1975	N/A
Dynamite	Williams	1946	N/A
Eager Beaver	Williams	1965	1301
Earthshaker	Williams	1989	N/A
Earthshaker [6]	Williams	1989	N/A
Easy Aces [7]	Gottlieb	1955	1100
Easy Steps [8]	Rock-Ola	1938	N/A
Eclipse	Pacific Amusement	1935	N/A
Eclipse	Gottlieb	1982	193
Egg Head	Gottlieb	1961	2100

1. Movie theme 2. First cyclonic kicker 3. Mechanical flippers 4. Mechanical animation 5. Double award
6. Falling station 7. First steel legs 8. Gives odds

Type	Play	Designer	Artist	Class 1	Class 2	Class 3
EM	2	SK	GM	$475	$325	$175
EM-P	1	N/A	RP	$1,450	$950	$500
EM	1	N/A	N/A	$425	$275	$150
EM	1	WN	RP	$1,375	$925	$500
EM-P	1	N/A	N/A	$600	$400	$225
EM	1	N/A	N/A	$675	$450	$250
M	1	N/A	N/A	$1,025	$675	$375
EM	1	HM	RP	$925	$625	$325
EM	2	N/A	N/A	$1,150	$750	$400
EM	1	TZ	CM	$2,500	$1,650	$875
EM	1	N/A	N/A	$450	$300	$175
SS	4	HW	N/A	$775	$525	$275
SS	4	EK	GOM	$650	$425	$225
EM	4	EK	GOM	$975	$650	$350
EM	1	WN	RP	$3,225	$2,150	$1,150
SS	4	JJ	DW	$500	$325	$175
EM-P	1	N/A	N/A	$725	$475	$250
EM	1	HW	GM	$650	$425	$225
EM	1	BR	N/A	$550	$350	$200
EM	1	EK	GM	$1,100	$725	$400
EM	1	HM	RP	$550	$375	$200
EM	1	N/A	N/A	$500	$325	$175
EM	2	WN	RP	$650	$450	$250
EM	2	WN	RP	$750	$500	$275
SS	4	WP	PM	$1,125	$750	$400
EM	2	EK	GOM	$575	$375	$200
EM	1	N/A	N/A	$425	$275	$150
M	1	N/A	N/A	$2,700	$1,800	$950
EM	1	JK	N/A	$850	$550	$300
SS	2	JAP	RB	$375	$250	$150
EM	1	N/A	N/A	$550	$375	$200
EM	2	NC	AS	$375	$250	$150
SS	4	PL	TE	$1,550	$1,025	$550
SS	4	PL	TE	$1,700	$1,125	$600
EM	1	WN	RP	$1,350	$900	$475
EM	1	N/A	N/A	$500	$325	$175
EM-P	1	N/A	N/A	$850	$550	$300
SS	4	JOB/AS	N/A	$850	$575	$300
EM	1	WN	RP	$875	$600	$325

Game	Manufacturer	Year	# Made
Eight and Six [1]	Silver Star Mfg Co.	1932	N/A
8 Ball	Williams	1952	N/A
8 Ball	Williams	1966	3250
Eight Ball	Bally	1977	20230
Eight Ball Champ	Bally	1985	1500
Eight Ball Deluxe	Bally	1981	8250
Eight Ball Deluxe	Bally	1984	N/A
Eight Ball Deluxe Limited Edition	Bally	1982	2388
El Dorado	Gottlieb	1975	2875
El Dorado City of Gold	Gottlieb/Premier	1984	905
El Paso	Williams	1948	N/A
El Toro	Exhibit Supply	1938	N/A
El Toro	Williams	1963	1850
El Toro [2]	Bally	1972	2065
Elektra	Bally	1981	2950
Elvira and the Party Monsters	Bally	1989	4000
Elvis	Stern	2004	N/A
Elvis Gold	Stern	2004	500
Embryon	Bally	1981	2250
Entry	Bally	1938	N/A
Entry	Bally	1946	N/A
Escape from the Lost World	Bally	1988	1500
Esquire	Stoner	1934	N/A
Eureka	Bally	1938	N/A
Eureka	Bally	1947	N/A
Evel Knievel [3]	Bally	1977	155
Evel Knievel	Bally	1977	1400
Excalibur	Gottlieb/Premier	1988	1710
Expo [4]	Williams	1969	N/A
Exposition	Chicago Coin	1938	147
Expressway	Bally	1971	1555
Extra Inning	Gottlieb	1971	350
Eye of the Tiger	Gottlieb	1978	730
F-14 Tomcat	Williams	1987	14502
Fair	Genco	1939	N/A
Fair Grounds [5]	Bally	1937	N/A
Fair Lady	Gottlieb	1956	550
Fairway	Williams	1953	N/A
Falstaff	Gottlieb	1957	850

1. 2 sizes 2. Add-A-Ball 3. Rare EM version 4. Mechanical animation 5. Large cabinet

Type	Play	Designer	Artist	Class 1	Class 2	Class 3
M	1	N/A	N/A	$600	$400	$225
EM	1	HW	GM	$900	$600	$325
EM	2	NC	N/A	$625	$400	$225
SS	4	GC	PF	$1,250	$825	$450
SS	4	GC	TR	$900	$600	$325
SS	4	GC	MH	$1,700	$1,125	$600
SS	4	GC	MH	$1,450	$975	$525
SS	4	GC	MH	$2,075	$1,375	$725
EM	1	EK	GOM	$1,600	$1,050	$575
SS	4	EK	LD	$1,025	$675	$375
EM	1	HW	GM	$525	$350	$200
EM	1	N/A	N/A	$575	$375	$200
EM	2	SK	GM	$500	$325	$175
EM	1	JP	DIW	$650	$425	$225
SS	4	CF	TR	$950	$625	$350
SS	4	DN/JP	GF	$2,050	$1,350	$725
SS	4	SR	JV/KO	$4,025	$2,650	$1,425
SS	4	SR	JVKO	$4,900	$3,225	$1,725
SS	4	CF	TR	$1,125	$750	$400
EM	1	N/A	N/A	$500	$350	$175
EM-P	1	N/A	N/A	$900	$600	$325
SS	4	DL	GF	$1,025	$675	$375
EM	1	N/A	N/A	$550	$375	$200
EM	1	N/A	N/A	$500	$325	$175
EM	1	N/A	N/A	$550	$375	$200
EM	4	GG	PF	$3,125	$2,050	$1,100
SS	4	GG	PF	$1,775	$1,175	$625
SS	4	JT/JN	COM	$700	$475	$250
EM	2	NC	CM	$500	$350	$175
EM	1	N/A	N/A	$725	$475	$250
EM	1	TZ	CM	$600	$400	$225
EM	1	EK	GOM	$750	$500	$275
EM	2	EK	GOM	$1,025	$700	$375
SS	4	SR	DW	$1,600	$1,050	$575
EM	1	N/A	N/A	$725	$475	$250
EM-P	1	N/A	N/A	$675	$450	$250
EM	2	WN	RP	$475	$325	$175
EM	1	HW	GM	$875	$575	$325
EM	4	WN	RP	$450	$300	$175

Game	Manufacturer	Year	# Made
Family Guy	Stern	2007	N/A
Fan-Tas-Tic	Williams	1972	5680
Fantasy	Stoner	1940	N/A
Far Out	Gottlieb	1974	4820
Fashion Show	Gottlieb	1962	2675
Fast Ball	Exhibit Supply	1946	N/A
Fast Draw	Gottlieb	1975	8045
Fathom	Bally	1981	3500
Favorite [1]	Buckley Mfg.	1932	N/A
Feed Bag [2]	Western Equipment	1938	N/A
Fence Buster	Gottlieb	1936	N/A
Festival	Chicago Coin	1966	N/A
Fiesta	Exhibit Supply	1946	N/A
Fiesta	Williams	1959	N/A
Fifth Inning	Bally	1939	N/A
50/50	Bally	1965	580
Fighting Irish	Chicago Coin	1950	N/A
Finance	Chicago Coin	1936	362
Fire Alarm	Gottlieb	1939	N/A
Fire Chief	Gottlieb	1935	N/A
Fire Cracker [3]	J. H. Keeney & Co.	1937	N/A
Fire Cracker	Chicago Coin	1963	N/A
Fire Queen	Gottlieb	1977	970
Fire!	Williams	1987	7700
Fire! Champagne Edition	Williams	1987	273
Fireball	Bally	1972	3815
Fireball II	Bally	1981	2300
Fireball Classic	Bally	1985	2000
Firecracker [4]	Bally	1971	2800
Firepower	Williams	1980	17410
Firepower II	Williams	1983	3400
Fish Tales	Williams	1992	13640
Five & Ten	Stoner	1935	N/A
Five & Ten	Gottlieb	1941	N/A
Five Star Final [5]	Gottlieb	1932	N/A
Five Star Final Jr. [5]	Gottlieb	1932	N/A
Five Star Final Sr.	Gottlieb	1932	N/A
Five Star Reserve	Gottlieb	1938	N/A
Flag-Ship	Gottlieb	1957	1250

1. Tabletop w/ optional legs   2. Full cabinet   3. Five-ball game   4. Free-ball gate   5. Tabletop

Type	Play	Designer	Artist	Class 1	Class 2	Class 3
SS	4	PL	JY/MH	$4,150	$2,750	$1,450
EM	4	NC	CM	$525	$350	$200
EM	1	N/A	N/A	$600	$400	$225
EM	4	EK	GOM	$800	$525	$275
EM	2	WN	RP	$450	$300	$175
EM	1	N/A	N/A	$725	$475	$250
EM	4	EK	GOM	$875	$575	$325
SS	4	WP	GF	$3,175	$2,100	$1,125
M	1	N/A	N/A	$425	$275	$150
EM-P	1	N/A	N/A	$725	$475	$250
EM-P	1	N/A	N/A	$1,200	$800	$425
EM	4	ALS/JEK/JG	N/A	$375	$250	$125
EM	1	N/A	N/A	$425	$275	$150
EM	2	HW	GM	$450	$300	$175
EM	1	N/A	N/A	$800	$550	$300
EM	2	TZ	N/A	$500	$325	$175
EM	1	N/A	RP	$1,150	$775	$425
EM	1	N/A	N/A	$975	$650	$350
EM	1	HM	RP	$725	$475	$250
EM	1	N/A	N/A	$500	$325	$175
EM	1	N/A	N/A	$675	$450	$250
EM	2	JG/AP/JEK/WM	RP	$625	$425	$225
EM	2	EK	GOM	$1,000	$675	$350
SS	4	BO	MS	$1,475	$975	$525
SS	4	BO	MS	$1,650	$1,100	$600
EM	4	TZ	DC	$2,275	$1,500	$800
SS	4	GG	DC	$1,350	$900	$475
SS	4	GC	DW	$1,600	$1,050	$575
EM	4	HW	CM	$625	$425	$225
SS	4	SR	COM	$875	$575	$325
SS	4	MR	COM	$800	$550	$300
SS	4	MR	PM	$2,200	$1,450	$775
EM	1	N/A	N/A	$500	$325	$175
EM	1	HM	RP	$500	$325	$175
M	1	N/A	N/A	$775	$525	$275
M	1	N/A	N/A	$725	$500	$275
M	1	N/A	N/A	$800	$550	$300
EM-P	1	N/A	N/A	$625	$400	$225
EM	2	WN	RP	$600	$400	$225

Game	Manufacturer	Year	# Made
Flagship	Exhibit Supply	1940	N/A
Flamingo	Williams	1947	N/A
Flash [1]	R.& H. Sales Company	1932	N/A
Flash	Rock-Ola	1935	N/A
Flash	Exhibit Supply	1939	N/A
Flash	Williams	1979	19505
Flash Gordon	Bally	1981	10000
Fleet	Bally	1938	N/A
Fleet	Bally	1940	N/A
Fleet Jr.	Bally	1934	N/A
Fleet Sr.	Bally	1934	N/A
Flicker	O. D. Jennings Co.	1936	N/A
Flicker [2]	Bally	1975	1585
Flight	Exhibit Supply	1938	N/A
Flight 2000	Stern	1980	6301
Flintstones, The	Williams	1994	4779
Flip Flop!	Bally	1976	5350
Flip-A-Card	Gottlieb	1970	1800
Flipper [2]	Gottlieb	1960	685
Flipper [3]	Gottlieb	1960	415
Flipper Clown [4]	Gottlieb	1962	1550
Flipper Cowboy [4]	Gottlieb	1962	1000
Flipper Fair [4]	Gottlieb	1961	1150
Flipper Football	Capcom	1996	750
Flipper Parade [4]	Gottlieb	1961	1500
Flipper Pool [4]	Gottlieb	1965	700
Floating Power	Genco	1948	N/A
Flying Carpet	Gottlieb	1972	3170
Flying Champ	Western Products	1941	N/A
Flying Chariots	Gottlieb	1963	3410
Flying Circus	Gottlieb	1961	2050
Flying High	Western Equipment	1936	N/A
Flying High	Gottlieb	1953	1400
Flying Saucers	Genco	1950	N/A
Flying Trapeze	Gottlieb	1947	1000
Flying Trapeze Jr.	Gottlieb	1934	N/A
Flying Trapeze Sr.	Gottlieb	1934	N/A
Flying Turf [5]	O. D. Jennings & Co.	1935	N/A
Flying Turns [6]	Midway Mfg.	1964	N/A

1. Neon 2. Add-A-Ball 3. Woodrail 4. Add-A-Ball/Mechanical animation 5. Similar to Sportsman
6. Mechanical animation

Type	Play	Designer	Artist	Class 1	Class 2	Class 3
EM	1	N/A	N/A	$550	$375	$200
EM	1	N/A	N/A	$500	$350	$175
M	1	OHR	N/A	$625	$425	$225
M	1	N/A	N/A	$675	$450	$250
EM	1	HW/LYD	N/A	$550	$375	$200
SS	4	SR	COM	$950	$625	$350
SS	4	CF	KO	$1,200	$800	$425
EM	1	N/A	N/A	$475	$325	$175
EM	1	N/A	N/A	$725	$475	$250
EM	1	HGB	N/A	$775	$525	$275
EM	1	HBG	N/A	$800	$550	$300
EM-P	1	N/A	N/A	$725	$475	$250
EM	2	JP	DIW	$750	$500	$275
EM	1	N/A	N/A	$600	$400	$225
SS	4	HW	DW(B)/GS(P)	$1,100	$750	$400
SS	4	JT/JN	KO	$2,200	$1,450	$775
EM	4	JP	DIW	$825	$550	$300
EM	1	EK	AS	$800	$525	$300
EM	1	WN	RP	$1,925	$1,275	$675
EM	1	WN	RP	$2,200	$1,450	$775
EM	1	WN	RP	$1,650	$1,100	$575
EM	1	WN	RP	$1,800	$1,200	$650
EM	1	WN	RP	$1,425	$950	$500
SS	6	BH/PA	HV	$1,100	$725	$400
EM	1	WN	RP	$1,400	$925	$500
EM	1	EK	RP	$1,100	$725	$400
EM	1	N/A	RP	$650	$450	$250
EM	1	EK	GOM	$850	$575	$300
EM	1	N/A	N/A	$675	$450	$250
EM	2	WN	RP	$550	$375	$200
EM	2	WN	RP	$825	$550	$300
EM-P	1	N/A	N/A	$975	$650	$350
EM	1	WN	RP	$1,300	$850	$475
EM	1	SK	RP	$825	$550	$300
EM	1	HM	RP	$600	$400	$225
EM	1	N/A	N/A	$625	$425	$225
EM	1	N/A	N/A	$675	$450	$250
EM-P	1	N/A	N/A	$1,600	$1,075	$575
EM	2	N/A	GM	$2,125	$1,400	$750

Game	Manufacturer	Year	# Made
Follies of 1940	Genco	1939	N/A
Football	O. D. Jennings and Co.	1934	N/A
Football	Exhibit Supply	1935	N/A
Football	Chicago Coin	1949	N/A
Football of 1937 [1]	Genco	1937	N/A
Force II	Gottlieb	1981	2000
Fore	Bally	1973	80
Formation	Genco	1940	N/A
Fortune	Rock-Ola	1936	N/A
Fortune [2]	J. H. Keeney & Co.	1941	N/A
41-Derby [2]	Bally	1941	N/A
42nd Street	Genco	1933	N/A
Forward March	Mills Novelty Co.	1937	N/A
Foto Finish	Gottlieb	1937	N/A
Foto Finish [3]	Gottlieb	1961	1000
4 Aces	Williams	1970	N/A
Four Aces	Genco	1942	N/A
4-Belles	Gottlieb	1954	400
Four Corners [4]	Williams	1952	N/A
Four Diamonds	J. H. Keeney & Co.	1941	N/A
Four-Five-Six	Baker Novelty	1940	N/A
4 Horsemen, The	Gottlieb	1950	1800
Four Million B.C.	Bally	1971	3550
4 Queens [5]	Bally	1970	1256
Four Roses	Genco	1940	N/A
4 Roses	Williams	1962	1250
Four Seasons	Gottlieb	1968	1500
4 Square	Gottlieb	1971	2200
4 Star	Williams	1958	N/A
Four Stars	Gottlieb	1952	950
Fox Hunt	Chicago Coin	1940	1503
Foxy Lady [6]	Game Plan	1978	N/A
Frankenstein, Mary Shelley's	Sega	1995	3000
Freddy: a Nightmare on Elm Street	Gottlieb/Premier	1994	2800
Free Fall [5]	Gottlieb	1974	650
Freedom	Bally	1976	5080
Freedom	Bally	1976	1500
Freefall	Stern	1981	1300
Freshie	Williams	1949	N/A

1. Light animation 2. Full cabinet 3. Metal rail (there's also a rare woodrail version) 4. Bingo type
5. Add-A-Ball 6. Cocktail table

Type	Play	Designer	Artist	Class 1	Class 2	Class 3
EM	1	N/A	N/A	$550	$375	$200
EM	1	N/A	N/A	$1,700	$1,125	$600
EM-P	1	N/A	N/A	$700	$475	$250
EM	1	N/A	N/A	$525	$350	$200
EM	1	N/A	N/A	$1,075	$725	$375
SS	4	JO	DM	$1,025	$675	$375
EM	1	JP	BT	$750	$500	$275
EM	1	N/A	N/A	$600	$400	$225
EM-P	1	N/A	N/A	$900	$600	$325
EM-P	1	N/A	N/A	$675	$450	$250
EM-P	1	N/A	N/A	$675	$450	$250
M	1	HH	N/A	$525	$350	$200
EM	1	N/A	N/A	$550	$375	$200
EM-P	1	N/A	RP	$1,200	$800	$425
EM	1	WN	RP	$1,500	$1,000	$525
EM	2	SK	N/A	$375	$250	$150
EM	1	N/A	N/A	$425	$275	$150
EM	1	WN	RP	$2,450	$1,625	$875
EM	1	HW	GM	$925	$600	$325
EM	1	N/A	N/A	$550	$375	$200
EM	1	N/A	N/A	$500	$325	$175
EM	1	WN	RP	$1,075	$725	$375
EM	4	TZ	DIW	$1,325	$875	$475
EM	1	JP	CM	$600	$400	$225
EM	1	N/A	N/A	$500	$325	$175
EM	1	SK	GM	$525	$350	$200
EM	4	EK	AS	$425	$275	$150
EM	1	EK	GOM	$675	$450	$250
EM	1	HW	GM	$750	$500	$275
EM	1	WN	RP	$1,200	$800	$425
EM	1	N/A	N/A	$575	$375	$200
SS	4	EC/WM	PL	$375	$250	$150
SS	4	JONB	PF	$1,700	$1,125	$600
SS	4	BP/RT	COM	$1,800	$1,200	$650
EM	1	EK	GOM	$700	$475	$250
EM-P	4	CF	CM	$700	$475	$250
SS	4	CF	CM	$500	$325	$175
SS	4	HW	N/A	$600	$400	$225
EM	1	HW/SS	GM	$825	$550	$300

Game	Manufacturer	Year	# Made
Friendship "7" [1]	Williams	1962	800
Frontier	Bally	1980	1850
Frontiersman	Gottlieb	1955	1000
Full House	Williams	1966	2900
Fun Cruise [2]	Bally	1965	675
Fun House	Williams	1956	N/A
Fun Land	Gottlieb	1968	3100
Fun Park [1]	Gottlieb	1968	580
Fun-Fair	Genco	1958	N/A
Fun-Fest	Williams	1973	6025
Funhouse	Williams	1990	10750
Future Spa	Bally	1979	6400
Galahad	Bally	1970	791
Galaxy	Stern	1980	5150
Galloping Ghost	Pacific Amusement	1934	N/A
Game Show, The Bally	Bally	1990	2500
Games, The	Gottlieb	1984	1768
Gator [3]	Bally	1969	2120
Gaucho	Gottlieb	1963	5350
Gay Cruise [2]	Bally	1965	60
Gay 90's	Williams	1970	N/A
Gay Paree [4]	Williams	1957	N/A
Gay Time	Genco	1938	N/A
Gemini	Gottlieb	1978	300
Genesis	Gottlieb/Premier	1986	3500
Genie [5]	Gottlieb	1979	6800
Georgia	Williams	1950	N/A
Getaway	Allied Leisure	1977	N/A
Getaway: High Speed II, The	Williams	1992	13259
Gigi	Gottlieb	1963	3575
Gilligan's Island	Bally	1991	4100
Gin	Chicago Coin	1974	N/A
Gin Rummy	Gottlieb	1949	500
Ginger	Chicago Coin	1936	967
Gizmo	Williams	1948	N/A
Gladiator	Gottlieb	1956	1200
Gladiators	Gottlieb/Premier	1993	1995
Glamor	Gottlieb	1951	300
Glamour	Bally	1940	N/A

1. Add-A-Ball   2. Flipperless   3. Add-A-Ball/Zipper flippers   4. 1st metal legs   5. Widebody

Type	Play	Designer	Artist	Class 1	Class 2	Class 3
EM	1	SK	N/A	$800	$525	$300
SS	4	GC	GF/MH/KO	$800	$550	$300
EM	1	WN	RP	$1,525	$1,000	$550
EM	1	NC	N/A	$600	$400	$225
EM	1	TZ	N/A	$225	$150	$75
EM	4	HW	GM	$2,300	$1,525	$800
EM	1	EK	AS	$625	$425	$225
EM	1	EK/STK	AS	$875	$575	$325
EM	1	HB	N/A	$700	$475	$250
EM	4	NC	CM	$525	$350	$200
SS	4	PL/LD	JY	$2,800	$1,850	$1,000
SS	4	GC	PF(B)/DC(P)	$825	$550	$300
EM	2	TZ	CM	$375	$250	$125
SS	4	HW	N/A	$725	$475	$250
EM	1	N/A	N/A	$550	$375	$200
SS	4	DL/PP	TE	$1,125	$750	$400
SS	4	JT/AS	LD/DN	$600	$400	$225
EM	4	TZ	JK	$550	$375	$200
EM	4	WN	RP	$475	$325	$175
EM	1	TZ	N/A	$300	$200	$100
EM	4	SK	CM	$425	$275	$150
EM	4	HW	GM	$575	$375	$200
EM	1	N/A	N/A	$450	$300	$175
EM	2	EK	GOM	$650	$450	$250
SS	4	JT	LD	$725	$475	$250
SS	4	EK	GOM	$1,000	$675	$350
EM	1	HW	GM	$600	$400	$225
SS	4	BB	MT	$900	$600	$325
SS	4	SR	DW/MS	$1,825	$1,225	$650
EM	1	WN	RP	$1,025	$675	$375
SS	4	WP/DL	JY	$1,750	$1,150	$625
EM	1	JEK/AP/WM	CM	$450	$300	$150
EM	1	HM	RP	$1,375	$925	$500
EM	1	N/A	N/A	$550	$375	$200
EM	1	HW/SS	GM	$525	$350	$200
EM	2	WN	RP	$825	$550	$300
SS	4	JN	COM/DM	$1,125	$750	$400
EM	1	WN	RP	$1,200	$800	$425
EM	1	N/A	N/A	$550	$375	$200

Game	Manufacturer	Year	# Made
Glider	Genco	1949	N/A
Global Warfare	Game Plan	1981	10
Globe Trotter	Gottlieb	1938	N/A
Globe Trotter	Gottlieb	1951	910
Go-Cart	J. H. Keeney & Co.	1963	N/A
Goal-Kick	Genco	1934	N/A
Gobs	Chicago Coin	1942	400
Godzilla	Sega	1998	N/A
Goin' Nuts	Gottlieb	1983	10
Gold Award	Rock-Ola	1935	N/A
Gold Ball	Chicago Coin	1947	2500
Gold Ball	Bally	1983	1750
Gold Cup [1]	Bally	1939	N/A
Gold Cup	Bally	1948	N/A
Gold Medal	Genco	1935	N/A
Gold Medal [1]	Bally	1939	N/A
Gold Record	Chicago Coin	1975	N/A
Gold Rush	Rock-Ola	1935	N/A
Gold Rush [2]	Bally	1966	1750
Gold Rush	Williams	1971	N/A
Gold Star	Gottlieb	1940	N/A
Gold Star [3]	Gottlieb	1954	700
Gold Strike	Gottlieb	1975	675
Gold Top Army and Navy	Rock-Ola	1935	N/A
Gold Wings	Gottlieb/Premier	1986	3260
Golden Arrow	Gottlieb	1977	1530
Golden Bells	Williams	1959	N/A
Golden Comet Ball [4]	Field Mfg.	1932	N/A
Golden Cue [5]	Sega	1998	10
Golden Gate [6]	Exhibit Supply	1934	N/A
Golden Gate	Exhibit Supply	1939	N/A
Golden Gloves	Chicago Coin	1949	N/A
Golden Gloves	Williams	1960	N/A
Golden Wheel	Bally	1937	N/A
GoldenEye	Sega	1996	2200
Gondola	Exhibit Supply	1949	N/A
Gondolier	Gottlieb	1958	900
Goofy Jr. [4]	Bally	1932	N/A
Goofy Sr.	Bally	1932	N/A

1. Full cabinet   2. 1st bagatelle in glass   3. Double award   4. Tabletop   5. Rare   6. 2 sizes

Type	Play	Designer	Artist	Class 1	Class 2	Class 3
EM	1	N/A	N/A	$375	$250	$150
SS	4	RS/EC	JT	$1,475	$975	$525
EM	1	N/A	N/A	$500	$325	$175
EM	1	WN	RP	$1,425	$950	$500
EM	1	EK	N/A	$450	$300	$175
EM	1	HH	N/A	$575	$375	$200
EM	1	N/A	N/A	$550	$375	$200
SS	6	JOEB	MW	$1,925	$1,275	$675
SS	4	AS	N/A	$2,000	$1,325	$700
EM-P	1	N/A	N/A	$725	$475	$250
EM	1	N/A	RP	$900	$600	$325
SS	4	GC	TR	$675	$450	$250
EM-P	1	N/A	N/A	$725	$475	$250
EM	1	N/A	N/A	$825	$550	$300
EM-P	1	N/A	N/A	$725	$500	$275
EM-P	1	N/A	N/A	$600	$400	$225
EM	4	AP/JEK/WM	CM	$350	$225	$125
EM-P	1	DR	GM	$725	$475	$250
EM	1	TZ	N/A	$725	$475	$250
EM	4	NC	CM	$675	$450	$250
EM	1	HM	RP	$1,525	$1,025	$550
EM	1	WN	RP	$1,125	$750	$400
EM	1	EK	GOM	$1,525	$1,025	$550
M	1	BHU	N/A	$5,850	$3,875	$2,050
SS	4	JT	LD(P)/DOM(B)	$1,000	$675	$350
EM	1	EK	GOM	$775	$525	$275
EM	1	HW	GM	$700	$450	$250
M	1	N/A	N/A	$550	$375	$200
SS	4	JN	MW	$3,050	$2,025	$1,075
EM	1	N/A	N/A	$550	$375	$200
EM	1	N/A	N/A	$1,325	$875	$475
EM	1	N/A	RP	$550	$375	$200
EM	1	HM	GM	$650	$425	$225
EM-P	1	N/A	N/A	$1,450	$950	$500
SS	6	WP	PF	$1,900	$1,250	$675
EM	1	N/A	N/A	$375	$250	$150
EM	2	WN	RP	$600	$400	$225
M	1	JF	N/A	$550	$375	$200
M	1	JF	NA	$600	$400	$225

Game	Manufacturer	Year	# Made
Gorgar	Williams	1979	14000
Granada [1]	Williams	1972	875
Grand Award	Chicago Coin	1949	700
Grand Champion	Williams	1953	N/A
Grand Lizard	Williams	1986	2750
Grand Prix	Williams	1976	10544
Grand Prix	Williams	1976	2
Grand Prix	Stern	2005	N/A
Grand Slam	Gottlieb	1953	1800
Grand Slam	Gottlieb	1972	3600
Grand Slam	Bally	1983	N/A
Grand Slam	Bally	1983	1000
Grand Tour	Bally	1964	1310
Grandstand [2]	Bally	1938	N/A
Grandstand	Bally	1950	N/A
Granny and the Gators	Bally	1984	N/A
Great Guns	J. H. Keeney and Co.	1937	N/A
Green Pastures	Gottlieb	1954	750
Gridiron	Genco	1934	N/A
Gridiron	Gottlieb	1977	1025
Groovy	Gottlieb	1970	1355
Grub Stake	L. B. Elliot Products	1936	N/A
Grub Stake	A.B.T. Mfg.	1936	N/A
Gulfstream	Williams	1973	4175
Gun Club	Daval	1939	N/A
Gun Club	Genco	1941	N/A
Gun Club [3]	Williams	1953	N/A
Gun Smoke [1]	Chicago Coin	1968	N/A
Guns N' Roses	Data East	1994	3000
Gusher	Exhibit Supply	1936	N/A
Gusher [4]	Williams	1958	N/A
Guys Dolls [5]	Gottlieb	1953	1500
Gypsy Queen	Gottlieb	1955	1400
Handicap	Exhibit Supply	1938	N/A
Handicap [6]	Williams	1952	N/A
Handicapper [7]	J. H. Keeney and Co.	1937	N/A
Hang Glider [1]	Bally	1976	2325
Happy Clown [6]	Gottlieb	1964	3235
Happy Days	Genco	1936	N/A

1. Add-A-Ball   2. Full cabinet   3. Reel scoring   4. Disappearing bumper   5. Posts move, no flippers
6. Mechanical animation   7. One-ball payout

Type	Play	Designer	Artist	Class 1	Class 2	Class 3
SS	4	BO	COM	$975	$650	$350
EM	1	NC	CM	$525	$350	$200
EM	1	JEK	RP	$725	$500	$275
EM	1	HW	GM	$600	$400	$225
SS	4	BO/PA	PA(B)/PF(P)	$925	$625	$325
EM	4	SK	CM	$725	$475	$250
SS	4	SK	CM	$2,675	$1,775	$950
SS	4	PL/LK	JY	$3,075	$2,025	$1,075
EM	1	WN	RP	$1,750	$1,150	$625
EM	1	EK	GOM	$825	$550	$300
SS	2	GK	DW	$775	$525	$275
SS	4	GK	DW	$600	$400	$225
EM	1	TZ	N/A	$575	$400	$225
EM-P	1	N/A	N/A	$725	$475	$250
EM-P	1	N/A	N/A	$950	$650	$350
SS	2	JP	MH/PM	$925	$600	$325
EM	1	N/A	N/A	$675	$450	$250
EM	1	WN	RP	$1,600	$1,075	$575
EM	1	HH	N/A	$700	$475	$250
EM	2	JO	GOM	$725	$475	$275
EM	4	EK	AS	$800	$525	$300
EM-P	1	N/A	N/A	$1,025	$675	$375
EM-P	1	N/A	N/A	$1,200	$800	$425
EM	1	NC	CM	$900	$600	$325
EM	1	N/A	N/A	$600	$400	$225
EM	1	N/A	N/A	$625	$425	$225
EM	1	HW	GM	$650	$425	$250
EM	2	AP/ES	CM	$550	$375	$200
SS	4	JK/JONB/LS/Slash	SS	$3,950	$2,600	$1,400
EM	1	N/A	N/A	$675	$450	$250
EM	1	HW	GM	$1,275	$850	$450
EM	1	WN	RP	$1,175	$800	$425
EM	1	WN	RP	$1,200	$800	$425
EM	1	N/A	N/A	$500	$325	$175
EM	1	HW	GM	$800	$550	$300
EM-P	1	N/A	N/A	$850	$550	$300
EM	1	JP	DIW	$800	$525	$275
EM	4	WN	RP	$725	$500	$275
EM	1	N/A	N/A	$550	$375	$200

Game	Manufacturer	Year	# Made
Happy Days [2]	Gottlieb	1952	1150
Happy Go Lucky	Gottlieb	1951	600
Harbor Lites	Gottlieb	1956	1500
Hardbody	Bally	1987	2000
Harlem Globetrotters On Tour	Bally	1979	14550
Harley-Davidson	Bally	1991	N/A
Harley-Davidson	Sega	1999	N/A
Harley-Davidson	Stern	1999	N/A
Harley-Davidson 2nd Edition	Stern	2002	600
Harley-Davidson Third Edition	Stern	2004	N/A
Harvest	Bally	1964	1075
Harvest Moon	Gottlieb	1948	500
Harvest Time	Genco	1950	N/A
Harvey	Williams	1951	N/A
Haunted House [3]	Gottlieb	1982	6835
Havana	United Mfg.	1947	N/A
Hawaii	United Mfg.	1947	N/A
Hawaiian Beauty [4]	Gottlieb	1954	900
Hawthorne [5]	Bally	1939	N/A
Hay-Ride [6]	Bally	1964	250
Hayburners [7]	Williams	1951	N/A
Hayburners II	Williams	1968	N/A
Headliner	Bally	1939	N/A
Hearts and Spades [6]	Gottlieb	1969	615
Hearts Spades [8]	Allied Leisure	1978	N/A
Heat Wave [1]	Williams	1964	N/A
Heat Wave	Bally	1967	N/A
Heavy Metal Meltdown [9]	Bally	1987	1600
Heavyweight	Pacific Mfg.	1937	N/A
Hee Haw	Chicago Coin	1973	N/A
Hell's Bells	Western Equipment	1934	N/A
Hercules [10]	Atari	1979	N/A
Hi Dolly	Gottlieb	1965	1600
Hi Straight	J. H. Keeney & Co.	1960	N/A
Hi-Ball	Peo Mfg.	1932	N/A
Hi-De-Ho [11]	Pacific Amusement	1937	N/A
Hi-Deal	Bally	1975	2085
Hi-Dive	Gottlieb	1941	N/A
Hi-Diver [1]	Gottlieb	1959	1650

1. Mech. animation 2. Light animation 3. Multi-level playfield 4. Double award 5. Full cabinet 6. Add-A-Ball
7. Mechanical horse race 8. Cocktail table 9. Speaker stacks 10. Largest machine ever made 11. Pool theme

Type	Play	Designer	Artist	Class 1	Class 2	Class 3
EM	1	WN	RP	$1,250	$825	$450
EM	1	WN	RP	$1,275	$850	$450
EM	1	WN	RP	$1,325	$875	$475
SS	4	WP	GF	$800	$525	$300
SS	4	GK	GF	$1,125	$750	$400
SS	4	BO	MS	$2,825	$1,875	$1,000
SS	6	N/A	NA	$3,000	$2,000	$1,050
SS	6	LR/JONB	N/A	$3,225	$2,125	$1,125
SS	6	LR/JONB	N/A	$3,525	$2,325	$1,250
SS	6	LR/JONB	N/A	$3,925	$2,600	$1,375
EM	1	TZ	N/A	$550	$375	$200
EM	1	HM	RP	$1,325	$875	$475
EM	1	N/A	N/A	$400	$275	$150
EM	1	HW	GM	$675	$450	$250
SS	4	JO	TD	$1,950	$1,300	$700
EM	1	N/A	N/A	$475	$300	$175
EM	1	N/A	N/A	$625	$400	$225
EM	1	WN	RP	$1,800	$1,200	$650
EM-P	1	N/A	N/A	$675	$450	$250
EM	1	TZ	N/A	$575	$375	$200
EM	1	HW/SS	GM	$1,500	$1,000	$525
EM	2	SK	N/A	$700	$475	$250
EM	1	N/A	N/A	$550	$375	$200
EM	1	EK	AS	$900	$600	$325
SS	2	BB	MT	$325	$225	$125
EM	1	SK	AS	$825	$550	$300
EM	1	N/A	N/A	$825	$550	$300
SS	4	DL	TR	$750	$500	$275
EM-P	1	N/A	N/A	$1,025	$675	$375
EM	4	JG	CM	$475	$300	$175
EM-P	1	N/A	N/A	$725	$475	$250
SS	4	SB	JIK	$1,475	$975	$525
EM	2	WN	RP	$750	$500	$275
EM	1	EK	RP	$425	$275	$150
M	1	N/A	N/A	$675	$450	$250
EM-P	1	N/A	N/A	$1,025	$675	$375
EM	1	JP	DIW	$625	$425	$225
EM	1	HM	RP	$550	$375	$200
EM	1	WN	RP	$1,675	$1,125	$600

Game	Manufacturer	Year	# Made
Hi-Flyer	Chicago Coin	1974	N/A
Hi-Hat	Genco	1941	N/A
Hi-Lo [1]	Genco	1938	N/A
Hi-Lo Ace [2]	Bally	1973	2500
Hi-Score	Gottlieb	1967	1900
Hi-Score Pool	Chicago Coin	1971	N/A
Hialeah [3]	Bally	1936	N/A
High Ace [2]	Williams	1974	N/A
High Card	Gottlieb	1936	N/A
High Hand	Bally	1935	N/A
High Hand	Gottlieb	1973	4950
High Roller Casino	Stern	2001	N/A
High Speed	Williams	1986	17080
High Stepper	Stoner	1941	N/A
High-Lite	Daval	1939	N/A
High-Low	Chicago Coin	1935	236
Highways	Williams	1961	600
Hit [4]	Genco	1938	N/A
Hit 'N' Run	Gottlieb	1952	1400
Hit Number	J. H. Keeney and Co.	1938	N/A
Hit Parade [4]	Gottlieb	1936	N/A
Hit Parade	Marvel Mfg. Co.	1948	N/A
Hit Parade	Chicago Coin	1951	N/A
Hit the Deck [5]	Gottlieb	1978	375
Hits and Runs	Genco	1951	N/A
Hockey	Chicago Coin	1941	1548
Hoe Down	Allied Leisure	1978	N/A
Hokus Pokus	Bally	1976	3086
Hold 'Em [6]	Stoner	1936	N/A
Hold Over	Stoner	1940	N/A
Hold Tight	Western Products	1939	N/A
Holiday	Chicago Coin	1948	700
Hollywood	Rock-Ola	1936	N/A
Hollywood	Marvel Mfg. Co.	1945	N/A
Hollywood	Williams	1961	550
Hollywood	Chicago Coin	1976	N/A
Hollywood Heat	Gottlieb/Premier	1986	3400
Home Run	Chicago Coin	1937	3093
Home Run	Chicago Coin	1941	1464

1. Light animation 2. Add-A-Ball 3. Horse racing theme 4. Baseball theme 5. Digital score reels
6. Football theme

Type	Play	Designer	Artist	Class 1	Class 2	Class 3
EM	2	WM/JEK	CM	$375	$250	$150
EM	1	N/A	N/A	$500	$325	$175
EM	1	N/A	N/A	$725	$475	$250
EM	1	JP	DIW	$675	$450	$250
EM	4	EK	AS	$675	$450	$250
EM	2	WM	CM	$525	$350	$200
EM-P	1	N/A	N/A	$850	$550	$300
EM	1	NC	CM	$400	$275	$150
EM-P	1	N/A	N/A	$1,150	$750	$400
EM	1	N/A	N/A	$525	$350	$200
EM	1	EK	GM	$775	$525	$275
SS	4	KJ	JY/KO	$2,225	$1,475	$775
SS	4	SR/PA	PA/MS	$1,625	$1,075	$575
EM	1	N/A	N/A	$500	$325	$175
EM	1	N/A	N/A	$675	$450	$250
EM	1	N/A	N/A	$675	$450	$250
EM	1	SK	GM	$575	$375	$200
EM	1	N/A	N/A	$850	$550	$300
EM	1	WN	RP	$875	$575	$325
EM	1	N/A	N/A	$500	$325	$175
EM-P	1	N/A	N/A	$1,325	$875	$475
EM	1	N/A	N/A	$425	$275	$150
EM	1	N/A	N/A	$500	$350	$175
EM	1	JO	GOM	$1,425	$950	$500
EM	1	N/A	RP	$550	$375	$200
EM	1	N/A	N/A	$600	$400	$225
SS	4	BB	N/A	$350	$250	$125
EM	2	GK	CM	$625	$425	$225
EM	2	N/A	N/A	$725	$475	$250
EM	1	N/A	N/A	$425	$275	$150
EM	1	N/A	N/A	$725	$475	$250
EM	1	N/A	N/A	$450	$300	$175
EM-P	1	N/A	N/A	$1,550	$1,025	$550
EM	1	N/A	N/A	$550	$375	$200
EM	2	SK	GM	$525	$350	$200
EM	2	AP/JEK/WM	N/A	$1,000	$650	$350
SS	4	JT	DOM(B)LD(P)	$850	$575	$300
EM	1	N/A	N/A	$900	$600	$325
EM	1	N/A	N/A	$900	$600	$325

Game	Manufacturer	Year	# Made
Home Run [1]	Gottlieb	1971	580
Home Run 1940 [2]	Chicago Coin	1940	2645
Honey [3]	Exhibit Supply	1938	N/A
Honey	Genco	1947	N/A
Honey	Williams	1972	6301
Hong Kong [4]	Williams	1952	N/A
Hook	Data East	1992	6705
Hoops	Gottlieb/Premier	1991	879
Hootenanny	Bally	1963	1051
Horoscope	Gottlieb	1941	N/A
Horse Shoes	Williams	1951	N/A
Horsefeathers	Williams	1952	N/A
Hot Diggity	Williams	1956	N/A
Hot Hand	Stern	1979	4117
Hot Line	Williams	1966	3651
Hot Shot	Gottlieb	1973	9000
Hot Shots	Gottlieb/Premier	1989	2342
Hot Springs [5]	Gottlieb	1937	N/A
Hot Tip [6]	J. H. Keeney & Co.	1937	N/A
Hot Tip [7]	J. H. Keeney & Co.	1947	N/A
Hot Tip	Williams	1977	1300
Hot Tip	Williams	1977	4903
Hot-Rods	Bally	1949	N/A
Hotdoggin'	Bally	1980	2050
Hula-Hula [8]	Chicago Coin	1965	N/A
Humpty Dumpty [9]	Gottlieb	1947	6500
Hurdy Gurdy [1,10]	Gottlieb	1966	3186
Hurricane [10]	Williams	1991	N/A
Hyde Park [1]	Gottlieb	1966	951
Ice Fever [10]	Gottlieb/Premier	1985	1585
Ice Show [1]	Gottlieb	1966	N/A
Ice-Revue	Gottlieb	1965	2050
Incredible Hulk, The	Gottlieb	1979	6150
Independence Day	Sega	1996	1500
Indiana Jones	Stern	2008	N/A
Indiana Jones: The Pinball Adventure	Williams	1993	12716
Indianapolis 500	Bally	1995	2249
Invasion Strategy [11]	Komputer Dynamics	1975	N/A
Iron Maiden	Stern	1981	1200

1. Add-A-Ball   2. Light animation   3. Tabletop   4. Bingo type   5. Non-payout   6. One-ball payout
7. Full cabinet   8. Animated hula dancer   9. First flipper game   10. Mechanical animation   11. Rare game

Type	Play	Designer	Artist	Class 1	Class 2	Class 3
EM	1	EK	GOM	$900	$600	$325
EM	1	N/A	N/A	$1,025	$675	$375
EM	1	N/A	N/A	$500	$325	$175
EM	1	N/A	N/A	$600	$400	$225
EM	4	SK	N/A	$750	$500	$275
EM	1	HW	GM	$900	$600	$325
SS	4	TIS	PF	$1,625	$1,075	$575
SS	4	RT	DM/COM	$750	$500	$275
EM	1	TZ	CM	$575	$375	$200
EM	1	HM	RP	$675	$450	$250
EM	1	HW	GM	$725	$475	$275
EM	1	HW	GM	$1,025	$675	$375
EM	1	HW	GM	$975	$650	$350
SS	4	HW	N/A	$675	$450	$250
EM	1	SK	N/A	$625	$425	$225
EM	4	EK	GOM	$725	$475	$250
SS	4	JN	COM	$825	$550	$300
EM	1	N/A	N/A	$1,025	$675	$375
EM-P	1	N/A	N/A	$675	$450	$250
EM-P	1	N/A	N/A	$775	$525	$275
EM	4	TK	CM	$775	$525	$275
SS	4	TK	CM	$700	$450	$250
EM	1	N/A	N/A	$2,500	$1,650	$875
SS	4	GG	GF	$750	$500	$275
EM	2	ALS/JEK/JG	RP	$575	$400	$200
EM	1	HM	RP	$1,600	$1,050	$575
EM	1	EK	RP	$1,250	$825	$450
SS	4	BO	JY/PA	$1,575	$1,050	$550
EM	2	EK	RP	$725	$500	$275
SS	4	JT	LD	$875	$575	$300
EM	1	EK	RP	$1,075	$700	$375
EM	1	EK	RP	$850	$575	$300
SS	4	EK	GOM	$1,125	$750	$400
SS	6	RH	JB	$1,525	$1,000	$550
SS	4	JB	KO	$4,425	$2,925	$1,550
SS	4	MR/DW	DW	$4,050	$2,675	$1,425
SS	4	DN	DH/PB	$2,225	$1,475	$800
SS	4	N/A	N/A	$3,300	$2,200	$1,175
SS	4	BRP	KP	$2,100	$1,375	$750

Game	Manufacturer	Year	# Made
Iron Man	Stern	2010	N/A
Iron Man Classic	Stern	2010	N/A
Island Queens [1]	Bally	1960	N/A
Jack and Jill	Bally	1933	N/A
Jack In The Box	Gottlieb	1973	8300
Jack 'N Jill [2]	Gottlieb	1948	2000
Jack·Bot	Williams	1995	2428
Jackpot	Williams	1971	6303
Jacks Open	Gottlieb	1977	2975
Jacks to Open	Gottlieb/Mylstar	1984	2350
Jalopy [3]	Williams	1951	N/A
Jamboree	Exhibit Supply	1948	N/A
James Bond 007	Gottlieb	1980	3625
Jeanie	Exhibit Supply	1950	N/A
Jet Spin	Gottlieb	1977	4761
Jig Saw [2]	Williams	1957	N/A
Jitterbug [4]	Genco	1938	N/A
Jitters	Western Equipment	1936	N/A
Jive Time [5]	Williams	1970	465
Jockey Club	Standard Mfg.	1933	N/A
Jockey Club [6]	Bally	1941	N/A
Jockey Club [7]	Gottlieb	1954	1150
Jockey Special	Bally	1948	N/A
Johnny Mnemonic	Williams	1995	2756
Joker	Gottlieb	1950	850
Joker	Bally	1968	110
Joker Poker	Gottlieb	1978	820
Joker Poker	Gottlieb	1978	9280
Jokerz!	Williams	1988	N/A
Jolly	Chicago Coin	1940	2209
Jolly Jokers [8]	Williams	1962	700
Jolly Roger	Williams	1967	3502
Joust	Bally	1969	1050
Joust [9]	Williams	1983	402
Jubilee	Gottlieb	1955	500
Jubilee [8]	Williams	1973	7303
Judge Dredd	Bally	1993	6990
Judy	Exhibit Supply	1950	N/A
Juggle Ball [10]	Rock-Ola	1932	N/A

1. 2-Shot or 5-Shot models 2. Light animation 3. Mechanical car race 4. Win extra ball 5. Mechanical animation 6. One-ball payout 7. Double award 8. Add-A-Ball 9. Head-to-head play 10. Tabletop

Type	Play	Designer	Artist	Class 1	Class 2	Class 3
SS	4	JONB	MG	$5,375	$3,550	$1,900
SS	4	JONB	MG	$3,800	$2,500	$1,350
EM	1	N/A	N/A	$400	$275	$150
M	2	N/A	N/A	$625	$400	$225
EM	4	EK	GOM	$700	$475	$250
EM	1	HM	RP	$1,300	$850	$475
SS	4	BO/LD	JY	$1,525	$1,000	$550
EM	1	NC	CM	$600	$400	$225
EM	1	EK	GOM	$1,175	$775	$425
SS	1	EK	DM	$975	$650	$350
EM	1	HW/SS	GM	$1,500	$1,000	$525
EM	1	N/A	N/A	$375	$250	$150
SS	4	AE	DW	$1,025	$700	$375
EM	1	N/A	N/A	$375	$250	$150
EM	4	EK	GOM	$825	$550	$300
EM	1	HW	GM	$1,075	$700	$375
EM	1	N/A	N/A	$675	$450	$250
EM-P	1	N/A	N/A	$675	$450	$250
EM	1	NC	CM	$450	$300	$175
M	1	SSIM	N/A	$925	$625	$325
EM-P	1	N/A	N/A	$800	$550	$300
EM	1	WN	RP	$1,150	$775	$425
EM	1	N/A	N/A	$600	$400	$225
SS	4	GEG	JY	$1,750	$1,175	$625
EM	1	WN	RP	$1,175	$775	$425
EM	4	TZ	JK	$575	$375	$200
EM	4	EK	GOM	$1,525	$1,000	$550
SS	4	EK	GOM	$975	$650	$350
SS	4	BO/PA	JY(B)MS(P)	$1,200	$800	$425
EM	1	N/A	N/A	$550	$375	$200
EM	1	SK	N/A	$500	$350	$175
EM	4	NC	CM	$400	$250	$150
EM	2	TZ	CM	$850	$575	$300
SS	2	BO	COM	$3,350	$2,225	$1,175
EM	4	WN	RP	$900	$600	$325
EM	4	SK	CM	$450	$300	$175
SS	4	JT	KO	$1,700	$1,125	$600
EM	1	N/A	N/A	$375	$250	$150
M	1	N/A	N/A	$750	$500	$275

Game	Manufacturer	Year	# Made
Juke Box	Chicago Coin	1976	N/A
Jumbo [2]	Bally	1935	N/A
Jumper [3]	Exhibit Supply	1939	N/A
Jumpin' Jack's	Williams	1963	1500
Jumpin' Jacks [4]	Genco	1952	N/A
Jumping Jack	Gottlieb	1973	4975
Jungle [5]	Genco	1938	N/A
Jungle	Genco	1941	N/A
Jungle [6]	Williams	1960	N/A
Jungle	Gottlieb	1972	5775
Jungle King [7]	Gottlieb	1973	825
Jungle Life	Gottlieb	1973	2731
Jungle Lord	Williams	1981	6000
Jungle Princess	Gottlieb	1977	1600
Jungle Queen	Gottlieb	1977	6795
Junior [1]	Genco	1937	N/A
Junk Yard	Williams	1996	3013
Jurassic Park	Data East	1993	9008
Just 21 [8]	Gottlieb	1950	N/A
K. C. Jones [9]	Gottlieb	1949	800
Kabuki	Data East/Fabulous Fantasies	1994	2
Keen-A-Ball	Gottlieb	1939	N/A
Keep-'Em-Flying	Gottlieb	1942	N/A
Kelly Pool Jr.	Gottlieb	1935	N/A
Kelly Pool Sr.	Gottlieb	1935	N/A
Kewpie Doll [10]	Gottlieb	1960	950
Key Lite	Bally	1939	N/A
Kick Off [11]	Bally	1977	1655
Kick-Off	Williams	1958	N/A
Kickoff [7]	Williams	1967	1150
Kicker	Chicago Coin	1966	N/A
Kicker	Gottlieb	1977	380
Kilroy	Chicago Coin	1947	N/A
King Arthur and his Round Table	Gottlieb	1949	1220
King Fish [12]	Genco	1935	N/A
King Kong	Data East	1990	9
King Kool	Gottlieb	1972	3325
King of Diamonds [13]	Gottlieb	1967	3200
King of Diamonds	Retro Pinball	2010	N/A

1. Tabletop 2. One-ball payout or ticket model 3. Tunnels under playfield 4. Vertical pinball
5. Light animation puzzle 6. Mechanical animation 7. Add-A-Ball 8. Turret shooter 9. Light animation

Type	Play	Designer	Artist	Class 1	Class 2	Class 3
EM	4	AP/JEK/WM	CM	$425	$300	$150
EM-P	1	GM	N/A	$750	$500	$275
EM	1	N/A	N/A	$725	$475	$250
EM	2	SK	N/A	$600	$400	$225
EM	1	HH	N/A	$500	$350	$175
EM	2	EK	GOM	$875	$575	$325
EM	1	N/A	N/A	$950	$625	$350
EM	1	HH	N/A	$800	$550	$300
EM	1	HM	N/A	$1,025	$700	$375
EM	4	EK	GOM	$850	$575	$300
EM	1	EK	GOM	$650	$425	$225
EM	1	EK	GOM	$550	$375	$200
SS	4	BO	COM	$875	$575	$325
EM	2	EK	GOM	$775	$525	$275
EM	4	EK	GOM	$875	$575	$325
EM	1	N/A	N/A	$500	$325	$175
SS	4	BO/DS	PM/PB	$3,150	$2,075	$1,100
SS	4	JK/EC/JB	M	$2,050	$1,350	$725
EM	1	HM	RP	$725	$475	$250
EM	1	WN	RP	$1,700	$1,125	$600
SS	4	JK/EC/LR/LS	N/A	$17,500		
EM	1	HM	RP	$475	$325	$175
EM	1	HM	RP	$575	$375	$200
EM	1	N/A	N/A	$750	$500	$275
EM	1	N/A	N/A	$850	$550	$300
EM	1	WN	RP	$1,125	$750	$400
EM	1	N/A	N/A	$425	$275	$150
EM	4	JP	DIW	$575	$400	$200
EM	1	HW	GM	$850	$575	$300
EM	1	SK	N/A	$575	$375	$200
EM	1	JG/JEK/ALS	N/A	$525	$350	$200
EM	1	JB	GOM	$525	$350	$200
EM	1	JEK	RP	$625	$400	$225
EM	1	HM	RP	$900	$600	$325
EM-P	1	N/A	N/A	$975	$650	$350
SS	4	JA	KO	$9,250	$6,125	$3,250
EM	2	EK	GOM	$675	$450	$250
EM	1	EK	AS	$1,550	$1,025	$550
SS	4	EK	AS	$3,700	$2,450	

10. Last woodrail game   11. Last Bally EM   12. One-ball payout   13. Retro

Game	Manufacturer	Year	# Made
King Pin [1]	Chicago Coin	1951	N/A
King Pin	Williams	1962	1250
King Pin	Gottlieb	1973	4350
King Rex	Bally	1970	275
King Rock	Gottlieb	1972	4000
King Tut	Richard Mfg.	1932	N/A
King Tut	Bally	1969	800
Kingpin	Capcom	1996	9
Kings	Genco	1935	N/A
Kings	Williams	1957	N/A
Kings & Queens	Gottlieb	1965	2875
Kings of Steel	Bally	1984	2900
Kings of the Turf [2]	H. C. Evans & Co.	1935	N/A
Kings of the Turf [3]	H. C. Evans & Co.	1935	N/A
Kismet	Williams	1961	700
Kiss	Bally	1979	17000
Klick	Genco	1938	N/A
Klondike [4]	Bally	1938	N/A
Klondike	Williams	1971	3302
Knock Out [5]	Gottlieb	1950	3000
Knockout	Exhibit Supply	1941	N/A
Knockout	Bally	1975	2085
Krull	Gottlieb	1983	10
Lady Luck [6]	Gottlieb	1954	700
Lady Luck	Williams	1968	3202
Lady Luck	Bally	1986	500
Lady Robin Hood	Gottlieb	1948	6000
Lady Sharpshooter [7]	Game Plan	1985	1200
Lancer	Exhibit Supply	1940	N/A
Lancers	Gottlieb	1961	1700
Landslide	Exhibit Supply	1940	N/A
Lariat	Gottlieb	1969	150
Laser Ball	Williams	1979	4500
Laser Cue	Williams	1984	2800
Laser War [8]	Data East	1987	N/A
Last Action Hero	Data East	1993	5505
Latonia	Stoner	1937	N/A
Lawman	Gottlieb	1971	1750
Lazer Lord [9]	Stern	1984	1

1. Mechanical animation 2. Five-ball payout 3. Regular 4. One-ball payout 5. Playfield animation
6. Double award 7. Cocktail table 8. First stereo sound 9. Prototype

Type	Play	Designer	Artist	Class 1	Class 2	Class 3
EM	1	N/A	N/A	$600	$400	$225
EM	1	NC	N/A	$725	$475	$250
EM	1	EK	GOM	$900	$600	$325
EM	1	TZ	DW	$625	$425	$225
EM	4	EK	GOM	$550	$375	$200
M	1	N/A	N/A	$500	$325	$175
EM	1	TZ	DIW	$575	$375	$200
SS	4	MR	SF	$28,500	$18,825	$9,975
EM	1	N/A	N/A	$875	$575	$325
EM	1	HW	GM	$950	$625	$350
EM	1	WN	RP	$1,850	$1,225	$650
SS	4	GK	DW	$700	$475	$250
EM-P	1	N/A	N/A	$1,200	$800	$425
EM	1	N/A	N/A	$800	$550	$300
EM	4	SK	GM	$425	$275	$150
SS	4	JP	KO	$3,750	$2,475	$1,325
EM	1	N/A	N/A	$425	$275	$150
EM-P	1	N/A	N/A	$725	$475	$275
EM	1	NC	CM	$850	$550	$300
EM	1	HM	RP	$4,000	$2,650	$1,400
EM	1	N/A	N/A	$500	$325	$175
EM	2	GK	DIW	$725	$475	$275
SS	4	JT	N/A	$8,750	$5,775	$3,075
EM	1	WN	RP	$1,325	$875	$475
EM	2	NC	LR/CM	$475	$325	$175
SS	4	GC	GF	$925	$600	$325
EM	1	HM	RP	$1,325	$875	$475
SS	4	N/A	N/A	$350	$225	$125
EM	1	N/A	N/A	$500	$325	$175
EM	2	WN	RP	$500	$350	$175
EM	1	N/A	N/A	$475	$325	$175
EM	2	EK	AS	$1,200	$800	$425
SS	4	BO	COM	$775	$525	$275
SS	4	ET	PE	$750	$500	$275
SS	4	JK	KO/MH	$1,050	$700	$375
SS	4	TS/JK/EC/JONB	M	$1,450	$975	$525
EM-P	1	N/A	N/A	$975	$650	$350
EM	2	EK	GOM	$675	$450	$250
SS	4	N/A	N/A	$10,000	$6,600	$3,500

Game	Manufacturer	Year	# Made
Lazy-Q [2]	Williams	1953	N/A
Lead Off	Bally	1940	1850
Leader	Exhibit Supply	1940	N/A
League Leader	Success Mfg.	1941	N/A
Leap Year	Marvel Mfg.	1948	N/A
Leathernecks, Pamco	Pacific Amusement	1936	N/A
Lectronamo	Stern	1978	2423
Legionnaire	Chicago Coin	1941	1100
Leland Sr. [3]	Stoner for Chicago Coin	1933	N/A
Leland Standard	Stoner for Chicago Coin	1933	N/A
Lethal Weapon 3	Data East	1992	N/A
Liberty	Daval	1939	N/A
Liberty	Gottlieb	1942	N/A
Liberty Bell	Williams	1977	3000
Liberty Belle	Gottlieb	1962	2950
Lightning (34)	Exhibit Supply	1934	N/A
Lightning (38)	Exhibit Supply	1934	N/A
Lightning	Exhibit Supply	1938	N/A
Lightning	Stern	1981	2350
Lightning Ball [4]	Gottlieb	1959	950
Lights...Camera...Action!	Gottlieb/Premier	1989	1708
Lime Light	Bally	1940	N/A
Line-up	Baker Novelty	1940	N/A
Lite-A-Card [5]	Gottlieb	1960	850
Lite-A-Line	Amusement Novelty Supply	1935	N/A
Lite-O-Card	Gottlieb	1939	N/A
Little Chief	Williams	1975	6300
Little Joe	Bally	1972	2080
Live Wire	Chicago Coin	1937	196
Loch Ness Monster [1]	Game Plan	1985	1
Log Cabin [3]	Caille Brothers	1903	N/A
Lone Star	Exhibit Supply	1940	N/A
Long Beach [6]	Genco	1937	N/A
Loop the Loop	Bally	1966	1055
Lord of the Rings	Stern	2003	5100
Lord of the Rings LE	Stern	2009	500
Lost In Space	Sega	1998	600
Lost World	Bally	1978	10330
Lost World Jurassic Park	Sega	1997	N/A

1. Prototype   2. Reel scoring   3. Tabletop   4. Mechanical animation   5. Carry over scoring
6. Light animation

Type	Play	Designer	Artist	Class 1	Class 2	Class 3
EM	1	HW	GM	$675	$450	$250
EM	1	N/A	N/A	$500	$350	$175
EM	1	N/A	N/A	$550	$375	$200
EM	1	N/A	N/A	$675	$450	$250
EM	1	N/A	N/A	$375	$250	$125
EM-P	1	N/A	N/A	$1,075	$725	$375
SS	4	MK	N/A	$550	$375	$200
EM	1	N/A	N/A	$425	$275	$150
M	1	N/A	N/A	$500	$325	$175
M	1	N/A	N/A	$450	$300	$175
SS	4	JK/EC	M	$1,450	$950	$525
EM	1	N/A	N/A	$500	$325	$175
EM	1	N/A	N/A	$550	$375	$200
EM	2	SK	CM	$575	$375	$200
EM	4	WN	RP	$600	$400	$225
EM	1	HW	N/A	$625	$425	$225
EM	1	HW	N/A	$650	$450	$250
EM	1	HW	LD	$625	$425	$225
SS	4	JJ	N/A	$700	$475	$250
EM	1	WN	RP	$1,800	$1,200	$650
SS	4	JN	BJ/COM	$950	$650	$350
EM	1	N/A	N/A	$425	$275	$150
EM	1	N/A	N/A	$550	$375	$200
EM	2	WN	RP	$675	$450	$250
EM	1	N/A	N/A	$750	$500	$275
EM	1	HM	RP	$425	$275	$150
EM	4	SK	CM	$800	$525	$275
EM	4	JP	CM	$650	$450	$250
EM	1	N/A	N/A	$675	$450	$250
SS	4	JK/EC	SM	$20,327		
M	1	AC	N/A	$3,250	$2,150	$1,150
EM	1	N/A	N/A	$550	$375	$200
EM	1	N/A	N/A	$600	$400	$225
EM	2	TZ	N/A	$500	$350	$175
SS	4	GEG/JK/CG	JV/KO/MH	$4,125	$2,725	$1,450
SS	4	GEG/JK/CG	JV/KO/MH	$5,000	$3,300	$1,750
SS	6	JONB	N/A	$2,175	$1,450	$775
SS	4	GG	PF	$1,100	$725	$400
SS	6	JONB	MW	$1,675	$1,125	$600

Game	Manufacturer	Year	# Made
Lot-O-Fun	Gottlieb	1939	N/A
Lot-O-Smoke	Gottlieb	1939	N/A
Love Bug [1]	Williams	1971	N/A
Lovely Lucy	Gottlieb	1954	850
Lucky [2]	Chicago Coin	1939	183
Lucky Ace	Williams	1974	2809
Lucky Draw [3]	Mirco Games	1978	N/A
Lucky Hand [1]	Gottlieb	1977	610
Lucky Inning [4]	Williams	1950	N/A
Lucky Seven [5]	Williams	1977	80
Lucky Seven [5]	Williams	1978	4252
Lucky Star	Gottlieb	1947	2600
Lucky Strike [6]	Genco	1940	N/A
Lucky Strike	Williams	1965	1800
Lucky Strike	Gottlieb	1975	1013
Lulu	Williams	1954	N/A
Lunar Shot [1]	Williams	1967	N/A
Machine: Bride of Pin•Bot, The	Williams	1991	8100
Mad Cap	Stoner	1936	N/A
Mad World	Bally	1964	2050
Mademoiselle	Gottlieb	1959	700
Madison Square Gardens [6]	Gottlieb	1950	900
Magic	Exhibit Supply	1948	N/A
Magic	Stern	1979	2466
Magic Circle	Bally	1965	580
Magic City	Williams	1967	2675
Magic Clock [7]	Williams	1960	N/A
Magic Clock	Bally	1965	N/A
Magic Lamp [8]	J. H. Keeney & Co.	1937	N/A
Magic Town [1]	Williams	1967	3950
Magnotron	Gottlieb	1974	6550
Maisie [6]	Gottlieb	1947	3500
Majestic [9]	Gottlieb	1957	1350
Major League	Pacific Amusement	1934	N/A
Majorettes [6]	Williams	1952	N/A
Majorettes [1]	Gottlieb	1964	425
Majors [10]	Chicago Coin	1939	2944
Majors [11]	Chicago Coin	1939	1610
Majors – 1941	Chicago Coin	1941	2900

1. Add-A-Ball   2. Standard/free play   3. Cocktail table   4. Mech. animation   5. Playfield animation   6. Light animation   7. Moving target   8. One-ball payout w/ photocell   9. 1st roto target   10. Free play   11. Novelty play

Type	Play	Designer	Artist	Class 1	Class 2	Class 3
EM	1	HM	RP	$500	$325	$175
EM	1	HM	RP	$725	$475	$250
EM	1	NC	CM	$575	$375	$200
EM	1	WN	RP	$1,200	$800	$425
EM	1	N/A	N/A	$625	$425	$225
EM	1	NC	CM	$575	$375	$200
SS	4	N/A	N/A	$300	$200	$125
EM	1	EK	GOM	$1,150	$775	$400
EM	1	HW	GM	$850	$575	$300
EM	2	CO	CM	$850	$575	$300
SS	4	CO	CM	$600	$400	$225
EM	1	HM	RP	$625	$425	$225
EM	1	N/A	N/A	$675	$450	$250
EM	1	NC	N/A	$600	$400	$225
EM	1	EK	GOM	$925	$600	$325
EM	1	HW	GM	$650	$450	$250
EM	1	NC	AS	$775	$525	$275
SS	4	JT/PA	JY	$1,575	$1,050	$550
EM	1	N/A	N/A	$625	$425	$225
EM	2	TZ	AS	$625	$425	$225
EM	2	WN	RP	$475	$325	$175
EM	1	HM	RP	$1,675	$1,100	$600
EM	1	N/A	N/A	$575	$375	$200
SS	4	MK	N/A	$975	$650	$350
EM	1	TZ	N/A	$625	$425	$225
EM	1	NC	GM	$775	$525	$275
EM	2	HM/SK	N/A	$450	$300	$175
EM	1	N/A	N/A	$450	$300	$175
EM-P	1	N/A	N/A	$1,000	$675	$350
EM	1	NC	GM	$750	$500	$275
EM	4	EK	GOM	$550	$375	$200
EM	1	HW	RP	$600	$400	$225
EM	4	WN	RP	$575	$375	$200
EM	1	HW	N/A	$1,500	$1,000	$525
EM	1	HW	RP	$700	$475	$250
EM	1	WN	RP	$1,750	$1,150	$625
EM	1	N/A	N/A	$750	$500	$275
EM	1	N/A	N/A	$900	$600	$325
EM	1	N/A	N/A	$875	$600	$325

Game	Manufacturer	Year	# Made
Majors of '49	Chicago Coin	1949	1500
Mam'selle	Exhibit Supply	1947	N/A
Man 'n the Moon	Daval	1935	N/A
Man-O-War [1]	Gottlieb	1938	N/A
Manhattan	Exhibit Supply	1935	N/A
Manhattan	United Mfg.	1948	N/A
Marathon	Gottlieb	1955	750
Marble Queen	Gottlieb	1953	1000
Mardi Gras	Genco	1948	N/A
Mardi Gras	Williams	1962	1100
Mariner	Bally	1971	2000
Mario Andretti	Gottlitb/Premier	1995	1120
Marjorie	Gottlieb	1947	1200
Mars [2]	Chicago Coin	1937	407
Mars God of War	Gottlieb	1981	5240
Marvel [3]	Chicago Coin	1938	N/A
Maryland	Williams	1949	N/A
Mascot	Bally	1940	N/A
Masquerade [2]	Gottlieb	1966	3662
Masterpiece	Pacific Amusement	1933	N/A
Mat-Cha-Skor	Peo Mfg.	1933	N/A
Mata Hari	Bally	1977	170
Mata Hari	Bally	1978	16260
Match Play	Gottlieb	1935	N/A
Maverick The Movie	Data East	1994	N/A
Mayfair	Gottlieb	1966	2120
Mazuma [4]	Pacific Amusement	1937	N/A
McCoy, The	Mills Novelty Co.	1936	N/A
Medieval Madness	Williams	1997	4016
Medusa	Bally	1981	3250
Melody [5]	Bally	1947	N/A
Melody [6]	Gottlieb	1967	550
Melody Lane	Gottlieb	1960	1000
Memory Lane	Stern	1978	2624
Mercury	Genco	1950	N/A
Mermaid [2]	Gottlieb	1951	600
Merry-Go-Round [7]	A.B.T. Mfg.	1933	N/A
Merry-Go-Round	Gottlieb	1934	N/A
Merry-Go-Round	Exhibit Supply	1940	N/A

1. Full cabinet 2. Mechanical animation 3. Ball color detector 4. One-ball payout 5. 1st Bally flipper game
6. Add-A-Ball 7. Tabletop

Type	Play	Designer	Artist	Class 1	Class 2	Class 3
EM	1	N/A	RP	$675	$450	$250
EM	1	N/A	N/A	$550	$375	$200
EM	1	N/A	N/A	$825	$550	$300
EM-P	1	N/A	N/A	$725	$475	$250
EM	1	N/A	N/A	$550	$375	$200
EM	1	IW	N/A	$500	$325	$175
EM	2	WN	RP	$425	$300	$150
EM	1	WN	RP	$1,700	$1,125	$600
EM	1	N/A	N/A	$750	$500	$275
EM	4	SK	N/A	$500	$325	$175
EM	4	TZ	CM	$600	$400	$225
SS	4	JN	COM	$1,600	$1,050	$575
EM	1	HM	RP	$600	$400	$225
EM	1	N/A	N/A	$1,075	$725	$375
SS	4	JOB	DM	$775	$500	$275
EM	1	N/A	N/A	$625	$425	$225
EM	1	N/A	N/A	$525	$350	$200
EM	1	N/A	N/A	$500	$325	$175
EM	4	EK	AS	$725	$475	$250
M	1	FM	N/A	$500	$350	$175
M	1	N/A	N/A	$800	$550	$300
EM	4	JP	DC	$2,600	$1,725	$925
SS	4	JP	DC	$1,000	$675	$350
EM-P	1	N/A	N/A	$750	$500	$275
SS	4	TS	MW	$1,475	$975	$525
EM	2	EK	RP	$1,025	$675	$375
EM-P	1	N/A	N/A	$1,025	$675	$375
EM-P	1	N/A	N/A	$875	$600	$325
SS	4	BE	JY/GF	$8,550	$5,650	$3,000
SS	4	WW	KO	$1,300	$875	$475
EM	1	N/A	N/A	$650	$450	$250
EM	1	EK	AS	$850	$575	$300
EM	2	WN	RP	$550	$375	$200
SS	4	SS/MK	N/A	$800	$525	$275
EM	1	SK	RP	$575	$400	$200
EM	1	WN	RP	$15,000	$9,900	$5,250
M	1	N/A	N/A	$400	$275	$150
M	1	N/A	N/A	$1,200	$800	$425
EM	1	N/A	N/A	$975	$650	$350

Game	Manufacturer	Year	# Made
Merry-Go-Round	Gottlieb	1960	750
Merry Widow	Genco	1948	N/A
Merry Widow	Williams	1963	2150
Meteor	Stern	1979	8362
Metro	Genco	1940	N/A
Metro	Williams	1961	700
Metropolitan	Pacific Amusement	1933	N/A
Mexico	United Mfg.	1947	N/A
Miami [1]	Chicago Coin	1938	515
Miami [2]	Chicago Coin	1938	461
Miami Beach	Gottlieb	1941	N/A
Mibs	Gottlieb	1969	2200
Middle Earth [3]	Atari	1978	N/A
Midget Racer	Bally	1946	N/A
Midway	Daval	1939	N/A
Millionaire	Williams	1987	3500
Mini Cycle	Gottlieb	1970	885
Mini Pool [4]	Gottlieb	1969	500
MiniZag	Bally	1968	1172
Minstrel Man [5]	Gottlieb	1951	1800
Miss America	Gottlieb	1937	N/A
Miss America	Stoner	1937	N/A
Miss America	Gottlieb	1947	1673
Miss Annabelle [6]	Gottlieb	1959	1300
Miss-O	Williams	1969	2351
Monarch	Bally	1933	N/A
Monday Night Football	Data East	1989	1492
Monicker	Bally	1941	N/A
Monopolee	Chicago Coin	1936	127
Monopoly	Stern	2001	3600
Monopoly-Platinum	Stern	2001	40
Monster Bash	Williams	1998	3361
Monte Carlo [7]	Genco	1932	N/A
Monte Carlo	Rock-Ola	1936	N/A
Monte Carlo	Bally	1964	1050
Monte Carlo	Bally	1973	5254
Monte Carlo	Gottlieb/Premiere	1987	4315
Monterrey	United Mfg.	1948	N/A
Moon Glow	United Mfg.	1948	N/A

1. Standard play 2. Free Play 3. Widebody 4. Add-A-Ball 5. Drop targets 6. Mechanical animation
7. Tabletop

Type	Play	Designer	Artist	Class 1	Class 2	Class 3
EM	2	WN	RP	$600	$400	$225
EM	1	N/A	N/A	$450	$300	$175
EM	4	SK	GM	$475	$300	$175
SS	4	STK	GEO	$800	$550	$300
EM	1	HH	RP	$850	$575	$300
EM	2	SK	GM	$625	$425	$225
M	1	FM	N/A	$500	$325	$175
EM	1	N/A	N/A	$425	$275	$150
EM	1	N/A	N/A	$600	$400	$225
EM	1	N/A	N/A	$625	$425	$225
EM	1	HM	RP	$500	$325	$175
EM	1	EK	AS	$650	$425	$225
SS	4	GS	GO	$800	$525	$300
EM	1	N/A	N/A	$950	$625	$350
EM	1	N/A	N/A	$425	$275	$150
SS	4	JA	TE	$750	$500	$275
EM	2	EK	AS	$575	$375	$200
EM	1	EK	AS	$775	$525	$275
EM	1	TZ	JK	$500	$325	$175
EM	1	HM	RP	$3,100	$2,050	$1,100
EM-P	1	N/A	N/A	$975	$650	$350
EM	1	N/A	N/A	$825	$550	$300
EM	1	HM	RP	$625	$425	$225
EM	1	WN	RP	$1,000	$675	$350
EM	1	NC	CM	$500	$350	$175
M	1	N/A	N/A	$500	$325	$175
SS	4	JK/EC	KO	$1,225	$800	$425
EM	1	N/A	N/A	$450	$300	$175
EM	1	N/A	N/A	$900	$600	$325
SS	4	PL	JY	$3,800	$2,500	$1,350
SS	4	PL	JY	$4,500	$2,975	$1,575
SS	4	GEG	KO	$9,550	$6,300	$3,350
M	1	N/A	N/A	$500	$350	$175
EM-P	1	N/A	N/A	$900	$600	$325
EM	1	TZ	N/A	$600	$400	$225
EM	4	JP	DC	$875	$575	$300
SS	4	JT	DOM(B)/LD(P)	$975	$650	$350
EM	1	N/A	N/A	$575	$375	$200
EM	1	N/A	N/A	$375	$250	$150

Game	Manufacturer	Year	# Made
Moon Shot	Bally	1963	1250
Moon Shot [1]	Chicago Coin	1969	N/A
Morocco	Exhibit Supply	1948	N/A
Motordome	Bally	1986	2000
Moulin Rouge	Williams	1965	1325
Mousin' Around!	Bally	1989	N/A
Mr. & Mrs. Pac-Man	Bally	1982	10600
Mr. Chips	Genco	1939	N/A
Music Man	Williams	1960	N/A
Mustang	Chicago Coin	1964	N/A
Mustang	Gottlieb	1977	2225
Mystery	Exhibit Supply	1947	N/A
Mystery Castle	Alvin G.	1993	500
Mystic	Bally	1980	3950
Mystic Marvel [2]	Gottlieb	1954	1050
Nags	Chicago Coin	1938	805
Nags [3]	Williams	1951	N/A
Nags [4]	Williams	1960	N/A
Naples	Williams	1957	N/A
NASCAR	Stern	2005	N/A
Natural	Bally	1936	N/A
Natural	Genco	1939	N/A
Navy [5]	J. H. Keeney & Co.	1937	N/A
NBA	Stern	2009	N/A
NBA Fastbreak	Bally	1997	4414
Neighbors	Mills Novelty Co.	1936	N/A
Neontact [6]	Pacific Amusement	1935	N/A
Neptune [7]	Gottlieb	1978	270
Nevada	United Mfg.	1947	N/A
New Champ, The	Gottlieb	1941	N/A
New Daily-Races [8]	Gottlieb	1947	N/A
New York [7]	Gottlieb	1976	300
New Yorker	Bally	1935	N/A
NFL [9]	Stern	2001	N/A
Niagara	Gottlieb	1951	N/A
Nifty	Williams	1950	N/A
Night Moves [10]	International Concepts	1989	N/A
Night Rider	Bally	1976	4155
Night Rider	Bally	1977	7000

1. Light animation 2. Double award 3. One-ball game 4. Mechanical animation 5. One-ball payout
6. Neon lighting 7. Add-A-Ball 8. Full cabinet 9. Custom team backglass 10. Cocktail table

Type	Play	Designer	Artist	Class 1	Class 2	Class 3
EM	1	TZ	N/A	$950	$625	$350
EM	4	ALS/JEK/JG	CM	$525	$350	$200
EM	1	N/A	N/A	$425	$275	$150
SS	4	GK	TR	$825	$550	$300
EM	1	NC	AS	$850	$575	$300
SS	4	WP	PM	$1,225	$825	$450
SS	4	GC	MH/PM	$900	$600	$325
EM	1	N/A	N/A	$425	$275	$150
EM	4	SK/HM	GM	$375	$250	$150
EM	2	ALS/JEK	RP	$475	$325	$175
EM	2	EK	GOM	$675	$450	$250
EM	1	N/A	N/A	$500	$350	$175
SS	4	WW/MG	DH	$1,975	$1,300	$700
SS	4	GC	KO	$775	$525	$275
EM	1	WN	RP	$1,975	$1,300	$700
EM	1	N/A	N/A	$750	$500	$275
EM	1	HW	N/A	$825	$550	$300
EM	1	HW	GM	$2,900	$1,925	$1,025
EM	2	HW	GM	$450	$300	$175
SS	4	LK/PL	JY	$3,225	$2,125	$1,125
EM-P	1	N/A	N/A	$1,000	$675	$350
EM	1	N/A	N/A	$475	$325	$175
EM-P	1	N/A	N/A	$875	$600	$325
SS	4	GAS/RT/JONB	KO	$4,400	$2,925	$1,550
SS	4	GEG	KO	$1,950	$1,275	$700
EM	1	N/A	N/A	$425	$275	$150
EM	1	N/A	N/A	$2,650	$1,750	$950
EM	1	JO	GOM	$1,050	$700	$375
EM	1	N/A	N/A	$475	$325	$175
EM	1	HM	RP	$500	$325	$175
EM-P	1	HM	RP	$725	$475	$250
EM	2	EK	GOM	$1,125	$750	$400
EM-P	1	N/A	N/A	$1,375	$925	$500
SS	4	N/A	N/A	$3,350	$2,225	$1,175
EM	1	WN	RP	$2,625	$1,750	$925
EM	1	HW	GM	$550	$375	$200
SS	4	JT	N/A	$425	$300	$150
EM	4	GK	PF	$825	$550	$300
SS	4	GK	PF	$775	$500	$275

Game	Manufacturer	Year	# Made
Nine Ball	Stern	1980	2279
Nine Sisters [1]	Williams	1953	N/A
Nip-It [2]	Bally	1973	95
Nip-It	Bally	1973	4485
Nippy	Chicago Coin	1939	1351
Nitro Ground Shaker	Bally	1980	7950
No Fear: Dangerous Sports	Williams	1995	4540
No Good Gofers!	Williams	1997	2711
North Star	Gottlieb	1964	2525
Now	Gottlieb	1971	1125
Nudgy [3]	Bally	1947	N/A
Nugent	Stern	1978	2671
Oasis	Exhibit Supply	1950	N/A
O-Boy	Chicago Coin	1939	1700
Ocean Park [4]	Chicago Coin	1939	968
Ocean Park [5]	Chicago Coin	1939	256
Odd Ball	Daval	1938	N/A
Odd Ball Jr.	Daval	1938	N/A
Odds & Evens	Bally	1973	2570
Official	Mills Novelty Co.	1932	N/A
Official Baseball	Genco	1934	N/A
Oh Boy	Williams	1964	1700
Oh! Johnny	Gottlieb	1940	N/A
Oklahoma	United Mfg.	1949	N/A
Oklahoma	Gottlieb	1961	1710
Old Chicago	Bally	1976	7155
Old Faithful	Gottlieb	1949	810
Old Plantation	J. H. Keeney and Co.	1961	N/A
Olde King Cole	Gottlieb	1948	1500
Olympic Hockey	Williams	1972	2555
Olympics [6]	Williams	1952	N/A
Olympics	Gottleib	1962	2200
Olympics	Chicago Coin	1975	N/A
On Beam	Bally	1969	1150
On Deck	Baker Novelty	1940	N/A
One Better	Rock-Ola	1936	N/A
One-Two-Three [7]	Mills Novelty Co.	1938	N/A
"1 2 3"	Mills Novelty Co.	1940	N/A
One-Two-Three	Genco	1948	N/A

1. Reel scoring, 1 flipper 2. Moving alligator 3. Standard and rolldown cabinet 4. Novelty play
5. Free play 6. Light animation 7. Slot reels

Type	Play	Designer	Artist	Class 1	Class 2	Class 3
SS	4	STK	JEO/RQ	$1,075	$725	$375
EM	1	HW	GM	$775	$500	$275
EM	4	TZ	DIW	$1,375	$925	$500
EM	4	TZ	DIW	$1,200	$800	$425
EM	1	N/A	N/A	$550	$375	$200
SS	4	GC	DC	$1,300	$850	$450
SS	4	SR	GF	$2,475	$1,650	$875
SS	4	PL/LK	JY	$2,925	$1,925	$1,025
EM	1	WN	RP	$1,550	$1,025	$550
EM	4	EK	GOM	$500	$350	$175
EM	1	N/A	N/A	$600	$400	$225
SS	4	MK	N/A	$1,200	$800	$425
EM	1	N/A	N/A	$425	$275	$150
EM	1	N/A	N/A	$600	$400	$225
EM	1	N/A	N/A	$625	$425	$225
EM	1	N/A	N/A	$625	$425	$225
EM	1	N/A	N/A	$475	$325	$175
EM	1	N/A	N/A	$425	$275	$150
EM	1	JP	DC	$700	$475	$250
M	1	N/A	N/A	$500	$350	$175
M	1	N/A	N/A	$1,325	$875	$475
EM	2	SK	GM	$725	$475	$250
EM	1	HM	RP	$550	$375	$200
EM	1	N/A	N/A	$500	$325	$175
EM	4	WN	RP	$600	$400	$225
EM	4	GK	DC	$1,000	$675	$350
EM	1	HM	RP	$1,475	$975	$525
EM	1	EK	N/A	$450	$300	$175
EM	1	HM	RP	$1,425	$950	$500
EM	2	SK	CM	$550	$375	$200
EM	1	HM/HW	RP	$700	$475	$250
EM	1	WN	RP	$925	$625	$325
EM	2	WM/JEK/AP	CM	$375	$250	$150
EM	1	BJ	CM	$550	$375	$200
EM	1	N/A	N/A	$575	$375	$200
EM-P	1	N/A	N/A	$725	$475	$250
EM-P	1	N/A	N/A	$1,500	$1,000	$525
EM-P	1	N/A	N/A	$575	$375	$200
EM	1	SK	RP	$750	$500	$275

Game	Manufacturer	Year	# Made
Op-Pop-Pop	Bally	1969	1050
Operation: Thunder	Gottlieb/Premier	1992	2513
Opportunity	Marvel	1946	N/A
Orbit	Gottlieb	1971	3200
Orbitor 1	Stern	1982	889
Oscar [1]	Genco	1938	N/A
Out of Sight	Gottlieb	1974	1750
Owl [2]	Mills Novelty Co.	1941	N/A
OXO	Williams	1973	7053
Pace Maker [3]	Bally	1939	N/A
Paddock [3]	Chicago Coin	1937	N/A
Paddock	Williams	1969	1952
Palace Guard [4]	Gottlieb	1968	625
Palisades	Williams	1953	N/A
Palm Springs	Bally	1938	N/A
Palooka [4]	Williams	1964	700
Pan American	Bally	1941	N/A
Panama	Daval	1936	N/A
Panthera	Gottlieb	1980	5200
Par Golf [5]	GM Labs	1935	N/A
Paradise	Gottlieb	1940	N/A
Paradise	United Mfg.	1948	N/A
Paradise [6]	Gottlieb	1965	2100
Paragon	Bally	1979	9120
Paramount [7]	Bally	1938	N/A
Paratrooper	Williams	1952	N/A
Parlay, Pamco	Pacific Amusement	1935	N/A
Parlay Jr., Pamco	Pacific Amusement	1936	N/A
Parlay Sr., Pamco	Pacific Amusement	1935	N/A
Party Animal	Bally	1987	2250
Party Zone [8]	Bally	1991	N/A
Pat Hand	Williams	1975	6500
Paul Bunyan [9]	Gottlieb	1968	1900
Pay Table	Mills Novelty Co.	1934	N/A
Peachy	Chicago Coin	1938	496
Pearl Harbor [10]	Mills Novelty Co.	1935	N/A
Pennant,The	Bally	1933	N/A
Peppy	Chicago Coin	1938	742
Perky	Williams	1956	N/A

1. Light animation 2. Free-play version of "1 2 3" 3. One-ball game 4. Add-A-Ball 5. 9-hole course
6. Mechanical animation 7. Captive ball 8. Pinball Wizard 9. Six flippers 10. One-ball payout

Type	Play	Designer	Artist	Class 1	Class 2	Class 3
EM	1	TZ	CM	$600	$400	$225
SS	4	RT	COM(B)/DM(P)	$950	$625	$350
EM	1	N/A	N/A	$450	$300	$175
EM	4	EK	GOM	$500	$350	$175
SS	4	JJ	N/A	$1,425	$950	$500
EM-P	1	N/A	N/A	$625	$425	$225
EM	2	EK	GOM	$600	$400	$225
EM	1	N/A	N/A	$1,025	$675	$375
EM	4	NC	CM	$625	$400	$225
EM	1	N/A	N/A	$750	$500	$275
EM-P	1	N/A	N/A	$625	$425	$225
EM	1	NC	CM	$475	$325	$175
EM	1	EK	AS	$725	$475	$250
EM	1	HW	GM	$650	$450	$250
EM	1	N/A	N/A	$450	$300	$175
EM	1	SK	AS	$650	$450	$250
N/A	1	N/A	N/A	$450	$300	$175
N/A	1	N/A	N/A	$700	$475	$250
SS	4	AE	DW	$600	$400	$225
EM	1	N/A	N/A	$1,075	$725	$375
EM	1	HM	RP	$750	$500	$275
EM	1	N/A	N/A	$625	$425	$225
EM	2	EK	RP	$950	$650	$350
SS	4	GK	PF	$1,200	$800	$425
EM	1	NA	N/A	$625	$425	$225
EM	1	HW	GM	$800	$525	$300
EM-P	1	BON	N/A	$825	$550	$300
EM-P	1	N/A	N/A	$725	$475	$275
EM-P	1	N/A	N/A	$825	$550	$300
SS	4	DN	PM	$900	$600	$325
SS	4	DN	GF	$1,600	$1,075	$575
EM	4	NC	CM	$625	$400	$225
EM	2	WN/EK/STK	AS	$550	$375	$200
M-P	1	N/A	N/A	$550	$375	$200
EM	1	N/A	N/A	$700	$475	$250
EM-P	1	N/A	N/A	$875	$600	$325
M	1	N/A	N/A	$575	$400	$225
EM	1	N/A	N/A	$625	$425	$225
EM	1	HW	RP	$1,050	$700	$375

Game	Manufacturer	Year	# Made
Peter Pan	Williams	1955	N/A
Phantom of the Opera	Data East	1990	2750
Pharaoh	Williams	1981	2500
Pheasant [1]	O. D. Jennings & Co.	1938	N/A
Phoenix	Williams	1949	400
Phoenix	Williams	1978	6198
Piccadilly	Williams	1956	N/A
Picnic	Gottlieb	1958	850
Pigskin [2]	Peo Mfg.	1934	N/A
Pilot, The	National Pin Games	1932	N/A
Pin Bowler [3]	Chicago Coin	1949	N/A
Pin Wheel	Gottlieb	1953	800
Pin·Bot	Williams	1986	12001
Pin-Up [4]	Gottlieb	1975	715
Pinball	Stern	1977	594
Pinball	Stern	1977	1694
Pinball Lizard	Game Plan	1980	1400
Pinball Magic	Capcom	1995	1200
Pinball Pool	Gottlieb	1979	7200
Pinch Hitter	United Mfg.	1949	N/A
Pink Panther	Gottlieb	1981	2840
Pinky [5]	Williams	1950	N/A
Pioneer	Gottlieb	1976	3625
Pippin	Chicago Coin	1935	1501
Pirate Gold	Chicago Coin	1969	N/A
Pirates of the Caribbean	Stern	2006	N/A
Pistol Poker	Alvin G	1993	200
Pit Stop	Williams	1968	2002
Planets	Williams	1971	N/A
Play Ball	Exhibit Supply	1935	N/A
Play Ball [6]	Exhibit Supply	1938	N/A
Play Ball	Bally	1941	N/A
Play Ball [7]	Gottlieb	1971	3076
Play Boy	Chicago Coin	1947	3700
Play-Boy [8]	Gottlieb	1932	N/A
Playboy	Bally	1978	18250
Playboy [9]	Stern	2002	N/A
Playboy 35th Anniversary	Data East	1989	2338
Playland	Exhibit Supply	1950	N/A

1. Full cabinet   2. Three versions   3. Light animation   4. Add-A-Ball   5. Asymmetrical playfield
6. Baseball format   7. Fireball shooter   8. Tabletop   9. Adult

Type	Play	Designer	Artist	Class 1	Class 2	Class 3
EM	1	HW	GM	$775	$525	$275
SS	4	JK/EC	PF	$1,350	$900	$475
SS	4	TK	SM	$1,600	$1,075	$575
EM-P	1	N/A	N/A	$875	$600	$325
EM	1	HW	GM	$825	$550	$300
SS	4	BO	COM	$800	$525	$275
EM	2	HW	GM	$475	$325	$175
EM	2	WN	RP	$725	$500	$275
EM	1	N/A	N/A	$875	$600	$325
M	1	N/A	N/A	$1,000	$675	$350
EM	1	N/A	RP	$875	$575	$325
EM	1	WN	RP	$1,000	$675	$350
SS	4	BO/PA	PA	$1,450	$950	$525
EM	1	EK	GOM	$875	$600	$325
EM	4	MK	N/A	$725	$475	$250
SS	4	MK	N/A	$625	$425	$225
SS	4	EC	JS	$700	$475	$250
SS	4	BH/RH	JB/HV	$2,075	$1,375	$725
SS	4	EK	GOM	$875	$575	$325
N/A	1	N/A	N/A	$2,000	$1,325	$700
SS	4	JOB	JES	$650	$425	$225
EM	1	HW	GM	$875	$575	$325
EM	2	EK/WN	GOM	$900	$600	$325
EM	1	N/A	N/A	$825	$550	$300
EM	1	JEK/AS/JG	CM	$600	$400	$225
SS	4	DN	KO	$5,225	$3,450	$1,850
SS	4	WW/MG	DH	$1,125	$750	$400
EM	2	NC	CM	$625	$425	$225
EM	2	SK	LR	$425	$275	$150
EM-P	1	N/A	N/A	$1,400	$925	$500
EM	1	N/A	N/A	$1,100	$725	$400
EM	1	N/A	N/A	$750	$500	$275
EM	1	EK	GOM	$825	$550	$300
EM	1	N/A	RP	$625	$425	$225
M	2	N/A	N/A	$950	$625	$350
SS	4	JP	PF	$1,500	$1,000	$525
SS	4	DS/GEG	KO	$2,775	$1,850	$975
SS	4	EC/JK	KO	$1,575	$1,050	$550
EM	1	N/A	N/A	$625	$425	$225

Game	Manufacturer	Year	# Made
PlayMates [1]	Gottlieb	1968	500
Playtime	Exhibit Supply	1949	N/A
Playtime	Chicago Coin	1968	N/A
Pleasure Isle [1]	Gottlieb	1965	235
Plus or Minus	Bally	1936	N/A
Pockets	Bally	1936	N/A
Poker Face	Gottlieb	1953	1700
Poker Face	J. H. Keeney & Co.	1963	N/A
Pokerino	Williams	1978	1501
Police Force	Williams	1989	4700
Policy	Western Equipment	1936	N/A
Polo	Chicago Coin	1940	1640
Polo	Gottlieb	1970	1140
Pontiac	Genco	1934	N/A
Pool Sharks	Bally	1990	N/A
Pop 'Em	L. B. Elliot Products	1937	N/A
Pop-A-Card [1]	Gottlieb	1972	825
Popeye Saves the Earth	Bally	1994	4217
Post Time [2]	Mills Novelty Co.	1937	N/A
Post Time [1]	Williams	1969	2002
Power Play	Bally	1978	13750
President	Bally	1933	N/A
Pretty Baby	Williams	1965	1300
Preview	Western Equipment	1937	N/A
Preview	Gottlieb	1962	1900
Pro Pool [1]	Gottlieb	1973	800
Pro-Football	Gottlieb	1973	4500
Progress [3]	Bally	1940	N/A
Prospector	Bally	1935	N/A
Prospector	Sonic	1977	N/A
Puddin' Head	Genco	1948	N/A
Punch	Genco	1939	N/A
Punchy	Chicago Coin	1950	N/A
Punk!	Gottlieb	1982	959
Push Over	Gottlieb	1934	N/A
Put 'N' Take [2]	Western Equipment	1935	N/A
Pylon [4]	Exhibit Supply	1940	N/A
Pyramid	Gottlieb	1939	N/A
Pyramid	Gottlieb	1978	950

1. Add-A-Ball   2. One-ball payout   3. Revolving targets   4. Mechanical animation

Type	Play	Designer	Artist	Class 1	Class 2	Class 3
EM	1	EK	AS	$725	$500	$275
EM	1	N/A	N/A	$375	$250	$150
EM	2	ALS/JEK/JG	CM	$425	$275	$150
EM	2	EK	RP	$1,275	$850	$450
EM-P	1	N/A	N/A	$1,000	$675	$350
EM	1	N/A	N/A	$1,125	$750	$400
EM	1	WN	RP	$1,400	$925	$500
EM	1	EK	N/A	$900	$600	$325
SS	4	SK	COM	$650	$425	$225
SS	4	MR/BO	PA/JY	$1,075	$725	$375
EM-P	1	N/A	N/A	$1,375	$925	$500
EM	1	N/A	N/A	$900	$600	$325
EM	4	EK	AS	$600	$400	$225
M	1	HH	N/A	$625	$425	$225
SS	4	TK	DW	$1,100	$750	$400
EM-P	1	N/A	N/A	$1,575	$1,050	$550
EM	1	EK	GOM	$1,025	$675	$375
SS	4	BO/PA	JY/PA/PM	$1,675	$1,125	$600
EM-P	1	N/A	N/A	$1,375	$925	$500
EM	1	NC	CM	$425	$275	$150
SS	4	GK	DC	$1,250	$825	$450
M	1	N/A	N/A	$600	$400	$225
EM	2	SK	N/A	$500	$350	$175
EM-P	1	N/A	N/A	$1,000	$675	$350
EM	2	WN	RP	$500	$350	$175
EM	1	EK	GOM	$750	$500	$275
EM	1	EK	GOM	$725	$475	$275
EM	1	N/A	N/A	$700	$475	$250
EM-P	1	GM	N/A	$1,350	$900	$475
EM	4	N/A	N/A	$725	$500	$275
EM	1	N/A	N/A	$500	$350	$175
EM	1	N/A	N/A	$575	$375	$200
EM	1	N/A	N/A	$625	$425	$225
SS	4	TS	DM/TD	$750	$500	$275
EM	1	N/A	N/A	$450	$300	$175
EM-P	1	N/A	N/A	$750	$500	$275
EM	1	N/A	N/A	$1,125	$750	$400
EM	1	HM	RP	$625	$425	$225
EM	2	EK	GOM	$800	$550	$300

Game	Manufacturer	Year	# Made
Q-Bert's Quest	Gottlieb	1983	884
Quarterback	Bally	1976	1050
Quartette [1]	Gottlieb	1952	1450
Queen Mary	Rock-Ola	1936	N/A
Queen of Diamonds	Gottlieb	1959	1700
Queen of Hearts [2]	Gottlieb	1952	2200
Quick Draw	Gottlieb	1975	2660
Quick Silver	J. H. Keeney & Co.	1935	N/A
Quicksilver	Stern	1980	1201
Quintette	Gottlieb	1953	1200
Race the Clock	Williams	1955	N/A
Race Time	Gottlieb	1959	950
Race Way	Midway	1963	N/A
Races [3]	Western Equipment	1936	N/A
Races	Stoner	1937	N/A
Rack 'Em Up!	Gottlieb	1983	1762
Rack-A-Ball	Gottlieb	1962	2700
Radical!	Bally	1990	1315
Radio Station	California Games	1934	N/A
Rag Mop [4]	Williams	1950	N/A
Ragtime	Genco	1938	N/A
Railroad	Mills Novelty Co.	1936	N/A
Rainbow	J. H. Keeney & Co.	1936	N/A
Rainbow	Williams	1948	N/A
Rainbow	Gottlieb	1956	1250
Rambler	Bally	1936	N/A
Ramona	United Mfg.	1949	N/A
Rancho	Bally	1948	N/A
Rancho	Williams	1977	1229
Ranger	Exhibit Supply	1947	N/A
Rapid Transit	Chicago Coin	1935	3266
Raven	Gottlieb/Premier	1986	3550
Rawhide	Stern	1977	1200
Ready...Aim...Fire!	Gottlieb	1983	390
Rebound [5]	California Games	1934	N/A
Rebound [6]	Exhibit Supply	1934	N/A
Rebound, 1940 [7]	Exhibit Supply	1939	N/A
Recorder [8]	Genco	1938	N/A
Red Arrow	Bally	1934	N/A

1. First trap holes 2. First drop-through holes 3. One-ball payout 4. Single flipper 5. Senior 6. Junior
7. Wire ramp 8. Free game register

Type	Play	Designer	Artist	Class 1	Class 2	Class 3
SS	4	JT	DM	$950	$650	$350
EM	2	JP	DIW	$500	$325	$175
EM	1	WN	RP	$1,100	$750	$400
EM-P	1	N/A	N/A	$1,250	$825	$450
EM	1	WN	RP	$1,575	$1,025	$550
EM	1	WN	RP	$1,850	$1,225	$650
EM	2	EK	GOM	$900	$600	$325
EM	1	HW	N/A	$1,500	$1,000	$525
SS	4	JJ	DW	$725	$475	$250
EM	1	WN	RP	$1,075	$725	$400
EM	4	HW	GM	$500	$350	$175
EM	2	WN	RP	$575	$375	$200
EM	2	IW	JK	$1,250	$825	$450
EM-P	1	N/A	N/A	$875	$600	$325
EM	1	N/A	N/A	$625	$425	$225
SS	4	JOB	DM	$775	$525	$275
EM	1	WN	RP	$1,175	$775	$425
SS	4	DL/PP	JY	$1,400	$925	$500
EM	1	N/A	N/A	$750	$500	$275
EM	1	HW	GM	$750	$500	$275
EM	1	N/A	N/A	$575	$375	$200
EM-P	1	BEM/FB	N/A	$1,600	$1,075	$575
EM-P	1	N/A	N/A	$875	$575	$325
EM	1	HW	GM	$600	$400	$225
EM	1	WN	RP	$1,375	$900	$500
EM-P	1	N/A	N/A	$950	$625	$350
EM	1	N/A	N/A	$450	$300	$175
EM	1	N/A	N/A	$600	$400	$225
EM	2	HW/CO	N/A	$550	$375	$200
EM	1	N/A	N/A	$575	$375	$200
EM	1	N/A	N/A	$825	$550	$300
SS	4	JT	LD	$775	$525	$275
EM	4	AP/JEK/WM	CM	$575	$375	$200
SS	4	AS	DM	$475	$325	$175
EM	1	JOR	N/A	$625	$425	$225
EM	1	N/A	N/A	$500	$350	$175
EM	1	N/A	N/A	$625	$425	$225
EM	1	N/A	N/A	$575	$375	$200
EM-P	1	N/A	N/A	$1,000	$650	$350

Game	Manufacturer	Year	# Made
Red Baron	Chicago Coin	1975	N/A
Red Man	O. D. Jennings & Co.	1936	N/A
Red Max, The	Bally	1971	70
Red Sails	Pacific Amusement	1936	N/A
Red Shoes	United Mfg.	1950	N/A
Regatta	Exhibit Supply	1938	N/A
Regatta	Williams	1955	N/A
Register	Gottlieb	1934	N/A
Register	Gottlieb	1956	900
Relay	Gottlieb	1934	N/A
Relay (Senior)	Gottlieb	1934	N/A
Reno [1]	Williams	1957	N/A
Repeater	J. H. Keeney & Co.	1936	N/A
Repeater	J. H. Keeney & Co.	1940	N/A
Re-Play	Chicago Coin	1937	971
Request	Exhibit Supply	1938	N/A
Rescue 911	Gottlieb/Premier	1994	4000
Reserve	Bally	1938	N/A
Reserve	Williams	1961	750
Revenge From Mars	Bally	1999	6878
Review	Exhibit Supply	1938	N/A
Rink	Genco	1939	N/A
Rio	United Mfg.	1947	N/A
Rip Snorter	Genco	1949	N/A
Ripley's Believe It or Not	Stern	2004	N/A
Ritz [2]	Stoner	1938	N/A
River Boat	Williams	1964	1650
Riverboat Gambler	Williams	1990	3200
Riviera	Chicago Coin	1973	N/A
Ro Go [3]	Bally	1974	75
Ro Go	Bally	1974	3000
Road Kings	Williams	1986	5500
Road Race	Gottlieb	1969	1425
Road Show, Red & Ted's	Williams	1994	6259
Robin Hood	Daval	1938	N/A
Robo-War	Gottlieb/Premier	1988	2130
RoboCop	Data East	1989	1500
Rock	Gottlieb/Premier	1985	1875
Rock 'N Roll [4]	Williams	1970	N/A

1. First match feature   2. Full cabinet   3. Sample game   4. Add-A-Ball

Type	Play	Designer	Artist	Class 1	Class 2	Class 3
EM	2	AP/JEK/WM	LDR	$775	$525	$275
EM-P	1	N/A	N/A	$1,625	$1,075	$575
EM	1	TZ	N/A	$1,000	$675	$350
EM-P	1	N/A	N/A	$1,075	$725	$375
EM	1	N/A	N/A	$425	$275	$150
EM	1	N/A	N/A	$575	$375	$200
EM	1	HW	GM	$675	$450	$250
M	1	N/A	N/A	$625	$425	$225
EM	4	WN	RP	$500	$325	$175
EM	1	N/A	N/A	$450	$300	$175
EM	1	N/A	N/A	$500	$350	$175
EM	1	HW	GM	$650	$425	$250
EM-P	1	N/A	N/A	$1,000	$675	$350
EM	1	N/A	N/A	$950	$625	$350
EM	1	N/A	N/A	$525	$350	$200
EM	1	N/A	N/A	$500	$325	$175
SS	4	BIP	COM	$1,675	$1,100	$600
EM	1	N/A	N/A	$625	$425	$225
EM	1	SK	GM	$525	$350	$200
SS	4	GEG	JY/GF	$3,025	$2,000	$1,075
EM	1	HW/LD	N/A	$500	$350	$175
EM	1	N/A	N/A	$500	$325	$175
EM	1	HW	GM	$425	$275	$150
EM	1	HH	N/A	$425	$275	$150
SS	4	PL/LK	JY	$3,150	$2,075	$1,100
EM-P	1	N/A	N/A	$725	$475	$250
EM	1	NC	N/A	$825	$550	$300
SS	4	WP	LID(P)/PM(B)	$1,400	$925	$500
EM	4	WM/JEK	CM	$425	$300	$150
EM	4	GK	DC	$725	$475	$250
EM	4	GK	DC	$600	$400	$225
SS	4	MR	TE	$1,125	$750	$400
EM	1	EK	AS	$625	$425	$225
SS	4	PL/TE/DS	JY	$2,350	$1,550	$825
EM	1	N/A	N/A	$600	$400	$225
SS	4	JN/JT	COM	$800	$525	$275
SS	4	EC/JK	KO	$875	$600	$325
SS	4	JT	LD	$900	$600	$325
EM	1	NC	CM	$525	$350	$200

Game	Manufacturer	Year	# Made
Rock On	Allied Leisure	1975	N/A
Rock Star [1]	Gottlieb	1978	268
Rocket	Bally	1933	N/A
Rocket, New	Bally	1938	N/A
Rocket	Bally	1947	N/A
Rocket	Genco	1950	N/A
Rocket	Williams	1959	N/A
Rocket III	Bally	1967	2603
Rocket Ship	Gottlieb	1958	2000
Rockelite	Bally	1935	N/A
Rockettes	Gottlieb	1950	1000
RockMakers	Bally	1968	2420
Rocky	Gottlieb	1982	1504
Rocky and Bullwinkle and Friends	Data East	1993	N/A
Rodeo	Exhibit Supply	1935	N/A
Rodeo	Midway	1964	N/A
Rola Score	Chicago Coin	1936	1001
Rola-Ball [2]	Unkown	19??	N/A
Roll Over	Genco	1937	N/A
Roller Coaster	Gottlieb	1971	1550
Roller Derby	Bally	1939	N/A
Roller Disco	Gottlieb	1980	2400
RollerCoaster Tycoon	Stern	2002	N/A
Rollergames	Williams	1990	N/A
Rolling Stones	Bally	1980	5700
Rolling Stones, The	Stern	2011	N/A
Rolling Stones LE, The	Stern	2011	350
Rondeevoo	United Mfg.	1948	N/A
Rose Bowl	Chicago Coin	1937	580
Rose-Bowl [3]	Gottlieb	1951	1000
Rotation	Stoner	1940	N/A
Rotation VIII [4]	Midway	1978	N/A
Roto	Williams	1969	N/A
Roto Pool	Gottlieb	1958	1800
Round 'n' Round	Shyvers Mfg.	1936	N/A
Round Up	Bally	1971	70
Roundup	Bally	1936	N/A
RoundUp	Gottlieb	1948	1500
Roxy	Chicago Coin	1940	2849

1. Add-A-Ball   2. Tabletop   3. Yards scoring   4. Cocktail table

Type	Play	Designer	Artist	Class 1	Class 2	Class 3
SS	4	N/A	N/A	$350	$225	$125
EM	1	JO	GOM	$1,125	$750	$400
EM-P	1	HGB	N/A	$1,800	$1,200	$650
EM	1	N/A	N/A	$500	$325	$175
EM	1	N/A	N/A	$1,000	$675	$350
EM	1	HH	N/A	$1,000	$675	$350
EM	1	HW	GM	$1,225	$825	$450
EM	1	TZ	CM	$725	$475	$275
EM	1	WN	RP	$2,350	$1,550	$825
EM	1	N/A	N/A	$575	$375	$200
EM	1	HM	RP	$1,025	$675	$375
EM	4	TZ	JK	$750	$500	$275
SS	4	JT	DM	$3,000	$1,975	$1,050
SS	4	TIS	KO	$1,725	$1,150	$600
EM-P	1	N/A	N/A	$825	$550	$300
EM	2	N/A	N/A	$775	$500	$275
EM	1	N/A	N/A	$575	$375	$200
M	1	N/A	N/A	$300	$200	$125
EM	1	N/A	N/A	$625	$425	$225
EM	2	EK	GOM	$625	$400	$225
EM	1	N/A	N/A	$550	$375	$200
SS	4	EK	GOM	$700	$475	$250
SS	4	PL	JY	$2,725	$1,800	$950
SS	4	SR	PM	$1,200	$800	$425
SS	4	JP	GF	$2,625	$1,750	$925
SS	4	N/A	N/A	$5,700	$3,775	$2,000
SS	4	N/A	N/A	$6,600	$4,375	$2,325
EM	1	N/A	N/A	$425	$275	$150
EM	1	N/A	N/A	$450	$300	$175
EM	1	WN	RP	$1,650	$1,100	$575
EM	1	N/A	N/A	$500	$325	$175
SS	4	RNH	RS	$875	$575	$325
EM	2	NC	CM	$525	$350	$200
EM	1	WN	RP	$2,050	$1,350	$725
EM-P	1	N/A	N/A	$950	$625	$350
EM	2	N/A	CM	$500	$325	$175
EM-P	1	N/A	N/A	$1,050	$700	$375
EM	1	HM	RP	$900	$600	$325
EM	1	N/A	N/A	$600	$400	$225

Game	Manufacturer	Year	# Made
Royal	Bally	1939	N/A
Royal Flash	Chicago Coin	1964	N/A
Royal Flush	Gottlieb	1957	3400
Royal Flush	Gottlieb	1976	12250
Royal Flush Deluxe	Gottlieb	1983	2044
Royal Guard	Gottlieb	1968	2900
Royal Races [1]	Pacific Amusement	1937	N/A
Royal Rumble, WWF	Data East	1994	N/A
Rugby	Chicago Coin	1936	279
Safari	Bally	1968	1100
Safe Cracker [2]	Bally	1996	1148
St. Louis	Williams	1949	N/A
St. Moritz	Chicago Coin	1938	1016
Sally	Chicago Coin	1948	1600
Salute	Baker Novelty	1941	N/A
Samba	Exhibit Supply	1948	N/A
San Francisco	Williams	1964	2000
Sara-Suzy	Stoner	1940	N/A
Saratoga [3]	Williams	1948	N/A
Satellite	Williams	1958	N/A
Satin Doll	Williams	1975	2400
Scared Stiff, Elvira	Bally	1996	4028
School Days	Gottlieb	1941	N/A
Scoop	Bally	1939	N/A
Score Board	Gottlieb	1933	N/A
Score Card	Gottlieb	1940	N/A
Score Champ	J. H. Keeney & Co.	1940	N/A
Score-A-Line	Gottlieb	1940	N/A
Score-Board	Gottlieb	1956	1300
Scoreboard, Electric [4]	Gottlieb	1937	N/A
Scorpion	Williams	1980	2000
Scram [5]	A.B.T. Mfg.	1932	N/A
Screamo	Williams	1954	N/A
Screwball	Genco	1948	N/A
Screwy [5]	Bally	1932	N/A
Scuba	Gottlieb	1970	1450
Sea Belles	Gottlieb	1956	1300
Sea Breeze	United Mfg.	1946	N/A
Sea Hawk	Gottlieb	1941	N/A

1. Tabletop   2. Timed game, token pin   3. 1st thumper bumper   4. Baseball theme   5. Tabletop

Type	Play	Designer	Artist	Class 1	Class 2	Class 3
EM	1	N/A	N/A	$525	$350	$200
EM	2	JEK/AS/JG	RP	$675	$450	$250
EM	1	WN	RP	$1,275	$850	$450
EM	4	EK	GOM	$1,575	$1,025	$550
SS	4	EK	TD/EM	$1,025	$675	$375
EM	1	EK	AS	$925	$625	$325
EM-P	1	N/A	N/A	$875	$600	$325
SS	4	JK/TIS	PF/M	$1,550	$1,025	$550
EM	1	N/A	N/A	$700	$475	$250
EM	2	TZ	N/A	$675	$450	$250
SS	4	PL	JY	$4,550	$3,000	$1,600
EM	1	HW	GM	$625	$425	$225
EM	1	N/A	N/A	$675	$450	$250
EM	1	N/A	N/A	$525	$350	$200
EM	1	N/A	N/A	$500	$350	$175
EM	1	N/A	N/A	$425	$300	$150
EM	2	SK	N/A	$675	$450	$250
EM	1	N/A	N/A	$500	$350	$175
EM	1	HW	GM	$750	$500	$275
EM	1	HW	GM	$1,425	$950	$500
EM	2	NC	CM	$500	$325	$175
SS	4	DM/MW	GF	$3,550	$2,350	$1,250
EM	1	HM	RP	$625	$400	$225
EM	1	N/A	N/A	$500	$350	$175
M	1	N/A	N/A	$500	$350	$175
EM	1	HM	RP	$475	$325	$175
EM	1	N/A	N/A	$500	$325	$175
EM	1	HM	RP	$500	$350	$175
EM	4	WN	RP	$675	$450	$250
EM	1	N/A	N/A	$1,075	$725	$375
SS	4	BO	COM/TR	$1,100	$725	$400
M	1	TH	N/A	$850	$550	$300
EM	1	HW/SS	GM	$1,100	$750	$400
EM	1	HH	RP	$575	$400	$200
M	1	RM	N/A	$500	$350	$175
EM	2	EK	AS	$600	$400	$225
EM	2	WN	RP	$750	$500	$275
EM	1	N/A	N/A	$600	$400	$225
EM	1	HM	RP	$500	$325	$175

Game	Manufacturer	Year	# Made
Sea Hunt [1]	Allied Leisure	1972	N/A
Sea Jockeys [2]	Williams	1951	N/A
Sea Ray	Bally	1971	1300
Sea Wolf [3]	Williams	1959	N/A
Sea-Shore	Gottlieb	1964	1780
Seawitch	Stern	1980	2503
Secret Service	Data East	1988	N/A
See Saw	Bally	1970	1517
Select-A-Card [4]	Gottlieb	1950	1500
Sensation	Chicago Coin	1934	1775
Sensation of 1937	Chicago Coin	1937	1097
Serenade	United Mfg.	1948	N/A
Serenade	Williams	1960	N/A
Set Up [5]	Williams	1969	N/A
Seven Flashers	Western Products	1941	N/A
Seven Seas	Gottlieb	1959	700
Seven Up	Williams	1969	N/A
Seven-Up	Genco	1941	N/A
Sexy Girl	Unknown	1980	N/A
Shadow, The	Bally	1994	4247
Shamrock	Williams	1956	N/A
Shanghai	Chicago Coin	1948	1350
Shangri-La	Williams	1967	4900
Shantytown	Exhibit Supply	1949	N/A
Shaq Attaq	Gottlieb/Premier	1995	3380
Sharkey's Shootout	Stern	2000	N/A
Sharp Shooter [6]	Exhibit Supply	1935	N/A
Sharpshooter	Gottlieb	1949	1840
Sharpshooter	Game Plan	1979	4200
Sharp Shooter II	Game Plan	1983	600
Sheba	Bally	1965	825
Shells	Western Equipment	1936	N/A
Sheriff	Gottlieb	1971	2900
Shindig	Gottlieb	1953	1200
Ship Ahoy [5]	Gottlieb	1976	1150
Ship-Mates	Gottlieb	1964	5115
Shoo Shoo	Williams	1951	N/A
Shoot the Moon	Williams	1951	N/A
Shooting Star	Daval Mfg Co.	1934	N/A

1. Shakerball game 2. Mechanical boats race 3. Disappearing bumper 4. Turret shooter 5. Add-A-Ball
6. Tabletop

Type	Play	Designer	Artist	Class 1	Class 2	Class 3
EM	1	RNH	RB	$400	$275	$150
EM	1	HW	GM	$1,550	$1,025	$550
EM	2	TZ	CM	$600	$400	$225
EM	1	HM	GM	$1,825	$1,200	$650
EM	2	WN	RP	$700	$475	$250
SS	4	MK	BT	$625	$425	$225
SS	4	JK	KO/MH	$975	$650	$350
EM	4	TZ	CM	$600	$400	$225
EM	1	HM	RP	$850	$550	$300
EM	1	SG	N/A	$625	$400	$225
EM	1	N/A	N/A	$950	$625	$350
EM	1	N/A	N/A	$400	$275	$150
EM	2	HM	GM	$750	$500	$275
EM	1	SK	N/A	$500	$350	$175
EM	2	N/A	N/A	$425	$275	$150
EM	2	WN	RP	$800	$525	$275
EM	1	SK	N/A	$425	$275	$150
EM	1	N/A	N/A	$525	$350	$200
SS	4	N/A	N/A	$1,025	$675	$375
SS	4	BE	DW	$2,050	$1,350	$725
EM	2	HW	GM	$450	$300	$175
EM	1	JEK	N/A	$400	$275	$150
EM	4	SK	CM	$650	$450	$250
EM	1	N/A	N/A	$450	$300	$175
SS	4	JN	COM	$1,475	$975	$525
SS	4	JONB	JY	$1,950	$1,300	$700
M	1	N/A	N/A	$725	$475	$250
EM	1	HM	RP	$1,075	$725	$375
SS	4	RS/JJ/EC	GM	$625	$425	$225
SS	4	RS/WM	PF	$525	$350	$200
EM	2	TZ	N/A	$425	$275	$150
EM-P	1	N/A	N/A	$1,500	$1,000	$525
EM	4	EK	GOM	$700	$475	$250
EM	1	WN	RP	$1,100	$725	$400
EM	1	EK	GOM	$1,000	$650	$350
EM	4	WN	RP	$725	$500	$275
EM	1	HW	GM	$825	$550	$300
EM	1	HW	GM	$650	$425	$225
EM	1	N/A	N/A	$600	$400	$225

Game	Manufacturer	Year	# Made
Shooting Stars	P & S Machine	1947	N/A
Short Sox	Stoner	1936	N/A
Short Stop	Exhibit Supply	1940	N/A
Short Stop	Exhibit Supply	1948	N/A
Show Boat	Chicago Coin	1941	1200
Show Boat	United Mfg.	1949	N/A
Show Boat	Genco	1957	N/A
Show Boat	Gottlieb	1961	1950
Show Girl	Williams	1946	N/A
Showtime	Chicago Coin	1974	N/A
Shrek	Stern	2008	N/A
Shuffle Ball [1]	Western Equipment	1932	N/A
Side Kick	Daval Mfg. Co.	1939	N/A
Signal	Bally	1934	N/A
Signal Jr.	Bally	1934	N/A
Silver	Gottlieb	1957	2150
Silver Cup	Genco	1933	N/A
Silver Flash [2]	Genco	1937	N/A
Silver King Twins	Standard Amusement	1932	N/A
Silver Skates	Bally	1941	N/A
Silver Skates	Williams	1953	N/A
Silver Slugger	Gottlieb/Premier	1990	2100
Silver Streak	Bally	1947	N/A
Silverball Mania	Bally	1978	10350
Simpsons, The	Data East	1990	5502
Simpsons Pinball Party, The	Stern	2003	N/A
Sinbad	Gottlieb	1978	12950
Sinbad	Gottlieb	1978	950
Sinbad [3]	Gottlieb	1978	N/A
Sing Along	Gottlieb	1967	3300
Singapore	United Mfg.	1947	N/A
Sittin' Pretty	Gottlieb	1958	1050
Six Million Dollar Man, The	Bally	1978	10320
Six Shooter	Bally	1966	100
Six Sticks	Bally	1966	1410
Skateball	Bally	1980	4150
Ski Club [4]	Williams	1965	550
Ski-Hi	Genco	1937	N/A
Skill Pool	Williams	1963	2250

1. Mechanical flippers 2. Future city theme 3. Metal cabinet 4. Add-A-Ball

Type	Play	Designer	Artist	Class 1	Class 2	Class 3
EM	1	N/A	N/A	$625	$425	$225
EM	1	N/A	N/A	$1,200	$800	$425
EM	1	N/A	N/A	$1,450	$950	$500
EM	1	N/A	N/A	$575	$375	$200
EM	1	N/A	N/A	$550	$375	$200
EM	1	N/A	N/A	$400	$275	$150
EM	1	N/A	N/A	$725	$475	$250
EM	1	WN	RP	$950	$625	$350
EM	1	N/A	N/A	$525	$350	$200
EM	4	AP/WM	CM	$450	$300	$175
SS	4	PL	JY	$3,650	$2,400	$1,275
M	1	N/A	N/A	$900	$600	$325
EM	1	N/A	N/A	$550	$375	$200
EM	1	HW	N/A	$875	$600	$325
EM	1	HW	N/A	$875	$600	$325
EM	1	WN	RP	$1,550	$1,025	$550
M	1	HH	N/A	$600	$400	$225
EM	1	N/A	N/A	$950	$625	$350
M	2	N/A	N/A	$575	$375	$200
EM	1	N/A	N/A	$1,150	$750	$400
EM	1	HW	GM	$975	$650	$350
SS	4	JT	COM(B)/DM(P)	$1,200	$800	$425
EM	1	N/A	N/A	$600	$400	$225
SS	4	JP	KO	$1,200	$800	$425
SS	4	JK/EC	KO/MH	$1,775	$1,175	$625
SS	4	KJ/JB	KO/MH	$3,950	$2,600	$1,400
SS	4	EK	GOM	$925	$625	$325
EM	4	EK	GOM	$1,100	$725	$400
EM	4	EK	GOM	$950	$650	$350
EM	1	EK	AS	$850	$575	$300
EM	1	N/A	N/A	$625	$425	$225
EM	1	WN	RP	$2,000	$1,325	$700
SS	6	GK	DC	$900	$600	$325
EM	6	TZ	N/A	$775	$525	$275
EM	6	TZ	N/A	$500	$350	$175
SS	4	CF	GF	$850	$575	$300
EM	1	SK	AS	$575	$400	$225
EM	1	N/A	N/A	$500	$350	$175
EM	1	SK	N/A	$725	$475	$250

Game	Manufacturer	Year	# Made
Skill Roll	Gottlieb	1935	N/A
Skill-Ball [1]	Williams	1961	650
Skill-Pool	Gottlieb	1952	2100
Skipper [2]	Bally	1937	N/A
Skipper	Gottlieb	1969	1675
Sky Blazer	Exhibit Supply	1941	N/A
Sky Chief	Exhibit Supply	1942	N/A
Sky Divers	Bally	1964	2250
Sky High	Bally	1936	N/A
Sky Jump	Gottlieb	1974	4200
Sky Kings	Bally	1974	2000
Sky Lark [3]	J. H. Keeney & Co.	1941	N/A
Sky Ray	J. H. Keeney & Co.	1941	N/A
Sky Ride [4]	Genco	1933	N/A
Sky Rider	Chicago Coin	1974	N/A
Sky-Line [5]	Gottlieb	1965	2000
Sky-Rocket	Exhibit Supply	1939/41	N/A
Skylab	Williams	1974	3651
Skyline	Chicago Coin	1940	1400
Skyrocket	Bally	1971	545
Skyscraper [6]	Bally	1934	N/A
Skyway	O. D. Jennings & Co.	1935	N/A
Skyway	Williams	1954	N/A
Slap Stick	Bally	1976	85
Slick Chick	Gottlieb	1963	4550
Slugfest [5]	Williams	1952	N/A
Slugger [7]	Gottlieb	1938	N/A
Slugger	United Mfg.	1950	N/A
Sluggers	Genco	1941	N/A
Sluggin' Champ	Gottlieb	1955	950
Sluggin' Champ Deluxe	Gottlieb	1955	N/A
Smart Set	Williams	1969	4500
Smarty	Williams	1946	N/A
Smarty [1]	Williams	1968	2201
Smoke Signal	Williams	1955	N/A
Smoky	Exhibit Supply	1947	N/A
Snafu	Williams	1955	N/A
Snappy	Bally	1936	N/A
Snappy	Chicago Coin	1938	2365

1. Add-A-Ball   2. Removable payout section   3. Full cabinet   4. Counter game   5. Mechanical animation
6. Light animation   7. Five-ball/spin disk odds

Type	Play	Designer	Artist	Class 1	Class 2	Class 3
EM-P	1	N/A	N/A	$1,350	$900	$475
EM	1	SK	GM	$725	$475	$250
EM	1	WN	RP	$1,375	$925	$500
EM-P	1	N/A	N/A	$625	$425	$225
EM	4	EK	AS	$450	$300	$175
EM	1	N/A	N/A	$450	$300	$175
EM	1	N/A	N/A	$500	$325	$175
EM	1	TZ	N/A	$700	$475	$250
EM-P	1	N/A	N/A	$900	$600	$325
EM	1	EK	GOM	$750	$500	$275
EM	1	JP	DIW	$625	$425	$225
EM-P	1	N/A	N/A	$600	$400	$225
EM	1	N/A	N/A	$550	$375	$200
M	1	HH	N/A	$625	$425	$225
EM	4	JEK/WM	CM	$425	$275	$150
EM	1	WN	RP	$1,425	$950	$500
EM	1	N/A	N/A	$600	$400	$225
EM	1	SK	CM	$700	$475	$250
EM	1	N/A	N/A	$1,175	$775	$425
EM	2	HW	N/A	$650	$450	$250
EM	1	EW	N/A	$2,000	$1,325	$700
EM-P	1	N/A	N/A	$875	$600	$325
EM	1	HW	GM	$1,600	$1,075	$575
EM	1	JP	DIW	$925	$625	$325
EM	1	WN	RP	$2,050	$1,350	$725
EM	1	HW	GM	$1,600	$1,075	$575
EM	1	N/A	N/A	$725	$475	$250
EM	1	N/A	N/A	$575	$400	$225
EM	1	N/A	N/A	$600	$400	$225
EM	1	WN	RP	$2,125	$1,400	$750
EM	1	WN	RP	$2,650	$1,750	$925
EM	4	NC	CM	$450	$300	$175
EM	1	N/A	N/A	$425	$275	$150
EM-P	1	NC	CM	$650	$425	$225
EM	1	HW	GM	$875	$600	$325
EM	1	N/A	N/A	$500	$350	$175
EM	1	HW/SS	GM	$600	$400	$225
EM-P	1	N/A	N/A	$700	$475	$250
EM	1	N/A	N/A	$550	$375	$200

Game	Manufacturer	Year	# Made
Snappy 41	Chicago Coin	1941	1695
Snooks	Stoner	1939	N/A
Snooks	Williams	1951	N/A
Snooky	Pacific Amusement	1937	N/A
Snow Derby	Gottlieb	1970	1050
Snow Queen	Gottlieb	1970	1480
Soccer [1]	G. M. Laboratories	1936	N/A
Soccer	Williams	1964	2850
Soccer	Gottlieb	1975	2900
Sockit [2]	Western Equipment	1936	N/A
Softball	Mills Novelty Co.	1938	N/A
Solar City	Gottlieb	1977	2525
Solar Fire	Williams	1981	782
Solar Ride	Gottlieb	1979	8800
Solar Ride	Gottlieb	1979	365
Solids N Stripes	Williams	1971	N/A
Sopranos, The	Stern	2005	N/A
Sorcerer	Williams	1985	3700
Sound Stage	Chicago Coin	1976	3000
South Pacific	Genco	1950	N/A
South Pacific	Chicago Coin	1964	N/A
South Park	Sega	1999	N/A
Southern Belle	Gottlieb	1955	1000
Space Invaders	Bally	1980	11400
Space Jam	Sega	1996	N/A
Space Mission	Williams	1976	11652
Space Odyssey	Williams	1976	4300
Space Riders	Atari	1978	N/A
Space Ship [3]	Williams	1961	800
Space Shuttle	Williams	1984	7000
Space Station	Williams	1987	3800
Space Time	Bally	1972	5000
Space Walk	Gottlieb	1979	215
Spacelab [4]	Williams	1974	30
Spanish Eyes	Williams	1972	3905
Spark Plugs [5]	Williams	1951	N/A
Sparky	Stoner	1941	N/A
Speakeasy [4]	Bally	1982	3000
Speakeasy 4 [4]	Bally	1982	1000

1. Mannikin players 2. Baseball theme/one-ball payout 3. Williams' last light-score game 4. Add-A-Ball
5. Mechanical horse race

Type	Play	Designer	Artist	Class 1	Class 2	Class 3
EM	1	N/A	N/A	$475	$325	$175
EM	1	N/A	N/A	$500	$325	$175
EM	1	SS	GM	$600	$400	$225
EM	1	N/A	N/A	$650	$425	$225
EM	2	EK	AS	$800	$525	$300
EM	4	EK	AS	$650	$425	$225
EM	1	N/A	N/A	$1,750	$1,175	$625
EM	1	NC	N/A	$950	$625	$325
EM	2	EK	GOM	$775	$500	$275
EM-P	1	N/A	N/A	$1,625	$1,075	$575
EM	1	N/A	N/A	$800	$550	$300
EM	2	EK	GOM	$900	$600	$325
SS	4	BO	COM	$1,125	$750	$400
SS	4	EK	GOM	$950	$650	$350
EM	4	EK	GOM	$1,000	$675	$350
EM	2	NC	CM	$625	$425	$225
SS	4	GEG	KO	$3,975	$2,625	$1,400
SS	4	MR	PE	$925	$600	$325
EM	2	AP/JEK/WM	N/A	$525	$350	$200
EM	1	HH	RP	$575	$400	$225
EM	2	JEK/ALS/JG	RP	$400	$275	$150
SS	6	JOEB/RH	N/A	$3,000	$1,975	$1,050
EM	1	WN	RP	$1,300	$850	$450
SS	4	JP	PF	$1,475	$975	$525
SS	6	JK/OD/LR	MW	$1,725	$1,150	$600
EM	4	SK	CM	$950	$625	$325
EM	2	SK	CM	$725	$475	$275
SS	4	GS	GO/GV	$525	$350	$200
EM	1	SK	GM	$1,125	$750	$400
SS	4	BO/JK	MS	$1,150	$775	$400
SS	1	BO	TE	$1,275	$850	$450
EM	4	JP	CM	$675	$450	$250
EM	2	EK	GOM	$925	$600	$325
EM	1	SK	CM	$725	$475	$250
EM	1	NC	CM	$700	$475	$250
EM	1	HW	GM	$1,350	$900	$475
EM	1	N/A	N/A	$475	$325	$175
SS	2	GC	GF	$900	$600	$325
SS	4	GC	GF	$850	$550	$300

Game	Manufacturer	Year	# Made
Special Entry [1]	Bally	1946	N/A
Special Force	Bally	1986	2750
Spectra IV [2]	Valley	1978	N/A
Spectrum	Bally	1982	994
Speed	Daval Mfg Co.	1937	N/A
Speed Demon	J. H. Keeney & Co.	1940	N/A
Speed Way [3]	Williams	1948	N/A
Speedway [4]	Gottlieb	1933	N/A
Speedway [5]	Gottlieb	1933	N/A
Speedway	J. H. Keeney & Co.	1940	N/A
Spell Bound	Chicago Coin	1946	4000
Spider Man, The Amazing	Gottlieb	1980	7625
Spider-Man	Stern	2007	N/A
Spider-Man (Black) LE	Stern	2007	500
Spin Out	Gottlieb	1975	2850
Spin Wheel	Gottlieb	1968	2850
Spin-A-Card	Gottlieb	1969	2650
Spinball [6]	Chicago Coin	1948	1493
Spinning Reels	Mills Novelty Co.	1940	N/A
Spirit	Gottlieb	1982	1230
Spirit of 76 [7]	Mirco Games	1975	N/A
Spirit of 76	Gottlieb	1975	10300
Spit Fire	Genco	1935	N/A
Spitfire	Williams	1954	N/A
Splash [8]	Genco	1938	N/A
Split Second	Stern	1981	N/A
Spokes	Chicago Coin	1938	295
Spooksville [9]	Allied Leisure	1973	N/A
Sport Event [10]	Bally	1940	N/A
Sport King [11]	Bally	1940	N/A
Sport Page [11]	Bally	1938	N/A
Sport Parade	Chicago Coin	1940	2894
Sports [12]	Chicago Coin	1939	131
Sports [13]	Chicago Coin	1939	1376
Sportsman	O. D. Jennings & Co.	1934	N/A
Sportsman	Genco	1951	N/A
Sportsman	Williams	1952	N/A
Sportsman Deluxe	O. D. Jennings & Co.	1937	N/A
Sporty	Chicago Coin	1940	2200

1. One-ball replay   2. Rotating cocktail table   3. Ball does 360° around PF   4. Car moves 3 laps
5. Car moves 5 laps   6. Playfield spinner   7. 1st electronic game   8. Light animation   9. Shakerball game

Type	Play	Designer	Artist	Class 1	Class 2	Class 3
EM	1	N/A	N/A	$575	$375	$200
SS	4	DN	TR	$775	$500	$275
SS	4	N/A	N/A	$400	$275	$150
SS	4	CF	MH	$1,225	$800	$425
EM	1	N/A	N/A	$650	$450	$250
EM	1	N/A	N/A	$500	$325	$175
EM	1	HW	GM	$700	$475	$250
M	1	N/A	N/A	$1,800	$1,200	$625
M	1	N/A	N/A	$2,000	$1,325	$700
EM	1	N/A	N/A	$600	$400	$225
EM	1	N/A	N/A	$575	$375	$200
SS	4	EK	GOM	$1,525	$1,025	$550
SS	4	SR	KO/MH/MG/MCS	$4,675	$3,075	$1,650
SS	4	SR	KO/MH/MG/MCS	$7,700	$5,075	$2,700
EM	1	EK	GOM	$800	$525	$300
EM	4	EK	AS	$525	$350	$200
EM	1	EK	AS	$775	$525	$275
EM	1	JEK	RP	$600	$400	$225
EM-P	1	N/A	N/A	$1,800	$1,200	$650
SS	4	JT	TD	$1,125	$750	$400
SS	2	N/A	N/A	$700	$450	$250
EM	4	EK	GOM	$1,000	$650	$350
EM	1	HH	N/A	$900	$600	$325
EM	1	HW	GM	$850	$575	$300
EM	1	N/A	N/A	$750	$500	$275
SS	4	HW	DN(B)/GS(P)	$650	$425	$225
EM	1	N/A	N/A	$750	$500	$275
EM	1	RNH	RB	$375	$250	$150
EM-P	1	N/A	N/A	$1,075	$725	$375
EM-P	1	N/A	N/A	$725	$475	$250
EM-P	1	N/A	N/A	$575	$375	$200
EM	1	N/A	N/A	$550	$375	$200
EM	1	N/A	N/A	$625	$425	$225
EM	1	N/A	N/A	$550	$375	$200
EM-P	1	CD	N/A	$2,150	$1,425	$775
EM	1	N/A	N/A	$625	$425	$225
EM	1	HW	GM	$700	$475	$250
EM-P	1	N/A	N/A	$1,100	$750	$400
EM	1	N/A	N/A	$625	$425	$225

10. Baseball theme   11. Full cabinet   12. Novelty play   13. Standard play

Game	Manufacturer	Year	# Made
Spot Bowler	Gottlieb	1950	1000
Spot Pool [1]	Gottlieb	1941	N/A
Spot-A-Ball [2]	Hercules Novelty	1932	N/A
Spot-A-Card	Gottlieb	1941	N/A
Spot-A-Card	Gottlieb	1960	1200
Spot-Ball	In and Outdoor Games	1932	N/A
Spot-Pool	Williams	1959	N/A
Spottem	Bally	1939	N/A
Spring Break	Gottlieb/Premier	1987	3550
Springtime	Chicago Coin	1937	432
Springtime	Genco	1952	N/A
Spy Hunter	Bally	1984	2300
Square Head [3]	Gottlieb	1963	975
Stable Mate [4]	J. H. Keeney & Co.	1938	N/A
Stadium [5]	Stoner	1937	N/A
Stage Coach	Gottlieb	1954	650
Stage Coach	Chicago Coin	1968	N/A
Stage Door Canteen	Gottlieb	1945	7500
Stampede	Stern	1977	1100
Standard	Exhibit Supply	1935	N/A
Star Action [3]	Williams	1974	1155
Star Attraction	Chicago Coin	1941	2303
Star Battle [6]	Century Consolidated	1978	N/A
Star Gazer	Stern	1980	869
Star Light	Williams	1984	100
Star Lite	Exhibit Supply	1935	N/A
Star Pool [7]	Williams	1954	N/A
Star Pool	Williams	1974	6950
Star Race [8]	Gottlieb	1980	870
Star Shooter [6]	Allied Leisure	1979	N/A
Star Trek [3]	Gottlieb	1971	1450
Star Trek	Bally	1979	16842
Star Trek	Data East	1991	4400
Star Trek: The Next Generation	Williams	1993	11728
Star Trip [6]	Game Plan	1979	N/A
Star Wars	Data East	1992	10400
Star Wars Episode I	Williams	1999	3525
Star Wars Trilogy	Sega	1997	N/A
Star-Jet	Bally	1963	1050

1. Light animation 2. Tabletop 3. Add-A-Ball 4. Horse race/free play 5. Gives odds 6. Cocktail table
7. 2nd coin "Star Feature"/free games 8. Widebody

Type	Play	Designer	Artist	Class 1	Class 2	Class 3
EM	1	WN	RP	$1,550	$1,025	$550
EM	1	HM	RP	$750	$500	$275
M	1	N/A	N/A	$625	$400	$225
EM	1	HM	RP	$575	$375	$200
EM	1	WN	RP	$975	$650	$350
M	1	N/A	N/A	$650	$425	$225
EM	1	HW	GM	$825	$550	$300
EM	1	N/A	N/A	$800	$525	$275
SS	4	JT	LD(P)DM(B)	$750	$500	$275
EM	1	N/A	N/A	$775	$525	$275
EM	1	N/A	RP	$525	$350	$200
SS	4	GK	TR	$875	$600	$325
EM	1	WN	RP	$1,125	$750	$400
EM	1	N/A	N/A	$550	$375	$200
EM-P	1	N/A	N/A	$475	$325	$175
EM	1	WN	RP	$1,350	$900	$475
EM	4	ES/AP	CM	$575	$375	$200
EM	1	HM	RP	$550	$375	$200
SS	2	AP/JEK/WM	CM	$700	$450	$250
EM-P	1	N/A	N/A	$675	$450	$250
EM	1	SK	CM	$450	$300	$175
EM	1	N/A	N/A	$500	$325	$175
SS	2	N/A	N/A	$325	$225	$125
SS	4	BRP	N/A	$875	$575	$325
SS	4	BO	TS(B)/LB(P)	$750	$500	$275
EM	1	FKM	N/A	$450	$300	$175
EM	1	HW	GM	$950	$625	$350
EM	4	SK	CM	$550	$350	$200
SS	4	JOB	N/A	$700	$450	$250
SS	4	BB	RMT	$300	$200	$125
EM	1	EK	GOM	$1,100	$725	$400
SS	4	GO	KO	$1,250	$825	$450
SS	4	EC/JK	KO/MH	$1,750	$1,150	$625
SS	4	SR/DS/GF	GF	$2,600	$1,725	$925
SS	4	EC	DIW	$375	$250	$150
SS	4	JONB	M	$2,250	$1,475	$800
SS	4	JP	KO/PB/DAM	$2,650	$1,750	$925
SS	6	JK/JOEB	MW	$2,500	$1,650	$875
EM	2	TZ	GM	$875	$575	$300

Game	Manufacturer	Year	# Made
Stardust	Williams	1971	5455
Starfire	Williams	1956	N/A
Stargate	Gottlieb/Premier	1995	3600
Starlite	Williams	1953	N/A
Stars	Exhibit Supply	1941	N/A
Stars	Stern	1978	5127
Starship Troopers	Sega	1997	N/A
State Fair	Genco	1947	N/A
Steeple-Chase	Williams	1957	N/A
Stellar Wars	Williams	1979	5503
Step Up	Genco	1934	N/A
Step-Up	Genco	1946	N/A
Stepper-Upper	J. H. Keeney & Co.	1938	N/A
Stingray	Stern	1977	3066
Stock Car [1]	Gottlieb	1970	350
Stop and Go [2]	J. H. Keeney & Co.	1936	N/A
Stop and Go	Genco	1938	N/A
Stop and Go [3]	Genco	1951	N/A
Stop and Sock [4]	Gottlieb	1931	N/A
Stop 'N' Go	Williams	1964	1675
Stormy	Williams	1948	N/A
Straight Flush	Gottlieb	1957	1700
Straight Flush	Williams	1970	N/A
Straight Shooter [5]	Gottlieb	1959	1150
Strange Science	Bally	1986	2350
Strange World	Gottlieb	1978	675
Strato-Flite	Williams	1974	5977
Strat-o-Liner	Chicago Coin	1940	2506
Streamline	Bally	1934	N/A
Street Fighter II	Gottlieb/Premier	1993	5550
Strike Zone	Williams	1970	N/A
Striker	Gottlieb	1982	910
Striker Xtreme	Stern	2000	N/A
Strikes and Spares	Bally	1978	12820
Strikes N' Spares	Gottlieb/Premier	1995	750
Struggle Buggies [6]	Williams	1953	N/A
Student Prince	Williams	1968	3502
Subway	Genco	1934	N/A
Subway [3]	Gottlieb	1966	3200

1. Add-A-Ball 2. One-ball payout 3. Mechanical animation 4. Tabletop 5. First rollunder 6. Reel scoring

Type	Play	Designer	Artist	Class 1	Class 2	Class 3
EM	4	NC	CM	$600	$400	$225
EM	1	HW	GM	$650	$425	$225
SS	4	RT/JN	COM	$1,575	$1,050	$550
EM	1	HW/SS	GM	$675	$450	$250
EM	1	N/A	N/A	$700	$475	$250
SS	4	STK	JO	$650	$425	$225
SS	6	JK/JB	MW	$1,650	$1,100	$575
EM	1	N/A	N/A	$550	$375	$200
EM	1	HW	GM	$850	$575	$300
SS	4	SR	COM	$750	$500	$275
M	1	N/A	N/A	$500	$350	$175
EM	1	N/A	N/A	$450	$300	$150
EM-P	1	N/A	N/A	$700	$475	$250
SS	4	MK/RS/SS	N/A	$650	$425	$225
EM	1	EK	AS	$725	$475	$250
EM-P	1	N/A	N/A	$1,375	$900	$500
EM	1	N/A	N/A	$725	$475	$250
EM	1	N/A	RP	$650	$425	$250
M	1	N/A	N/A	$475	$325	$175
EM	2	NC	AS	$900	$600	$325
EM	1	HW	GM	$575	$375	$200
EM	1	WN	RP	$1,450	$975	$525
EM	1	NC	CM	$625	$425	$225
EM	1	WN	RP	$1,350	$900	$475
SS	4	DL	GF	$1,125	$750	$400
EM	1	JO	GOM	$1,275	$850	$450
EM	4	NC	CM	$700	$475	$250
EM	1	N/A	N/A	$650	$425	$225
M	1	N/A	N/A	$650	$450	$250
SS	4	RT/MV/BP/JN	COM(B)/DM(P)	$1,125	$750	$400
EM	2	NC	CM	$600	$400	$225
SS	4	JT/AE	DM	$1,025	$675	$375
SS	4	JOEB/JONB/RT	KO	$1,625	$1,075	$575
SS	4	GG	KO	$1,300	$850	$450
SS	4	RT/JOB	COM	$1,100	$725	$400
EM	1	HW	GM	$800	$550	$300
EM	4	SK	CM	$575	$375	$200
EM	1	HH	N/A	$875	$575	$300
EM	1	EK	AS	$1,375	$925	$500

Game	Manufacturer	Year	# Made
Subway Special	Genco	1934	N/A
Summer Time	Gottlieb	1940	N/A
Summer Time	United Mfg.	1948	N/A
Summer Time	Williams	1973	N/A
Sun Beam	Exhibit Supply	1941	N/A
Sun Valley	Chicago Coin	1962	N/A
Sunny [1]	Williams	1947	N/A
Sunset	Gottlieb	1962	2275
Sunshine	Gottlieb	1958	1100
Sunshine Baseball	Gottlieb	1936	N/A
Sunshine Derby [2]	Gottlieb	1936	N/A
Super Chubbie	Stoner	1941	N/A
Super Circus	Gottlieb	1957	1500
Super '8'	Stoner	1934	N/A
Super Hockey	Chicago Coin	1949	N/A
Super Jumbo [3]	Gottlieb	1954	500
Super Mario Brothers	Gottlieb/Premier	1992	4200
Super Mario Bros: Mushroom World [4]	Gottlieb/Premier	1992	519
Super Nova	Game Plan	1980	1000
Super Orbit	Gottlieb	1983	2100
Super Score	Chicago Coin	1946	3000
Super Score	Williams	1956	N/A
Super Score	Gottlieb	1967	2925
Super Six of '40	J. H. Keeney & Co.	1939	N/A
Super Soccer	Gottlieb	1975	7130
Super Spin	Gottlieb	1977	1352
Super Star	Williams	1972	3801
Super Star	Chicago Coin	1975	N/A
Super-Flite	Williams	1974	1901
Superliner	Gottlieb	1946	4000
Superman	Atari	1979	N/A
Supersonic	Bally	1979	10340
Sure Shot	Gottlieb	1976	3700
Surf Champ	Gottlieb	1976	1070
Surf 'N Safari	Gottlieb/Premier	1991	2006
Surf Queens	Bally	1946	N/A
Surf Rider	Williams	1956	N/A
Surf Side	Gottlieb	1967	1750
Surfer	Gottlieb	1976	2700

1. Williams' first flipper game 2. One-ball payout 3. 1st Gottlieb 4-player/score reels 4. Kid-size

Type	Play	Designer	Artist	Class 1	Class 2	Class 3
EM	1	HH	N/A	$975	$650	$350
EM	1	HM	RP	$500	$350	$175
EM	1	N/A	N/A	$450	$300	$175
EM	1	NC	CM	$475	$300	$175
EM	1	N/A	N/A	$425	$275	$150
EM	2	JEK/JG	RP	$750	$500	$275
EM	1	HW	GM	$700	$475	$250
EM	2	WN	RP	$675	$450	$250
EM	1	WN	RP	$1,100	$725	$400
EM-P	1	N/A	N/A	$1,375	$925	$500
EM-P	1	N/A	N/A	$1,125	$750	$400
EM	1	FWM	N/A	$450	$300	$175
EM	2	WN	RP	$700	$450	$250
EM	1	WB	N/A	$600	$400	$225
EM	1	N/A	N/A	$475	$325	$175
EM	4	WN	RP	$800	$525	$300
SS	4	JN	COM(B)/DM(P)	$1,400	$925	$500
SS	4	RT	DM/COM	$900	$600	$325
SS	4	AG	GM	$500	$350	$175
SS	4	EK	DM	$525	$350	$200
EM	1	N/A	N/A	$475	$300	$175
EM	1	HW	GM	$800	$550	$300
EM	2	EK	AS	$750	$500	$275
EM	1	N/A	N/A	$450	$300	$175
EM	4	EK	GM	$775	$500	$275
EM	2	EK	GOM	$750	$500	$275
EM	1	SK	CM	$550	$375	$200
EM	1	WM/JEK/AP	CM	$425	$275	$150
EM	2	NC	CM	$550	$350	$200
EM	1	HM	RP	$575	$375	$200
SS	4	SR	GO	$1,225	$800	$425
SS	4	GK	KO	$625	$425	$225
EM	1	EK	GOM	$775	$525	$275
EM	4	EK	GOM	$950	$650	$350
SS	4	JN	COM/DM	$1,375	$900	$475
EM	1	N/A	N/A	$475	$325	$175
EM	4	HW	GM	$575	$375	$200
EM	2	EK	AS	$600	$400	$225
EM	2	EK	GOM	$875	$575	$325

Game	Manufacturer	Year	# Made
Surfers [1]	Bally	1967	908
Suspense	Bally	1938	N/A
Suspense	WIlliams	1946	N/A
Suspense	Williams	1969	2303
Swanee	Exhibit Supply	1949	N/A
Sweepstakes	Williams	1952	N/A
Sweet Add-A-Line	Gottlieb	1955	800
Sweet Hearts	Gottlieb	1963	4450
Sweet Sioux	Gottlieb	1959	1350
Sweetheart [2]	Williams	1950	N/A
Swing	Chicago Coin	1938	1352
Swing Along	Gottlieb	1963	4710
Swing Time	Genco	1937	N/A
Swing Time [3]	Williams	1963	700
Swinger	Williams	1972	3229
Swords of Fury	Williams	1988	2705
System	Chicago Coin	1936	308
Tag-Team Pinball	Gottlieb/Premier	1985	1220
Tahiti	Chicago Coin	1949	N/A
Tailspin	Bingo Novelty	1933	N/A
Take Five [4]	Allied Leisure	1978	N/A
Tales from the Crypt	Data East	1993	4500
Tales of the Arabian Nights	Williams	1996	3128
Tally Ho	Exhibit Supply	1947	N/A
Tampico	United Mfg.	1949	N/A
Taps [5]	Harry Hoppe Corp.	1939	N/A
Target Alpha	Gottlieb	1976	7285
Target Pool	Gottlieb	1969	2425
Target Skill	Baker Novelty	1941	N/A
Taxi [6]	Williams	1988	N/A
Taxi [7]	Williams	1988	N/A
Teacher's Pet	Williams	1965	1600
Team One [3]	Gottlieb	1977	650
Tee'd Off	Gottlieb/Premier	1993	3500
Teenage Mutant Ninja Turtles	Data East	1991	3750
Telecard	Gottlieb	1949	1700
Temptation	Chicago Coin	1948	900
Ten Spot [8]	Williams	1961	900
Ten Strike [9]	J. H. Keeney and Co.	1937	N/A

1. Standard and Add-A-Ball   2. 10 Kick-out holes   3. Add-A-Ball   4. Cocktail table   5. Mechanical animation
6. Lola version   7. Marilyn version   8. Moving target   9. Bowling

Type	Play	Designer	Artist	Class 1	Class 2	Class 3
EM	1	TZ	JK	$750	$500	$275
EM	1	N/A	N/A	$575	$375	$200
EM	1	HW	N/A	$425	$275	$150
EM	2	NC	CM	$700	$475	$250
EM	1	N/A	N/A	$450	$300	$175
EM	2	HW	GM	$600	$400	$225
EM	1	WN	RP	$1,300	$850	$450
EM	1	WN	RP	$1,275	$850	$450
EM	4	WN	RP	$575	$400	$225
EM	1	HW	GM	$700	$475	$250
EM	1	N/A	N/A	$600	$400	$225
EM	2	WN	RP	$650	$450	$250
EM	1	N/A	N/A	$700	$475	$250
EM	1	SK	N/A	$625	$400	$225
EM	2	NC	CM	$650	$425	$225
SS	4	STK/TK/DW	DW	$1,125	$750	$400
EM	1	N/A	N/A	$700	$475	$250
SS	4	TR	LD	$675	$450	$250
EM	1	N/A	N/A	$400	$275	$150
M	1	N/A	N/A	$425	$275	$150
SS	2	JAP/BB	RB	$375	$250	$125
SS	4	JB	KA/M	$2,050	$1,350	$725
SS	4	JOP	PM	$3,725	$2,475	$1,325
EM	1	N/A	N/A	$400	$275	$150
EM	1	N/A	N/A	$425	$275	$150
EM	1	N/A	N/A	$975	$650	$350
EM	4	EK	GOM	$925	$625	$325
EM	1	EK	AS	$775	$525	$275
EM	1	N/A	N/A	$550	$375	$200
SS	4	MR/PA	PA	$1,325	$875	$475
SS	4	MR/PA	PA	$1,500	$1,000	$525
EM	1	SK	N/A	$575	$400	$225
EM	1	JB	GOM	$825	$550	$300
SS	4	RT/JN	COM/DM	$1,575	$1,050	$550
SS	4	EC/JK	PF(B)/KO(P)	$1,150	$750	$400
EM	1	HM	RP	$1,050	$700	$375
EM	1	N/A	N/A	$375	$250	$150
EM	1	SK	GM	$550	$350	$200
EM-P	1	N/A	N/A	$900	$600	$325

Game	Manufacturer	Year	# Made
Ten-Spot	Genco	1941	N/A
Tennessee	Williams	1948	N/A
Terminator 2: Judgment Day	Williams	1991	15202
Terminator 3: Rise of the Machines	Stern	2003	N/A
Texan	Gottlieb	1960	1100
Texas Mustang	Gottlieb	1941	N/A
Theatre of Magic	Bally	1995	6600
Thing	Chicago Coin	1951	N/A
Thistledowns [1]	Bally	1938	N/A
Thoro Bred	Gottlieb	1965	1750
3 Coins	Williams	1962	1100
3-D [2]	Williams	1958	N/A
Three Deuces	Williams	1955	N/A
Three Feathers	Genco	1949	N/A
"300"	Gottlieb	1975	7925
3 Jokers [3]	Williams	1970	N/A
Three Musketeers	Gottlieb	1949	800
Three Score	Gottlieb	1940	N/A
Three Up	Rock-Ola	1938	N/A
3-In-Line	Bally	1963	1000
3-Ring Circus [4]	Bally	1932	N/A
Thrill	Chicago Coin	1948	1300
Thriller	Chicago Coin	1936	303
Thunderball	Williams	1982	10
Thunderbird	Williams	1954	N/A
Thunderbolt	Bally	1938	N/A
Thunderbolt	Allied Leisure	1977	N/A
Tic-Tac-Toe	Williams	1959	N/A
Tim-Buc-Tu	Williams	1956	N/A
Time	Pacific Amusement	1935	N/A
Time Fantasy	Williams	1983	608
Time Line	Gottlieb	1980	3167
Time Machine	Data East	1988	2896
Time Tunnel	Bally	1971	70
Time 2000	Atari	1977	N/A
Time Warp	Williams	1979	8875
Time Zone	Bally	1973	2500
Times Square	Chicago Coin	1935	130
Times Square	Williams	1953	N/A

1. One-ball horserace game   2. Light animation   3. Add-A-Ball   4. Counter game

Type	Play	Designer	Artist	Class 1	Class 2	Class 3
EM	1	N/A	N/A	$475	$325	$175
EM	1	HW	GM	$550	$375	$200
SS	4	SR	DW	$1,600	$1,050	$575
SS	4	SR	KO	$2,800	$1,850	$975
EM	4	WN	RP	$550	$375	$200
EM	1	HM	RP	$475	$325	$175
SS	4	JOP	LD	$3,975	$2,625	$1,400
EM	1	N/A	RP	$825	$550	$300
EM-P	1	N/A	N/A	$750	$500	$275
EM	2	WN	RP	$700	$475	$250
EM	1	SK	GM	$500	$325	$175
EM	1	HW	GM	$925	$625	$325
EM	1	HW	GM	$725	$475	$275
EM	1	N/A	N/A	$475	$325	$175
EM	4	EK	GOM	$750	$500	$275
EM	1	NC	CM	$525	$350	$200
EM	1	HM	RP	$1,200	$800	$425
EM	1	HM	RP	$450	$300	$175
EM-P	1	N/A	N/A	$700	$475	$250
EM	4	TZ	N/A	$475	$325	$175
M	1	RM	N/A	$500	$350	$175
EM	1	N/A	N/A	$450	$300	$175
EM	1	N/A	N/A	$675	$450	$250
SS	2	MRJOK	COM	$5,000	$3,300	$1,750
EM	1	HW	GM	$675	$450	$250
EM	1	N/A	N/A	$575	$400	$225
SS	4	JP	RB	$375	$250	$150
EM	1	HW	GM	$725	$500	$275
EM	1	HW	GM	$625	$425	$225
EM	1	FKM	N/A	$625	$425	$225
SS	4	BO	SM(B)/COM(P)	$675	$450	$250
SS	4	AE	JES	$600	$400	$225
SS	4	JK/EC	KO/MH	$1,150	$750	$400
EM	4	JP	CM	$825	$550	$300
SS	4	MAR	GO/JIK	$425	$275	$150
SS	4	BO	COM	$750	$500	$275
EM	2	JP	CM	$700	$475	$250
EM	1	N/A	N/A	$825	$550	$300
EM	1	HW	GM	$1,050	$700	$375

Game	Manufacturer	Year	# Made
Tiny [1]	Western Equipment	1935	N/A
Tit for Tat	Chicago Coin	1935	1443
Title Fight [2]	Gottlieb/Premier	1990	1000
T.K.O.	Gottlieb	1979	125
T.N.T.	Allied Leisure	1976	N/A
Toledo	Williams	1975	3001
Tom Tom	Williams	1963	1300
Tommy, The Who's Pinball Wizard	Data East	1994	4700
Top Card	Gottlieb	1974	3100
Top Hand	Williams	1966	2600
Top Hat	Stoner	1935	N/A
Top Hat	Williams	1958	N/A
Top It	A.B.T. Mfg.	1936	N/A
Top Score	Gottlieb	1975	3200
Top Ten	Chicago Coin	1975	N/A
Topic	Bally	1941	N/A
Topper [3]	Chicago Coin	1939	1702
Topper [4]	Chicago Coin	1939	650
Torch	Gottlieb	1980	3880
Torchy	WIlliams	1947	N/A
Toreador	Gottlieb	1956	975
Torpedo Alley	Data East	1988	N/A
Totalite	Rock-Ola	1936	N/A
Totem	Gottlieb	1979	6643
Touch Off	Chicago Coin	1936	296
Touchdown [2]	Williams	1967	2253
Touchdown	Gottlieb/Premier	1984	711
Tournament	Mills Novelty Co.	1937	N/A
Tournament	Gottlieb	1955	600
Tout [5]	Pacific Amusement	1936	N/A
Track Odds	Chicago Coin	1936	20
Track Record [6]	Gottlieb	1939	N/A
Track Stars	Chicago Coin	1937	N/A
Trade Winds	Genco	1948	N/A
Trade Winds	Williams	1962	1250
Traffic [7]	Bally	1935	N/A
Trail Drive [2]	Bally	1970	1305
Trans-Atlantic	Rock-Ola	1936	N/A
Transformers (Pro)	Stern	2011	125

1. Counter game 2. Mechanical animation 3. Free play 4. Novelty play 5. One-ball payout
6. Full cabinet/payout 7. 3 models

Type	Play	Designer	Artist	Class 1	Class 2	Class 3
EM-P	1	N/A	N/A	$625	$425	$225
EM	1	SG	N/A	$600	$400	$225
SS	4	RT	CN(B)/DM(P)	$1,050	$700	$375
EM	1	EK	GOM	$5,750	$3,800	$2,025
SS	4	N/A	N/A	$475	$300	$175
EM	2	HW	CM	$525	$350	$200
EM	2	SK	GM	$600	$400	$225
SS	4	JK/EC/LR/LS	KA/M	$2,350	$1,550	$825
EM	1	JB	GOM	$1,050	$700	$375
EM	1	NC	N/A	$525	$350	$200
EM	1	N/A	N/A	$400	$275	$150
EM	2	HW	GM	$600	$400	$225
EM	1	N/A	N/A	$550	$375	$200
EM	2	EK	GOM	$750	$500	$275
EM	2	AP/JEK/WM	CM	$650	$425	$225
EM	1	N/A	N/A	$425	$275	$150
EM	1	N/A	N/A	$700	$475	$250
EM	1	N/A	N/A	$775	$525	$275
SS	4	JOB	GOM	$625	$425	$225
EM	1	N/A	N/A	$625	$425	$225
EM	2	WN	RP	$525	$350	$200
SS	4	CF	KO/MH	$800	$525	$300
EM	1	N/A	N/A	$550	$375	$200
SS	4	EK	GOM	$800	$525	$275
EM	1	N/A	N/A	$675	$450	$250
EM	1	SK	N/A	$450	$300	$175
SS	4	JT	LD	$850	$575	$300
EM	1	N/A	N/A	$600	$400	$225
EM	2	WN	RP	$600	$400	$225
EM-P	1	N/A	N/A	$875	$600	$325
EM-P	1	N/A	N/A	$950	$625	$350
EM-P	1	HM	RP	$700	$475	$250
EM	1	N/A	N/A	$625	$425	$225
EM	1	N/A	N/A	$475	$300	$175
EM	1	SK	N/A	$750	$500	$275
EM-P	1	HW	N/A	$1,500	$1,000	$525
EM	1	TZ	CM	$600	$400	$225
EM	1	N/A	N/A	$850	$550	$300
SS	4	GEG	N/A	$4,975	$3,300	—

Game	Manufacturer	Year	# Made
Transformers Autobot Crimson LE	Stern	2011	125
Transformers Decepticon Violet LE	Stern	2011	125
Transformers LE (Combo)	Stern	2011	500
Transmitter [1]	Stoner	1935	N/A
Transporter the Rescue	Bally	1989	859
Trap Lite	Exhibit Supply	1936	N/A
Trap Shot [2]	Rock-Ola	1936	N/A
Trapeze	Gotttlieb	1940	N/A
Travel Time	Williams	1973	3450
Tri Zone	Williams	1979	7250
Tri-Score	Genco	1951	N/A
Trident	Stern	1979	4019
Trigger	Exhibit Supply	1951	N/A
Trinidad	Chicago Coin	1948	2100
Trio	Bally	1965	750
Triple Action	Genco	1948	N/A
Triple Action	Williams	1974	3828
Triple Play	Genco	1938	N/A
Triple Strike	Williams	1975	3376
Triple Threat	Daval Mfg Co.	1939	N/A
Triplets	Gottlieb	1950	750
Triumph	Bally	1940	N/A
Tron: Legacy LE, Disney	Stern	2011	400
Tron: Legacy (PRO), Disney	Stern	2011	N/A
Trophy [3]	Chicago Coin	1938	400
Trophy [4]	Chicago Coin	1938	100
Trophy [5]	Bally	1948	N/A
Tropic Fun [6]	Williams	1973	1100
Tropic Isle	Gottlieb	1962	2700
Tropic Queens [7]	Bally	1960	N/A
Tropicana	United Mfg.	1948	N/A
Truck Stop	Bally	1988	N/A
Tucson	Williams	1949	N/A
Tumbleweed	Exhibit Supply	1949	N/A
Turf Champ	Williams	1958	N/A
Turf Champs	Stoner	1936	N/A
Turf King	Chicago Coin	1937	1100
Turf King [8]	Bally	1941	N/A
Turf Queen	Chicago Coin	1938	347

1. Tabletop   2. Animal targets   3. Novelty play   4. Replay   5. One-ball payout   6. Add-A-Ball
7. Flipperless one-ball   8. Full cabinet/payout

Type	Play	Designer	Artist	Class 1	Class 2	Class 3
SS	4	GEG	N/A	$7,050	$4,650	—
SS	4	GEG	N/A	$7,150	$4,725	—
SS	4	GEG	N/A	$6,375	$4,225	—
EM	1	N/A	N/A	$900	$600	$325
SS	4	GK/TK	TE	$1,000	$675	$350
EM-P	1	N/A	N/A	$575	$375	$200
EM	1	N/A	N/A	$1,000	$675	$350
EM	1	HM	RP	$550	$375	$200
EM	1	NC	CM	$575	$375	$200
SS	4	TK	CM	$700	$450	$250
EM	1	N/A	N/A	$550	$375	$200
SS	4	MK	N/A	$750	$500	$275
EM	1	N/A	N/A	$450	$300	$175
EM	1	JEK	RP	$375	$250	$150
EM	1	TZ	N/A	$450	$300	$175
EM	1	SK	N/A	$900	$600	$325
EM	1	SK	CM	$575	$375	$200
EM	1	N/A	N/A	$475	$325	$175
EM	1	SK	CM	$550	$350	$200
EM	1	N/A	N/A	$1,200	$800	$425
EM	1	HM	RP	$850	$550	$300
EM	1	N/A	N/A	$675	$450	$250
SS	4	JONB	JY	$4,700	$3,125	$1,650
SS	4	JONB	JY	$5,850	$3,875	$2,050
EM	1	N/A	N/A	$550	$375	$200
EM	1	N/A	N/A	$625	$400	$225
EM-P	1	N/A	N/A	$700	$475	$250
EM	1	NC	CM	$475	$325	$175
EM	1	WN	RP	$1,075	$700	$375
EM	1	N/A	N/A	$450	$300	$175
EM	1	N/A	N/A	$350	$225	$125
SS	4	STK/JP/DL	PM	$1,025	$675	$375
EM	1	HW	GM	$800	$525	$300
EM	1	N/A	N/A	$525	$350	$200
EM	1	HM/HW	GM	$1,800	$1,200	$650
EM-P	1	KK	N/A	$2,100	$1,400	$750
EM	1	N/A	N/A	$575	$375	$200
EM-P	1	N/A	N/A	$750	$500	$275
EM	1	N/A	N/A	$500	$325	$175

Game	Manufacturer	Year	# Made
24	Stern	2009	N/A
Twenty Grand	Williams	1952	N/A
21	Williams	1960	N/A
Twilight Zone	Bally	1993	15235
Twin Bill	Gottlieb	1955	800
Twin Six	J. H. Keeney & Co.	1941	N/A
Twin Win	Bally	1974	1570
Twinkle	Baker Novelty	1939	N/A
Twinky	Chicago Coin	1967	N/A
Twister	Sega	1996	N/A
2 in 1	Bally	1964	1060
2001	Gottlieb	1971	2200
TX-Sector	Gottlieb/Premier	1988	2336
Tycoon	Mills Novelty Co.	1936	N/A
UltraPin [1]	Global VR	2006	200
Ump	Stoner	1941	N/A
Universe [2]	Gottlieb	1959	1150
Up and Up	J. H. Keeney & Co.	1939	N/A
USA [3]	Bally	1958	N/A
U.S.A. Football [4]	Alvin G	1992	100
Utah	United Mfg.	1949	N/A
Vacation	Bally	1940	N/A
Vagabond [5]	Williams	1962	600
Valencia [6]	Williams	1975	N/A
Valiant	Williams	1962	1050
Vampire	Bally	1971	799
Vanities	Exhibit Supply	1947	N/A
Variety	Bally	1939	N/A
Varkon	WIlliams	1982	90
Vector	Bally	1982	3500
Vegas [7]	Game Plan	1979	N/A
Vegas	Gottlieb/Premier	1990	1500
Velvet	J. H. Keeney & Co.	1941	N/A
Venus	Chicago Coin	1941	1300
Victory	Genco	1941	N/A
Victory	Gottlieb/Premier	1987	3315
Victory Derby [8]	Bally	1946	N/A
Victory Special [8]	Bally	1945	N/A
Viking [9]	Williams	1960	N/A

1. Simulated pinball games 2. Mechanical animation 3. Extra coin buys extra balls 4. Head-to-head play
5. Add-A-Ball 6. Rare 7. Cocktail table 8. Full cabinet 9. 1960s cabinet style

Type	Play	Designer	Artist	Class 1	Class 2	Class 3
SS	4	SR	KO	$4,275	$2,825	$1,500
EM	1	HW	GM	$625	$425	$225
EM	1	HW	GM	$550	$375	$200
SS	4	PL/LD/TE	JY	$4,700	$3,100	$1,650
EM	1	WN	RP	$2,000	$1,325	$700
EM	1	N/A	N/A	$475	$325	$175
EM	2	JP	DC	$750	$500	$275
EM	1	N/A	N/A	$500	$325	$175
EM	2	N/A	CM	$425	$275	$150
SS	6	JB	PF	$1,475	$975	$525
EM	2	TZ	CM	$525	$350	$200
EM	1	EK	GOM	$900	$600	$325
SS	4	JT	COM	$675	$450	$250
EM-P	1	NA	N/A	$900	$600	$325
VID	4	BRM	MM	$2,850	$1,900	$1,000
EM	1	N/A	N/A	$625	$425	$225
EM	1	WN	RP	$2,025	$1,350	$725
EM	1	N/A	N/A	$1,075	$725	$375
EM	1	N/A	N/A	$400	$275	$150
SS	2	JA	TE	$775	$525	$275
EM	1	N/A	N/A	$425	$275	$150
EM	1	N/A	N/A	$625	$400	$225
EM	1	SK	N/A	$775	$525	$275
EM	4	HW	CM	$450	$300	$175
EM	2	SK	GM	$500	$350	$175
EM	2	TZ	DIW	$675	$450	$250
EM	1	N/A	N/A	$550	$375	$200
EM	1	N/A	N/A	$450	$300	$175
SS	2	TK	SM	$2,175	$1,425	$775
SS	4	GK	GF	$800	$525	$275
SS	4	EC	DIW	$400	$275	$150
SS	4	JN	COM(B)/DM(P)	$700	$475	$250
EM	1	N/A	N/A	$425	$275	$150
EM	1	N/A	N/A	$450	$300	$175
EM	1	N/A	N/A	$475	$325	$175
SS	4	JT	COM	$775	$525	$275
EM-P	1	N/A	N/A	$850	$550	$300
EM	1	N/A	N/A	$475	$325	$175
EM	2	HM	GM	$625	$425	$225

Game	Manufacturer	Year	# Made
Viking	Bally	1980	2600
Viper	Stern	1981	N/A
Viper Night Drivin'	Sega	1998	1100
Virginia	Williams	1948	N/A
Vogue	Bally	1939	N/A
Volcano	Gottlieb	1981	3655
Volley	Gottlieb	1976	2900
Voltan Escapes Cosmic Doom	Bally	1979	365
Vulcan	Gottlieb	1977	3575
Wagon Train	Gottlieb	1960	1100
War [1]	Viza	1978	N/A
Warlok	Williams	1982	412
Waterworld	Gottlieb/Premier	1995	1500
West Wind	Exhibit Supply	1941	N/A
Wheel of Fortune [2]	Western Equipment	1936	N/A
Wheel of Fortune	Stern	2007	N/A
Whiffle Board	Automatic Industries	1931	N/A
Whirl Wind	Gottlieb	1957	1100
Whirlwind	Williams	1990	7300
White Sails	Bally	1939	N/A
White Water	Williams	1993	7008
Whiz Kids	Chicago Coin	1952	N/A
Whizz Bang Model A	Gottlieb	1932	N/A
Whizz Bang Model B	Gottlieb	1932	N/A
Whizz Bang Model C	Gottlieb	1932	N/A
WHO dunnit	Bally	1995	2416
Whoopee	Williams	1964	2075
Whoopee Game	In and Outdoor Games	1931	N/A
Wiggler, The	Bally	1967	3410
Wild Card	Williams	1977	901
Wild Fire	J. H. Keeney & Co.	1941	N/A
Wild Fyre	Stern	1978	2400
Wild Life	Gottlieb	1972	3875
Wild West	Gottlieb	1951	800
Wild Wheels	Bally	1966	580
Wild Wild West	Gottlieb	1969	1350
Windy City	Buckley Mfg.	1933	N/A
Wing Ding [3]	Williams	1964	626
Wing Lite	Chicago Coin	1935	723

1. Cocktail table/head-to-head play 2. One-ball payout 3. Add-A-Ball

Type	Play	Designer	Artist	Class 1	Class 2	Class 3
SS	4	JP	KO	$850	$575	$300
SS	4	JJ	KP	$850	$575	$300
SS	6	RH	MW	$2,000	$1,325	$700
EM	1	HW	GM	$525	$350	$200
EM	1	N/A	N/A	$575	$375	$200
SS	4	JO	DM	$925	$625	$325
EM	1	EK	GOM	$700	$450	$250
SS	4	GC	DC	$1,300	$875	$475
EM	4	EK	GOM	$700	$475	$250
EM	1	WN	RP	$875	$575	$300
SS	2	N/A	N/A	$675	$450	$250
SS	4	MK	COM(B)/SM(P)	$1,000	$650	$350
SS	4	RT/JN	COM/SCM	$1,275	$850	$450
EM	1	N/A	N/A	$425	$275	$150
EM-P	1	N/A	N/A	$975	$650	$350
SS	4	DN	KO/MH	$3,375	$2,225	$1,175
M	1	EF	ALP	$550	$375	$200
EM	2	WN	RP	$825	$550	$300
SS	4	PL	JY	$1,625	$1,075	$575
EM	1	N/A	N/A	$550	$375	$200
SS	4	DN	JY	$2,600	$1,725	$925
EM	1	JEK/JG/ALS	N/A	$550	$375	$200
M	1	N/A	N/A	$575	$375	$200
M	1	N/A	N/A	$625	$425	$225
M	1	N/A	N/A	$575	$375	$200
SS	4	DS/BO	LD/PB	$1,675	$1,100	$600
EM	4	SK	N/A	$400	$275	$150
M	1	N/A	N/A	$600	$400	$225
EM	4	TZ	JK	$650	$425	$225
EM	1	SK	CM	$450	$300	$175
EM	1	N/A	N/A	$400	$275	$150
SS	4	HW	N/A	$650	$425	$225
EM	2	EK	GOM	$650	$450	$250
EM	1	HM	RP	$975	$650	$350
EM	2	TZ	GM	$425	$275	$150
EM	2	EK	AS	$575	$375	$200
M	1	N/A	N/A	$625	$425	$225
EM	1	SK	N/A	$575	$400	$200
EM	1	N/A	N/A	$550	$375	$200

Game	Manufacturer	Year	# Made
Wings	Rock-Ola	1933	N/A
Wings	Exhibit Supply	1940	N/A
Winner, The [2]	Western Equipment	1937	N/A
Winner	Williams	1972	2100
Wipe Out	Gottlieb/Premier	1993	2150
Wisconsin	United Mfg.	1948	N/A
Wishing Well	Gottlieb	1955	1050
Wizard [1]	Gottlieb	1971	N/A
Wizard!	Bally	1975	10005
Wonderland	Williams	1955	N/A
World Beauties	Gottlieb	1959	900
World Challenge Soccer	Gottlieb/Premier	1994	1470
World Champ	Gottlieb	1957	2300
World Cup	Williams	1978	6253
World Cup Soccer	Bally	1994	8743
World Fair	Gottlieb	1964	4650
World Poker Tour	Stern	2006	N/A
World Series [1]	Gottlieb	1972	775
World Tour	Alvin G	1992	1000
World's Fair	Bally	1938	N/A
World's Fair Jig-Saw	Rock-Ola	1933	N/A
World's Series	Rock-Ola	1934	N/A
!WOW! [3]	Mills Novelty Co.	1932	N/A
Wow	Stoner	1941	N/A
WWF Royal Rumble	Data East	1994	3500
X Files, The	Sega	1997	N/A
X-Men Magneto LE	Stern	2012	N/A
X-Men Pro	Stern	2012	N/A
X-Men Wolverine LE	Stern	2012	N/A
X's & O's	Bally	1984	3300
Xenon	Bally	1980	11000
Yacht Club	Chicago Coin	1940	1506
Yanks	Chicago Coin	1942	794
Yanks [4]	Williams	1948	N/A
Yukon [1]	Williams	1971	730
Zephyr	Bally	1938	N/A
Zig Zag	Genco	1941	N/A
Zig Zag [4]	Williams	1964	1674
Zip	Genco	1938	N/A

1. Add-A-Ball   2. Mechanical race horse   3. Tabletop   4. Mechanical animation

Type	Play	Designer	Artist	Class 1	Class 2	Class 3
M	1	DR	BH	$625	$425	$225
EM	1	N/A	N/A	$600	$400	$225
EM-P	1	N/A	N/A	$725	$475	$250
EM	2	SK	CM	$725	$500	$275
SS	4	RT	DM/COM	$1,225	$825	$450
EM	1	N/A	N/A	$550	$375	$200
EM	1	WN	RP	$975	$650	$350
EM	1	EK	GOM	$675	$450	$250
EM	4	GK	DC	$1,450	$950	$500
EM	1	HW	GM	$1,475	$975	$525
EM	1	WN	RP	$1,050	$700	$375
SS	4	JN	DM/COM	$1,125	$750	$400
EM	1	WN	RP	$1,225	$825	$425
SS	4	ET	CM	$650	$425	$225
SS	4	JOP/LD	KO	$1,800	$1,200	$650
EM	1	WN	RP	$1,400	$925	$500
SS	4	SR/KJ	BR	$3,025	$2,000	$1,075
EM	1	EK	GOM	$950	$625	$350
SS	1	JA	DH	$1,425	$950	$500
EM	1	N/A	N/A	$1,000	$675	$350
M	1	DR	N/A	$2,200	$1,475	$775
M	1	N/A	N/A	$1,800	$1,200	$650
M	1	N/A	N/A	$600	$400	$225
EM	1	N/A	N/A	$475	$325	$175
SS	4	TIS/JK	PF/M	$1,375	$925	$500
SS	6	RH	MW	$1,750	$1,150	$625
SS	4	JB	KO/SJ	$7,200	—	—
SS	4	JB	KO/SJ	$4,975	—	—
SS	4	JB	KO/SJ	$7,200	—	—
SS	4	GK	PM	$750	$500	$275
SS	4	GK	PF	$1,300	$875	$475
EM	1	N/A	N/A	$550	$375	$200
EM	1	N/A	N/A	$400	$275	$150
EM	1	HW	GM	$1,075	$725	$375
EM	1	NC	CM	$625	$425	$225
EM	1	N/A	N/A	$550	$375	$200
EM	1	N/A	N/A	$400	$275	$150
EM	1	SK	GM	$550	$375	$200
EM	1	N/A	N/A	$400	$275	$150

Pinball Game Price Charts

Game	Manufacturer	Year	# Made
Zip	Exhibit Supply	1939	N/A
Zip-A-Doo	Bally	1970	1083
Zodiac	Williams	1971	704
Zombie	Exhibit Supply	1940	N/A
Zoom	Stoner	1935	N/A

Type	Play	Designer	Artist	Class 1	Class 2	Class 3
EM	1	HW/LYD	N/A	$650	$450	$250
EM	2	TZ	CM	$575	$375	$200
EM	2	SK	LR	$450	$300	$175
EM	1	N/A	N/A	$500	$350	$175
EM	1	N/A	N/A	$600	$400	$225

APPENDICES

Designers

AC	Adolph A. Caille	EC	Ed Cebula
AE	Allen Edwall	ET	Ed Thomaszewski
AG	Al Greg	EW	Edward J. Wohlfeld
ALS	Al Schlappa	FB	Fred Bull
AP	Albin Peters	FKM	Frank K. Maitland
AS	Adolph Seitz Jr.	FM	Fred McClellan
BB	Bob Betor	FWM	Fred W. Moxey
BE	Brian Eddy	GAS	Gary Stern
BEM	Bert E. Mills	GC	George Christian
BH	Brian Hansen	GEG	George Gomez
BHU	Bill Huenergardt	GES	Gerry Stellenberg
BIP	Bill Parker	GG	Gary Gayton
BJ	Bob Jonesi	GH	Gordon Horlock
BM	Brian Matthews	GK	Greg Kmiec
BO	Barry Oursler	GM	George H. Miner
BOM	Bon MacDougall	GS	Gary Slater
BP	Bill Pfutzenreuter	HB	H. Berninger
BR	Bruno Radtke	HGB	Herbert G. Breitenstein
BRP	Brian Poklacki	HH	Harvey Heiss
BS	Barry Slater	HM	Harry Mabs
CD	Cliff Dumble	HS	Harry Stoner
CF	Claude Fernandez	HW	Harry Williams
CG	Chris Granner	IW	Iggy Wolverton
CO	Chris Otis	JA	Jerry Armstrong
DC	Dick Casper	JAP	Jack Pearson
DL	Dan Langlois	JB	Jeff Brenner
DN	Dennis Nordman	JEK	Jerry Koci
DR	David Rockola	JF	Jack Firestone
DS	Dwight Sullivan	JG	John Gore

Designers

JJ	Joe Joos Jr.	PAL	Paul Leslie
JK	Joe Kaminkow	PEP	Pete Piotrowski
JN	Jon Norris	PL	Pat Lawlor
JO	John Osborne	PP	Peter Perry
JOB	John Buras	RF	Ralph Flecher
JOEB	Joe Balcer	RH	Rob Hurtado
JOK	John Kotlarik	RM	Raymond T. Moloney
JONB	John Borg	RNH	Ron Halliburton
JOP	John Popaduik	RP	Roland Berrios
JOR	Joe Orcutt	RS	Roger Sharpe
JP	Jim Patla	RT	Ray Tanzer
JT	John Trudeau	SB	Steve Bicker
JW	Joe Warner	SE	Steve Epstein
KJ	Keith P. Johnson	SG	Sam Gensburg
KK	Karl Knickerbocker	SK	Steve Kordek
KS	Ken Shyvers	SR	Steve Ritchie
LD	Larry Demar	SS	Sam Stern
LK	Louis Koziarz	SSIM	S. Simonson
LR	Lonnie Ropp	STK	Steve Kirk
LS	Lyman F. Sheats Jr.	TES	Ted Estes
LYD	Lyndon Durant	TF	Todd Ferris
MAR	Marty Rosenthal	TH	Thomas S. Hutchison
MC	Matt Coriale	TIS	Tim Seckel
MG	Michael Gottlieb	TK	Tony Kramer
MK	Mike Kubin	TOK	Tom Kopera
MR	Mark Ritchie	TS	Tom Szafransky
MT	Mike Tori	TZ	Ted Zale
MV	Mike Vettros	WB	Wendell Bartelt
MW	Mark Weyna	WM	Wendel McAdams
NC	Norm Clark	WN	Wayne Neyens
OD	Orin Day	WP	Ward Pemberton
PA	Python Angelo	WW	Wally Welch

Artists

AS	Art Stenholm	KP	Keith Parkinson
BJ	Brian Johnson	LAD	Linda Doane
BT	Bob Timm	LB	L. Blazek
CM	Christian Marche	LD	Larry Day
COM	Constantino Mitchell	LID	Linda Deal
DC	Dave Christensen	LR	Louis Rennard
DH	Dan Hughes	M	Markus
DIW	Dick White	MH	Margaret Hudson
DM	David Moore	MS	Mark Sprenger
DOM	Don Marshall	MW	Morgan Weistling
DW	Doug Watson	PA	Python Angelo
GEO	George Obregon	PB	Paul Barker
GF	Greg Freres	PE	Pam Erickson
GM	George Molentin	PF	Paul Faris
GO	George Opperman	PL	Paul Loreli
GOM	Gordon Morrison	PM	Pat McMahon
GS	Gerry Simkus	RB	Roland Berrios
HV	Hugh Van Zanten	RP	Roy Parker
JB	Jeff Busch	RQ	Robert Quinn
JD	Jason Dominiak	RT	Richard Tracy
JIK	Jim Kelly	SF	Stan Fukuoka
JK	Jerry Kelly	SM	Seamus McLaughlin
JS	Jim Sullivan	TD	Terry Doerzaph
JY	John Youssi	TE	Tim Elliot
KA	Kurt Anderson	TR	Tony Ramunni
KO	Kevin O'Connor	TS	Tom Smeltzer

Manufacturers

ABT	A.B.T. Mfg. Co.		JS	Joseph Schneider Inc.
AKR	Akron		KEE	Keeney Inc.
ALG	Alvin G. & Co.		KOM	Komputer Dynamics
ALI	Allied Leisure Ind.		LBE	L.B. Elliot Products Co.
AMM	American Mill & Manufacturing Co.		MAR	Marvel
ATA	Atari		MIL	Mills Novelty Co.
AUT	Automatic Industries		MIR	Mirco
BAK	Baker Novelty		MULT	Multimorphic
BAL	Bally		MUT	Int'l Mutoscope
BIN	Bingo Novelty		MWY	Midway
BUC	Buckley		NAT	National Pin Games
CG	California Games		ODJ	O. D. Jennings and Co.
CAP	Capcom		PAM	Pacific Amusement Co.
CCIC	Century Consolidated Industries Co.		PMC	Pacific Manufacturing Corp.
CCI	Computer Concepts Inc.		PEO	Peo Mfg.
CCM	Chicago Coin		PNS	P and S Machine
DAV	Daval		PMI	PinBall Manufacturing Inc.
DE	Data East		RHS	R.& H. Sales Co.
DRO	Dave Robbins		RP	Retro Pinball
EXS	Exhibit Supply		RMC	Richard Manufacturing Co.
FII	Fascination Int'l Inc.		ROC	Rockola
FF	Fabulous Fantasies		SEG	Sega/Data East
FMC	Field Manufacturing Corp.		SHY	Shyvers Mfg.
GML	GM Labs		SON	Sonic
GNC	Genco		STA	Standard Amusement.Co.
GOT	D. Gottlieb & Co.		STM	Standard Mfg. Co.
GPRE	Gottlieb/Premier		STN	Stern Electronics
GPN	Game Plan		STO	Stoner
GVR	Global VR		SUC	Success Mfg.
GTN	Goodtime Novelty		UNT	United Mfg.
HCE	H.C. Evans		VAL	Valley Co.
HER	Hercules Novelty		WCC	Wico
HOP	Harry Hoppe Inc.		WEM	Western Mfg.
ICI	International Concepts Inc.		WEP	Western Products Inc.
INO	In and Outdoor Games		WES	Western Equipment
JJ	Jersey Jack		WIL	Williams Electronics

CPSIA information can be obtained at www.ICGtesting.com
Printed in the USA
LVOW05s2245270114

371236LV00010B/200/P

9 780615 731537